Teacher's Guide

Reading Words

Editorial Offices: Glenview, Illinois • Parsippany, New Jersey • New York, New York
Sales Offices: Parsippany, New Jersey • Duluth, Georgia • Glenview, Illinois
Coppell, Texas • Ontario, California • Mesa, Arizona

References

The following resources provide a foundation for the research upon which this program is based.

Adams, M. J., Foorman, B. R., Lundberg, I., and Beeler, T. (1998b). *Phonemic awareness in young children.* Baltimore, MD: Paul H. Brookes.

Ball, E. W., and Blachman, B. A. (1991). "Does Phoneme Awareness Training in Kindergarten Make a Difference in Early Word Recognition and Developmental Spelling?" *Reading Research Quarterly, 26(1),* 49–66.

Blachman, B. A. et al., (2000). *Road to the code: A phonological awareness program for young children.* Baltimore, MD: Paul H. Brookes.

Blevins, W. (1999). *Phonemic awareness activities.* New York, NY: Scholastic.

Byrne, B. and Fielding-Barnsley, R. (1993). *Sound foundation kit.* Artarmon, Australia: Peter Lynden Publishing.

Carnine, D. W., Silbert, J., and Kame'enui, E. J. (1997). *Direct instruction reading (3rd ed.).* Upper Saddle River, NJ: Merrill/Prentice-Hall.

Cunningham, P. M. (1991a). *Phonics they use: Words for reading and writing.* New York: HarperCollins.

Cunningham, P. M. (1991b). "Research Directions: Multimethod, Multilevel Literacy Instruction in First-Grade." *Language Arts, 68,* 578–584.

Cunningham, P. M. and Hall, D. P. (1994). *Making words: multilevel, hands-on, developmentally appropriate spelling and phonics activities.* Torrance, CA: Good Apple.

Engelmann, S. and Bruner, E. C. (1995). *Reading mastery I* (Rainbow edition). Columbus, OH: SRA/McGraw-Hill.

Gaskings, I. et al., (1997). "Procedures for Word Learning: Making Discoveries About Words." *The Reading Teacher, 50,* 312–327.

Henderson, E. (1990). *Teaching spelling.* Boston: Houghton Mifflin.

Lindamood, P. and Lindamood, P. (1998). *Lindamood phonemic sequencing program for reading, spelling, and speech: Teacher's manual for the classroom and the clinic.* Austin, TX: PRO-ED.

Notari-Syverson, A., O'Connor, R. E., and Vadasy, P. F. (1998). *Ladders to literacy: A kindergarten activity book.* Baltimore, MD: Paul H. Brookes.

Smith, S. B. et al., (2001). "An Analysis of Phonological Awareness Instruction in Four Kindergarten Basal Reading Programs." *Reading and Writing Quarterly, 17,* 25–51.

Smith, S., Simmons, D. C., and Kame'enui, E. J. (1998). "Phonological awareness: Research bases." In D. C. Simmons and E. J. Kame'enui (Eds.), *What reading research tells us about children with diverse learning needs: Bases and basics* (pp. 61–127). Mahwah, NJ: Lawrence Erlbaum Associates.

Smith, S., Simmons, D. C., and Kame'enui, E. J. (1998). "Phonological Awareness: Instructional and Curricular Basics and Implications." In D. C. Simmons and E. J. Kame'enui (Eds.), *What reading research tells us about children with diverse learning needs: Bases and basics* (pp. 129–140). Mahwah, NJ: Lawrence Erlbaum Associates.

Torgesen, J. K. and Bryant, B. T. (1994). *Phonological awareness training for reading.* Austin, TX: PRO-ED.

Yopp, H. K. (1992) "Developing Phonemic Awareness in Young Children." *The Reading Teacher, 45(9),* 696–703.

Activity Acknowledgments

The authors of this program would like to acknowledge the people who developed the following activities used in the program:

First Sound Song, H.K. Yopp, 1992. Part 1: 36, 52, 128, 154, 178, 204, 237; Part 3: 107.

If You Land on Me, Say My First Sound, modified from Blevins's (1977) *Phonemic Awareness Activities for Early Reading Progress.* Part 1: 290; Part 2: 50, 107, 147, 157.

Say It and Move It with Two-Square Strips, based on an activity from Ball and Blachman, 1999. Part 2: 12.

Regular and Irregular Words, modification of an activity from Carnine, Silbert, and Kame'enui, 1977. Part 3: 5, 17, 29, 41, 53, 75, 85, 97, 109, 121, 151, 161, 171, 181, 199, 211, 223, 235, 245, 254, 255; Part 4: 5, 6, 18, 19, 30, 31, 43, 44, 56, 57, 68, 78, 90, 91, 102, 103, 115, 126, 127, 138, 147, 148, 157, 158, 169, 170, 181, 193, 205, 215, 225, 226, 235, 236, 245, 246, 255, 256, 265, 273, 283, 293, 303, 304, 313, 325.

Sentence Page, modification of an activity from Carnine, Silbert, and Kame'enui, 1977. Part 4: 9, 22, 34, 47, 60, 81, 93, 106, 118, 129, 151, 161, 173, 185, 198, 218, 228, 238, 248, 258, 276, 286, 296, 306, 317.

Illustrations by Karen Bell

About the illustrator: Karen Bell and her family live on a ranch in Malibu, California, with a large collection of assorted dogs, cats, chickens, goats, turtles, and horses. Unfortunately, there are no dinosaurs.

ISBN: 0-328-04787-2
This product may appear as part of package ISBN: 0-328-05045-8.

6 7 8 9 10 V003 11 10 09 08 07 06 05 04

Scott Foresman Early Reading Intervention is based on Project Optimize, a five-year longitudinal research study by Dr. Edward J. Kame'enui and Dr. Deborah C. Simmons. It identifies at-risk children in kindergarten and grade 1 and provides intervention to improve reading achievement.

Scientifically Research-Based

Research shows 97% of kindergarten children who were taught with Scott Foresman Early Reading Intervention experienced faster achievement rates and were able to sustain that level of achievement into second grade.

Comprehensive Assessment

Scott Foresman Early Reading Intervention helps you make placement decisions and monitor progress, so you can focus instruction based on children's needs.

Validated Instructional Design

The instructional design of Scott Foresman Early Reading Intervention ensures the time, duration, and instructional delivery necessary for student success.

Program Authors

Deborah C. Simmons, Ph.D.

Associate Professor and Co-Director

Institute for Development of Educational Achievement
University of Oregon

Dr. Simmons is a well-respected researcher in the areas of literacy acquisition and development and intervention for children at risk of reading failure. Over the years, she has published numerous books, book chapters, and research articles, with her articles appearing in *The Journal of Educational Psychology, Reading and Writing Quarterly, Reading Today, Journal of Learning Disabilities,* and *Journal of Educational Research.*

Dr. Simmons serves on Editorial Boards for several professional journals, including *Journal of Special Education, Learning Disabilities Quarterly, Exceptional Children,* and *Reading and Writing Quarterly.* She also served on the Assessment Group of the Reading First Initiative for the U.S. Department of Education.

Edward J. Kame'enui, Ph.D.

Professor and Director

Institute for Development of Educational Achievement
University of Oregon

Dr. Kame'enui has published several college textbooks on various topics related to teaching reading and curriculum design. He also has published research and issue articles in publications including *The Exceptional Child, Reading Research Quarterly, Journal of Educational Research,* and *Journal of Reading Behavior.*

Dr. Kame'enui serves on Editorial Boards for several professional journals, including *Reading Research, Learning Disabilities Research and Practice,* and *Journal of Special Education.* He has served as the team leader of the Assessment Group of the Reading First Initiative for the U.S. Department of Education and has also served on Advisory Boards for the PBS television show *Between the Lions* and the International Dyslexia Association.

Project Optimize

Project Optimize, which has become Scott Foresman Early Reading Intervention, is just one of many collaborations between Dr. Simmons and Dr. Kame'enui. They are currently working on several research projects concentrating on accelerating literacy and improving reading competence for at-risk children.

Authors and Consultants

Consulting Authors

Michael D. Coyne, Ph.D.
Neag School of Education
University of Connecticut

Lana Edwards, Ph.D.
Assistant Professor
Lehigh University, Bethlehem, PA

Carrie Thomas-Beck, Ph.D.
Curriculum Specialist
Springfield Public Schools, Springfield, Oregon

Special Thanks

This program reflects the collaboration of researchers and practitioners and the contributions of many. The authors gratefully acknowledge and sincerely appreciate the effort, input, and support of the following individuals and organizations:

Bethel School District (Eugene, Oregon) Administrators, Principals, Teachers, Educational Assistants, and Students

Springfield School District (Springfield, Oregon) Principals, Kindergarten Teachers, Educational Assistants, and Students

Additionally, the authors would like to thank the following individuals for their continued and significant contributions in the implementation and refinement of the Early Reading Intervention program:

Amy Riepma, Rhonda Wolter, and **Melissa Allen**

Consultants

Beth Harn, Ph.D.
Assistant Professor of Psychology
California State University, Fresno

Diane O'Keefe
Business Manager
Institute for the Development
of Educational Achievement
University of Oregon

Naomi Rahn, M.S.
Instructor/Field Experience Coordinator
Early Intervention Program
University of Oregon

Tanya Sheehan
Research Assistant
Institute for Development
of Educational Achievement
University of Oregon

Sylvia Barrus Smith, Ph.D.
Research Associate
Institute for Development
of Educational Achievement
University of Oregon

Katie Tate
Editor
Institute for the Development
of Educational Achievement
University of Oregon

Joshua Wallin
Research Assistant
Institute for Development
of Educational Achievement
University of Oregon

Scientifically Research-Based

Project Optimize

Project Optimize is a five-year longitudinal research program that investigates the effectiveness of instructional emphasis and specificity on early reading and vocabulary development of kindergarten children.

What prompted the study?

National Education Reform

The President has mandated that all children will read at or above grade level by grade 3. We need proven instruction to help struggling readers meet that goal.

Findings of Other Researchers

Interventions delivered in grade 3 and beyond fail to close the achievement gap. The later the onset of intervention, the poorer the probability that children will read at grade 3.

Research Questions

What types of instruction and intervention strategies are most effective with the bottom 25% of kindergartners?

How intensive should the intervention be (time, duration, and instructional delivery) for students to reach satisfactory goals and maintain them over time?

Funding

Project Optimize was funded by the U.S. Department of Education and the Office of Special Education Programs.

Corporate Sponsors

Pacific Corporation and Washington Mutual

The Sample

- 441 kindergarten children from seven schools in the Pacific Northwest were screened on onset recognition fluency and letter naming fluency.
- The bottom 25% on both criteria were invited to participate in an "extended-day" kindergarten intervention.
- Children were randomly assigned to one of the three interventions.

The Demographics

- All Title I schools
- Free and reduced lunch: 37% to 63%
- District mobility: 15% to 20%
- Gender mix: 58% male, 42% female
- Sample size: 112 beginning sample, 96 end of kindergarten, 77 end of grade 1

The Interventions

- 30 minutes of additional instruction per day
- Instruction was delivered in small groups of 2–5 children.
- Instruction was delivered by either a certified teacher or a teaching assistant.
- Pre- and post-data were collected.
- Progress was monitored monthly.

Instructional Interventions

Intervention A
Scott Foresman Early Reading Intervention

Code Emphasis/ High Specificity

- 15 minutes of instruction on select phonological awareness skills, alphabetic understanding, and word reading
- 15 minutes of instruction on further development of phonological awareness, writing development, and integrating phonological awareness and orthography (letter-sound to whole word writing)

Intervention B
Phonological Awareness/ Vocabulary Comprehension

Code and Comprehension Emphasis/High Specificity

- 15 minutes of instruction on select phonological awareness skills, alphabetic understanding, and word reading
- 15 minutes focused on literature development, repeated reading procedure, explicit vocabulary instruction, and explicit story grammar and retell instruction

Intervention C
Basal Publisher: Sounds and Letters Module

Code Emphasis/ Moderate Specificity

- 30 total minutes of instruction focusing on a range of phonological awareness skills, alphabetic understanding, and word reading, plus writing instruction

Results

Growth in Phonological Awareness

Test: Phonemic Segmentation Fluency **Benchmark:** 35 Phonemes per Minute

Children in all three interventions exceeded the benchmark. Children in Intervention A exceeded the benchmark at least two months earlier and showed greater achievement than children in Interventions B and C.

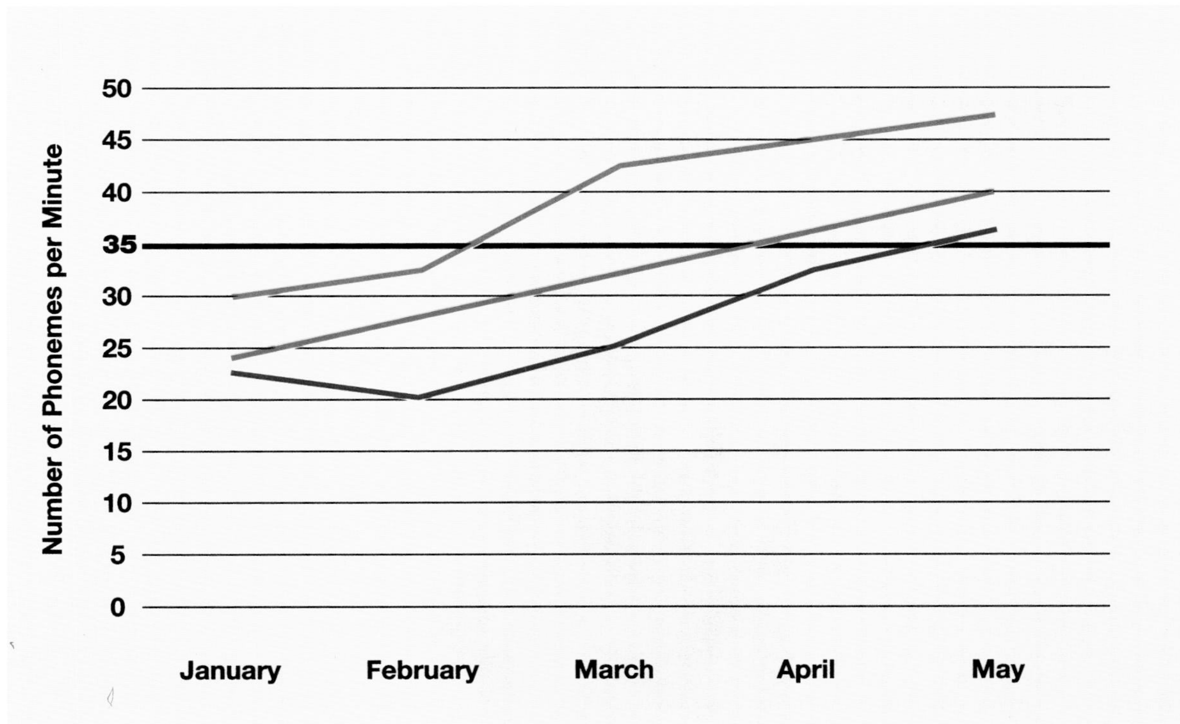

Intervention A *Scott Foresman Early Reading Intervention*
Intervention B *Phonological Awareness/Vocabulary Comprehension*
Intervention C *Basal Publisher: Sounds and Letters Module*

Scientifically Research-Based

Results

Growth in Alphabetic Principle

Test: Nonsense Word Fluency **Benchmark:** 25 Letter-Sound Correspondences per Minute

Children in Interventions A and B exceeded the benchmark.

Children in Intervention A showed the greatest achievement, surpassing the benchmark by 56%.

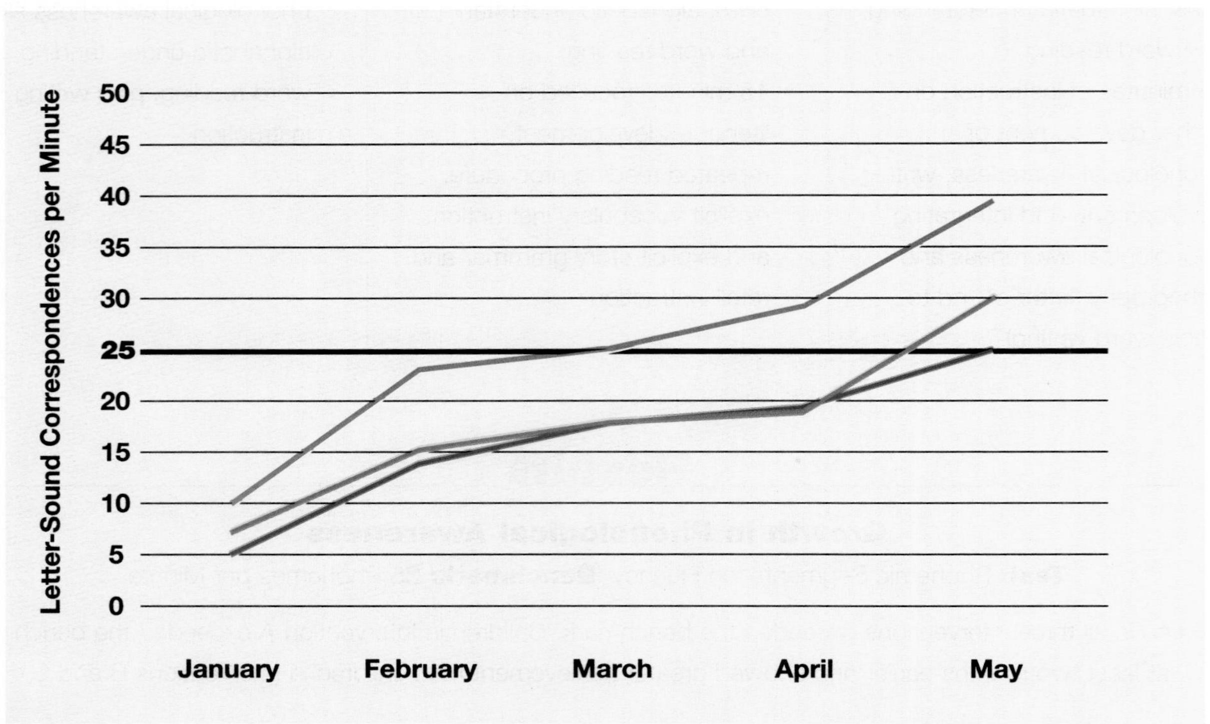

Intervention A *Scott Foresman Early Reading Intervention*
Intervention B *Phonological Awareness/Vocabulary Comprehension*
Intervention C *Basal Publisher: Sounds and Letters Module*

Results

Where Students with Similar Entry Levels Finished Kindergarten

Test: Phonemic Segmentation Fluency (PSF) **Median:** 21–30

87% of the children who received Intervention A achieved the benchmark. In most districts with similar children who did not receive an intervention, fewer than 30% of the children achieved the benchmark.

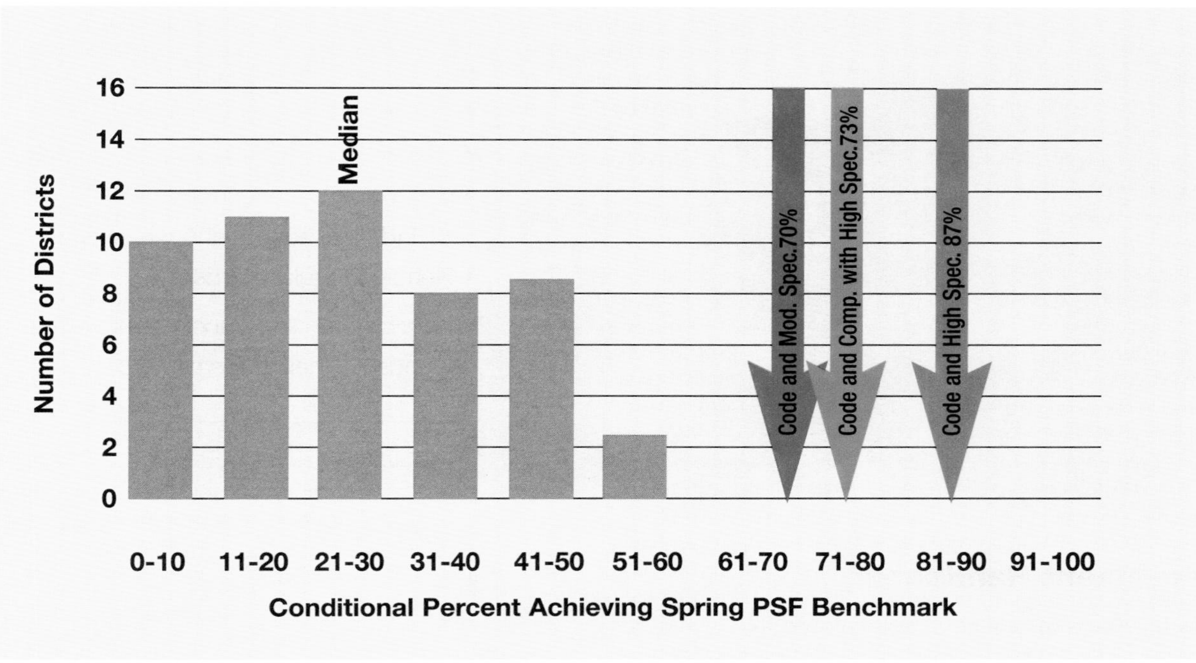

Intervention A *Scott Foresman Early Reading Intervention*
Intervention B *Phonological Awareness/Vocabulary Comprehension*
Intervention C *Basal Publisher: Sounds and Letters Module*

Research Conclusions

Research shows that 97% of kindergarten children who were taught with Scott Foresman Early Reading Intervention experienced faster achievement rates and were able to sustain that level of achievement into second grade.

Specificity Matters

Children in Interventions A and B, who received 15 minutes of highly specified instruction, made comparable gains to those in Intervention C, who received a full 30 minutes of less specific instruction.

Emphasis Matters

How instructional time is used affects outcomes. Emphasis on phonologic and alphabetic tasks affected achievement.

Emphasis and Specificity Matter

The combination of emphasis and specificity resulted in greater levels of early reading achievement than either of the factors alone.

Comprehensive Assessment

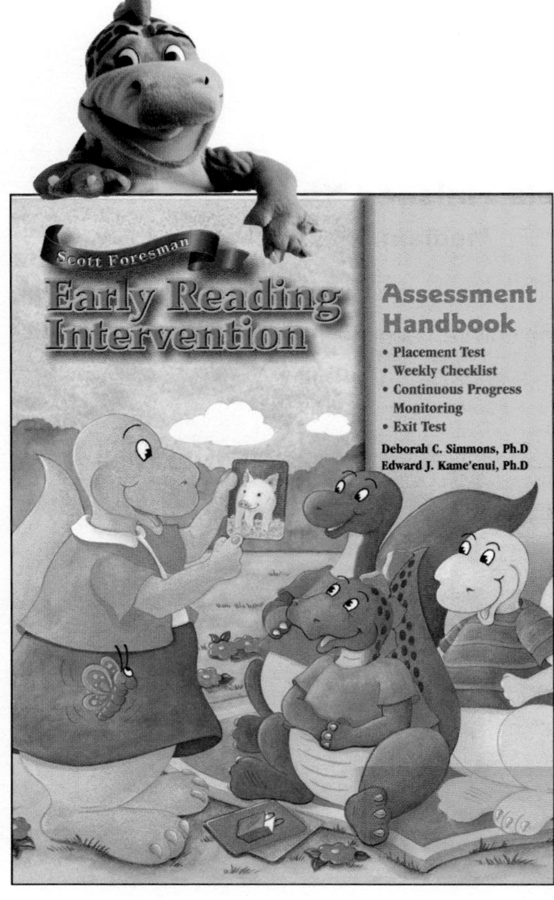

Assessment Handbook

The Assessment Handbook helps you make placement decisions and monitor progress, so you can focus instruction on children's needs.

Everything teachers need to place and monitor students in the program is contained in the Assessment Handbook.

- A Placement Test with directions
- Four Progress-Monitoring Tests
- Progress-Monitoring Checklists
- An Exit Test to ensure that children have mastered all skills

Before

The Placement Test

The Placement Test is used to determine where a child best fits within the program. Children are assessed in the following areas:

- Letter names and sounds
- Isolating initial sounds
- Segmenting whole words
- Letter-sound correspondences—initial sound, final sound, and whole word
- Reading regular words

Where children are placed in the program depends on their placement scores.

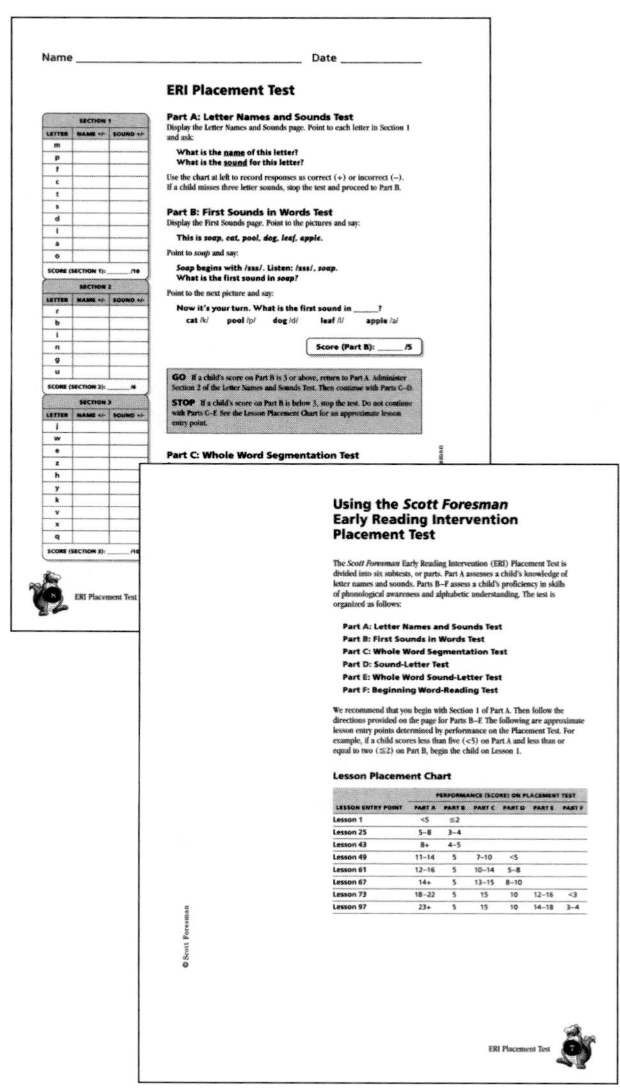

Name ______ Date ______

ERI Placement Test

SECTION 1		
LETTER	NAME +/-	SOUND +/-
m		
p		
f		
c		
t		
s		
d		
l		
a		
o		
SCORE (SECTION 1): ____ /10		

SECTION 2		
LETTER	NAME +/-	SOUND +/-
r		
b		
i		
n		
g		
u		
SCORE (SECTION 2): ____ /6		

SECTION 3		
LETTER	NAME +/-	SOUND +/-
j		
w		
e		
z		
h		
y		
k		
v		
x		
q		
SCORE (SECTION 3): ____ /10		

Part A: Letter Names and Sounds Test
Display the Letter Names and Sounds page. Point to each letter in Section 1 and ask:

What is the name of this letter?
What is the sound for this letter?

Use the chart at left to record responses as correct (+) or incorrect (–). If a child misses three letter sounds, stop the test and proceed to Part B.

Part B: First Sounds in Words Test
Display the First Sounds page. Point to the pictures and say:

This is *soap, cat, pool, dog, leaf, apple*.

Point to *soap* and say:

***Soap* begins with /sss/. Listen: /sss/, *soap*.**
What is the first sound in *soap*?

Point to the next picture and say:

Now it's your turn. What is the first sound in ____?
cat /k/ **pool** /p/ **dog** /d/ **leaf** /l/ **apple** /a/

Score (Part B): ____ /5

GO If a child's score on Part B is 3 or above, return to Part A. Administer Section 2 of the Letter Names and Sounds Test. Then continue with Parts C–D.

STOP If a child's score on Part B is below 3, stop the test. Do not continue with Parts C–F. See the Lesson Placement Chart for an approximate lesson entry point.

Part C: Whole Word Segmentation Test

ERI Placement Test

Using the *Scott Foresman* Early Reading Intervention Placement Test

The *Scott Foresman* Early Reading Intervention (ERI) Placement Test is divided into six subtests, or parts. Part A assesses a child's knowledge of letter names and sounds. Parts B–F assess a child's proficiency in skills of phonological awareness and alphabetic understanding. The test is organized as follows:

Part A: Letter Names and Sounds Test
Part B: First Sounds in Words Test
Part C: Whole Word Segmentation Test
Part D: Sound-Letter Test
Part E: Whole Word Sound-Letter Test
Part F: Beginning Word-Reading Test

We recommend that you begin with Section 1 of Part A. Then follow the directions provided on the page for Parts B–F. The following are approximate lesson entry points determined by performance on the Placement Test. For example, if a child scores less than five (<5) on Part A and less than or equal to two (≤2) on Part B, begin the child on Lesson 1.

Lesson Placement Chart

	PERFORMANCE (SCORE) ON PLACEMENT TEST					
LESSON ENTRY POINT	PART A	PART B	PART C	PART D	PART E	PART F
Lesson 1	<5	≤2				
Lesson 25	5–8	3–4				
Lesson 43	8+	4–5				
Lesson 49	11–14	5	7–10	<5		
Lesson 61	12–16	5	10–14	5–8		
Lesson 67	14+	5	13–15	8–10		
Lesson 73	18–22	5	15	10	12–16	<3
Lesson 97	23+	5	15	10	14–18	3–4

ERI Placement Test

During

Ongoing Assessment

Ongoing assessment features appear routinely throughout the Teacher's Guide. You can use these features to:

- Quickly assess whether children have learned a skill
- Correctly determine the appropriate instructional strategy to help children learn

Progress-Monitoring Tests

There are four progress-monitoring tests, one for each part of the program. Administering these tests lets you know:

- If children are ready to move on to the next part of the program
- If children need any additional instruction

Student Progress Checklists

There are progress-monitoring checklists for every six lessons. Use the checklists:

- To monitor progress on a weekly basis
- As a record of skills that children have learned
- To determine if children may need more intensive instruction

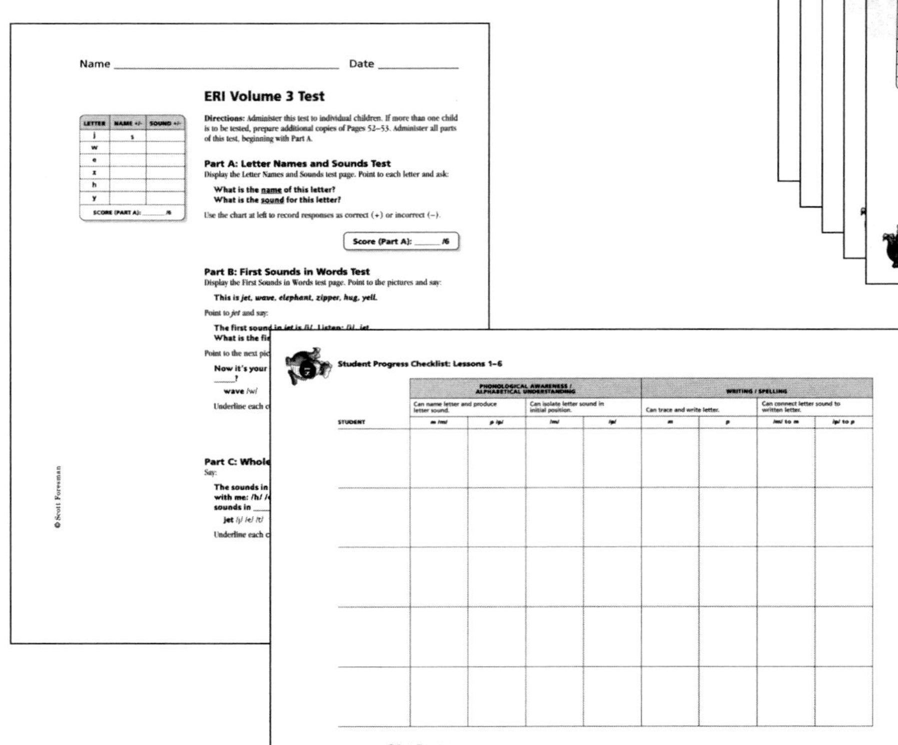

Name ______________________ Date ____________

ERI Volume 3 Test

Directions: Administer this test to individual children. If more than one child is to be tested, prepare additional copies of Pages 52–53. Administer all parts of this test, beginning with Part A.

LETTER	NAME +/-	SOUND +/-
j	s	
w		
e		
z		
h		
y		
SCORE (PART A): ____ /6		

Part A: Letter Names and Sounds Test
Display the Letter Names and Sounds test page. Point to each letter and ask:

What is the name of this letter?
What is the sound for this letter?

Use the chart at left to record responses as correct (+) or incorrect (–).

Score (Part A): ____ /6

Part B: First Sounds in Words Test
Display the First Sounds in Words test page. Point to the pictures and say:

This is *jet, wave, elephant, zipper, hug, yell.*

Point to *jet* and say:

Student Progress Checklist: Lessons 1–6

STUDENT	PHONOLOGICAL AWARENESS / ALPHABETICAL UNDERSTANDING: Can name letter and produce letter sound.		Can isolate letter sound in initial position.		WRITING / SPELLING: Can trace and write letter.		Can connect letter sound to written letter.	
	m /m/	p /p/	/m/	/p/	m	p	/m/ to m	/p/ to p

After

The Exit Test

The Exit Test allows you to determine whether or not your children have appropriately mastered the skills in the program and are ready to end their intervention lessons. During the Exit Test, children are assessed on:

- Letter names and sounds
- Isolating initial sounds
- Segmenting whole words
- Letter-sound correspondences—initial sound, final sound, and whole word
- Reading regular words
- Reading irregular words

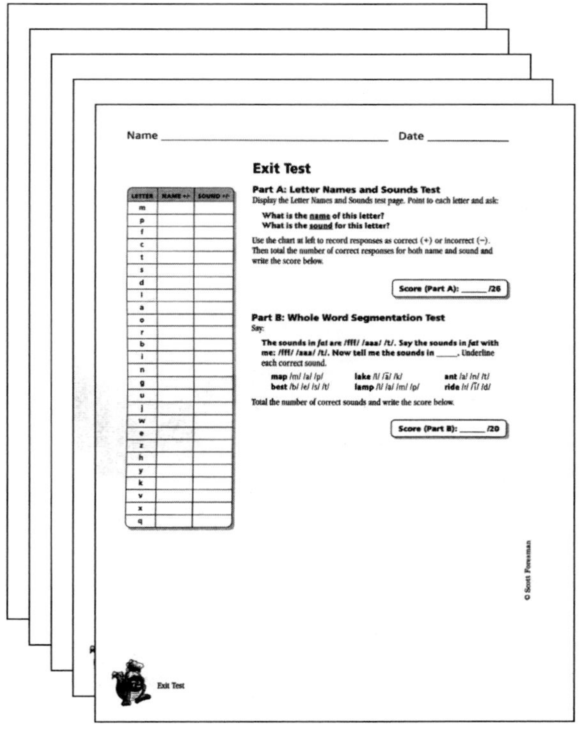

Name ______________________ Date ____________

Exit Test

Part A: Letter Names and Sounds Test
Display the Letter Names and Sounds test page. Point to each letter and ask:

What is the name of this letter?
What is the sound for this letter?

Use the chart at left to record responses as correct (+) or incorrect (–). Then total the number of correct responses for both name and sound and write the score below.

LETTER	NAME +/-	SOUND +/-
m		
p		
f		
c		
t		
s		
d		
l		
a		
o		
r		
b		
i		
n		
g		
u		
j		
w		
e		
z		
h		
y		
k		
v		
x		
q		

Score (Part A): ____ /26

Part B: Whole Word Segmentation Test
Say:

The sounds in *fat* are /fff/ /aaa/ /t/. Say the sounds in *fat* with me: /fff/ /aaa/ /t/. Now tell me the sounds in ____. Underline each correct sound.

map /m/ /a/ /p/ **lake** /l/ /ā/ /k/ **ant** /a/ /n/ /t/
best /b/ /e/ /s/ /t/ **lamp** /l/ /a/ /m/ /p/ **ride** /r/ /ī/ /d/

Total the number of correct sounds and write the score below.

Score (Part B): ____ /20

Exit Test

Components

Teacher Resources

Teacher's Guides

A proven research base ensures success for at-risk readers. 126 lessons in an easy-to-follow format give you the flexibility to teach one 30-minute or two 15-minute sessions.

Teacher Resource Package

A wealth of additional resources for every lesson! These heavy-duty cards have a teacher-friendly design that makes managing materials even easier.

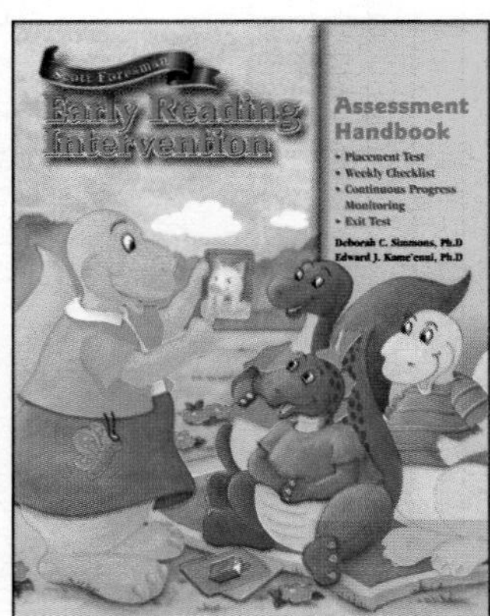

Assessment Handbook

The materials you need to accurately assess all your students are conveniently located in one book. Contains the Placement Test, four Progress-Monitoring Tests, Progress-Monitoring Checklists, and an Exit Test.

Hi, I'm Diz and I'm a Stegosaurus. Meet me and my friends Nat the Triceratops, Ron the Brontosaurus, and Rex the Tyrannosaurus Rex.

Diz the Dinosaur

This plush puppet with moveable mouth and arms helps you implement instruction in any lesson.

Student Materials

Diz Student Storybooks

These 10 decodable storybooks use engaging recurring characters to blend practice and application of sound-spelling patterns. (6 copies of each) Also available in a take-home version.

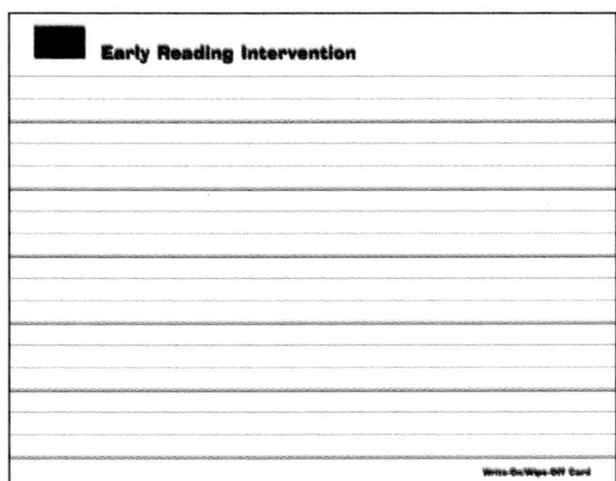

Write-On/Wipe-Off Cards

These cards have a write-on/wipe-off surface on the lined front side for practicing careful writing and a blank reverse side for writing large letters.

Student Activity Books

No more photocopying! The student resources for every lesson include separate D'Nealian™ and Ball and Stick pages.

Components

Manipulatives

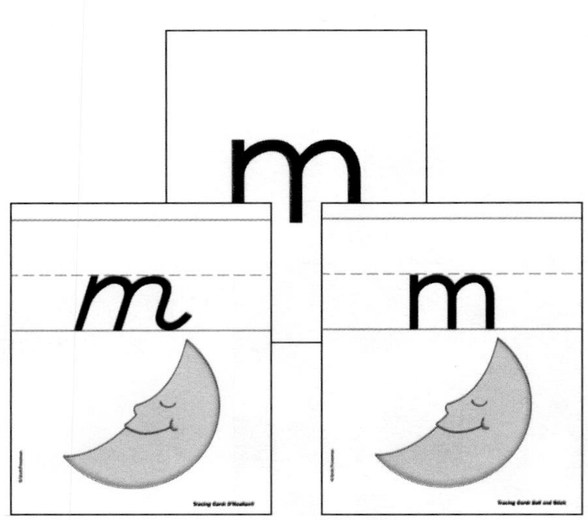

Alphabet Card Package

This unique package contains Alphabet Cards for learning letter names and sounds, Tracing Cards for connecting sounds to letters and learning letter shapes, and a Teacher's Sound Production Cue Card for prompting sound production.

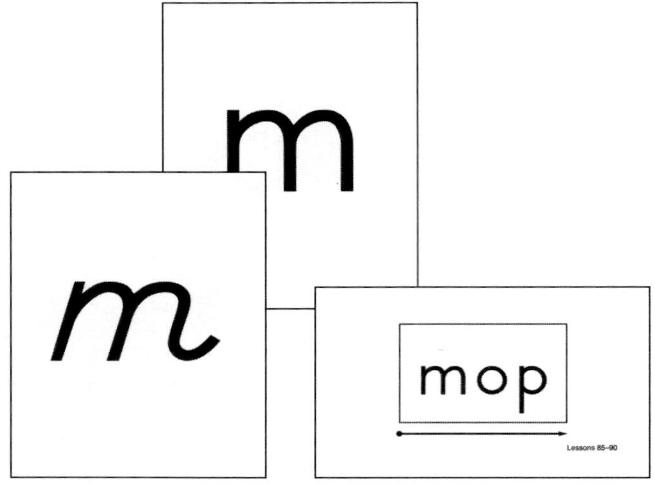

Letter and Word Cards Package

Use Letter Cards in D'Nealian™ and Ball and Stick formats for naming and tracing letters, Game Cards for games that practice letter names and sounds, and Word Cards to practice word reading strategies.

Letter Tiles

Sturdy, plastic, manipulative tiles are easy for little fingers to handle and allow children to practice segmenting and blending.

Picture Cards

Identify and isolate initial and final sounds with these full-color photographs.

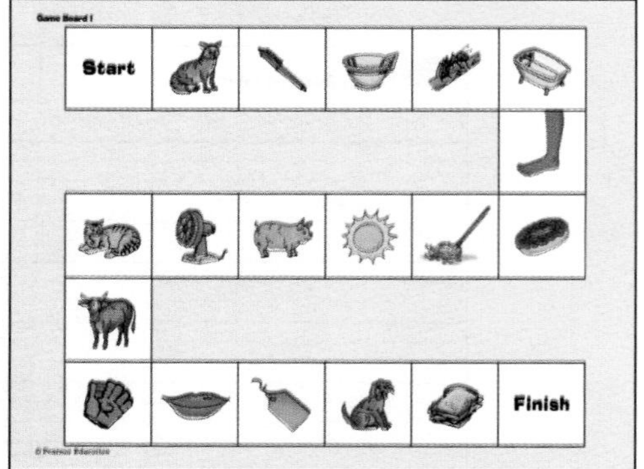

Game Boards and 2- and 3-Square Strips

Game boards help students identify initial and final sounds in an engaging format while the 2- and 3-Square Strips assist them in segmenting, blending, and reading words.

Professional Development Videos

Scott Foresman Early Reading Intervention videos are ideal for staff training and/or teacher inservice.

Research: A Message from the Authors

Featuring program authors, Dr. Deborah Simmons and Dr. Edward Kame'enui, this video discusses the scientific research foundation for the program and displays the results of Project Optimize, showing the remarkable achievements of children using Scott Foresman Early Reading Intervention.

Classroom Demonstration Lesson

View real-time video lessons of a real teacher and students using actual lessons from Scott Foresman Early Reading Intervention and then hear reactions to the program from real teachers and administrators.

Components

Use the Diz Clubhouse box to help organize all of your materials. Labeled compartments will help you find materials quickly and easily.

- Teacher's Guides:
  - Part 1: Learning Letter Names and Sounds
  - Part 2: Segmenting, Blending, and Integrating
  - Part 3: Word Reading
  - Part 4: Sentence Reading
- Teacher's Resource Packages (4)
- Student Activity Books (4 titles, 6 copies of each)
- Assessment Handbook
- Diz Student Storybooks (10 titles, 6 copies of each)
- Diz Take-Home Storybooks (6 books, 10 titles in each)
- Diz Dinosaur Puppet
- Picture Cards (174)
- Write-On/Wipe-Off Cards (6)
- Letter Tiles (26 letters, 6 tiles of each)
- Alphabet Card Package (26 D'Nealian Tracing Cards, 26 Ball and Stick Tracing Cards, 26 Alphabet Cards, and a Sound Production Cue Card)
- Letter and Word Cards Package (158 Letter Cards, 230 Word Cards, and 54 Game Cards)
- Game Boards and 2- and 3-Square Strips (3 Game Boards and 15 2- and 3-Square Strips)
- Professional Development Videos
  - Classroom Demonstration Lesson
  - Research: A Message from the Authors

Management

Getting Started

Scott Foresman Early Reading Intervention contains everything you need to intervene early and successfully.

Identify Children At-Risk

The beginning of the school year is the best time to informally assess which children are at risk for reading difficulties. At some point during the fourth to sixth week of the year, take the time to administer a formal screening assessment to determine which children fall into the bottom 25% of all readers. These children are the most at risk of experiencing reading difficulties. Scott Foresman Early Reading Intervention allows you to intervene and dramatically increase these children's chance for reading success.

DIBELS

When using a screening test at the beginning of the year, you may want to consider DIBELS—Dynamic Indicators of Basic Early Literacy Skills. This test may be downloaded from the Internet for free. For the test and scoring information, see: dibels.uoregon.edu.

Form Intervention Groups

The Placement Test must be administered to each child individually and only takes a few minutes per child. It will allow you to determine the entry point in the program for each student. Once all the children have been assessed, you can place them into groups. Each group should be made up of two to five children. After you have determined where children fit into the program, they will receive the instruction as a supplement to their regular reading and literacy instruction.

Scott Foresman Early Reading Intervention

Works in a Half-Day or Whole-Day Environment

Scott Foresman Early Reading Intervention is appropriate for small group instruction and is designed for flexible use based on the structure of your school day. You can choose to give the instruction in one 30-minute period or in two 15-minute periods. The instruction can come either before or after school or as part of an extended-day program.

Daily Preparation

Scott Foresman Early Reading Intervention is designed to minimize the time that it takes to prepare for each group.

Daily Preparation

Every lesson starts with a lesson overview with this important planning information:

- the activities children will engage in that day
- a list of materials needed for each activity
- an estimate of the amount of time for each activity

This information is designed to make daily preparation easier. When you first begin the program, preparation time should be approximately 15 minutes. That amount will significantly decrease as you and your students become more familiar with the program.

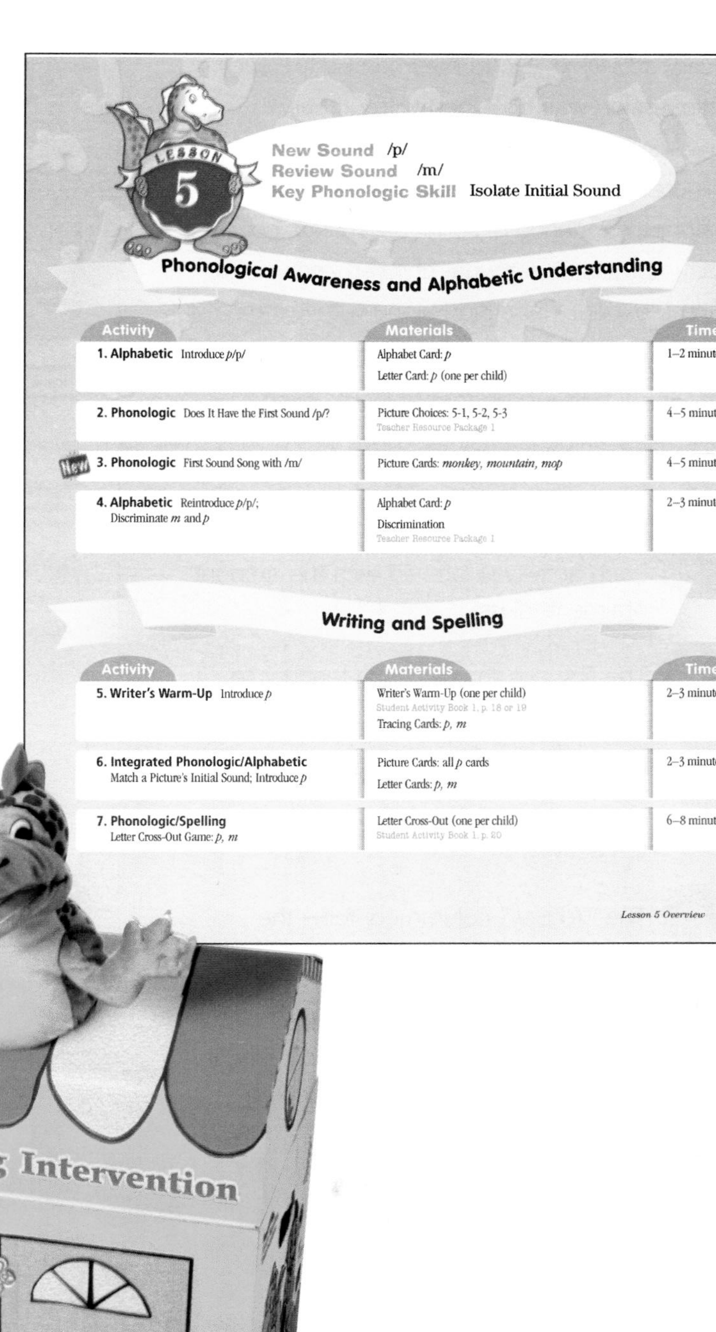

LESSON 5

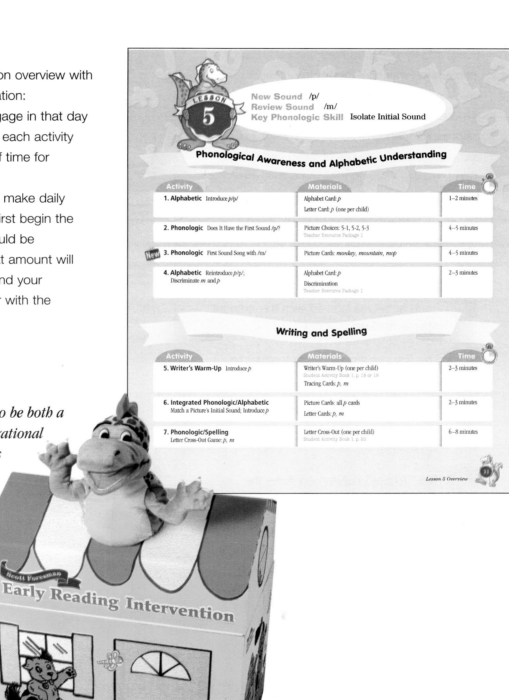

New Sound /p/
Review Sound /m/
Key Phonologic Skill Isolate Initial Sound

Phonological Awareness and Alphabetic Understanding

Activity	Materials	Time
1. **Alphabetic** Introduce *p*/p/	Alphabet Card: *p* Letter Card: *p* (one per child)	1–2 minutes
2. **Phonologic** Does It Have the First Sound /p/?	Picture Choices: 5-1, 5-2, 5-3 Teacher Resource Package 1	4–5 minutes
New 3. **Phonologic** First Sound Song with /m/	Picture Cards: *monkey, mountain, mop*	4–5 minutes
4. **Alphabetic** Reintroduce *p*/p/; Discriminate *m* and *p*	Alphabet Card: *p* Discrimination Teacher Resource Package 1	2–3 minutes

Writing and Spelling

Activity	Materials	Time
5. **Writer's Warm-Up** Introduce *p*	Writer's Warm-Up (one per child) Student Activity Book 1, p. 18 or 19 Tracing Cards: *p, m*	2–3 minutes
6. **Integrated Phonologic/Alphabetic** Match a Picture's Initial Sound; Introduce *p*	Picture Cards: all *p* cards Letter Cards: *p, m*	2–3 minutes
7. **Phonologic/Spelling** Letter Cross-Out Game: *p, m*	Letter Cross-Out (one per child) Student Activity Book 1, p. 20	6–8 minutes

Lesson 5 Overview 31

The program box is designed to be both a storage system and an organizational system. Labeled compartments inside the box indicate where to find the materials needed for the day's instruction.

Management

Daily Instruction

Scott Foresman Early Reading Intervention is an activity-based program proven to have the right instruction for at-risk children.

Every activity in Scott Foresman Early Reading Intervention was designed with primary children in mind. The activities last only minutes and are organized in a carefully planned sequence of skills that makes no assumptions about what children know. This direct, explicit instruction along with systematic review ensures student success.

The three-part lesson format inside each Teacher's Guide is easy to follow.

1. Each activity is labeled with the amount of time it takes.
2. The first column cues the teacher to what children will be doing.
3. The "To Do" column gives directions about what the teacher does during the activity.
4. The "To Say" column contains the direct, explicit instruction.
5. The lesson format also includes opportunities for Ongoing Assessment and gives an immediate reteaching strategy for children who don't grasp the material the first time through.

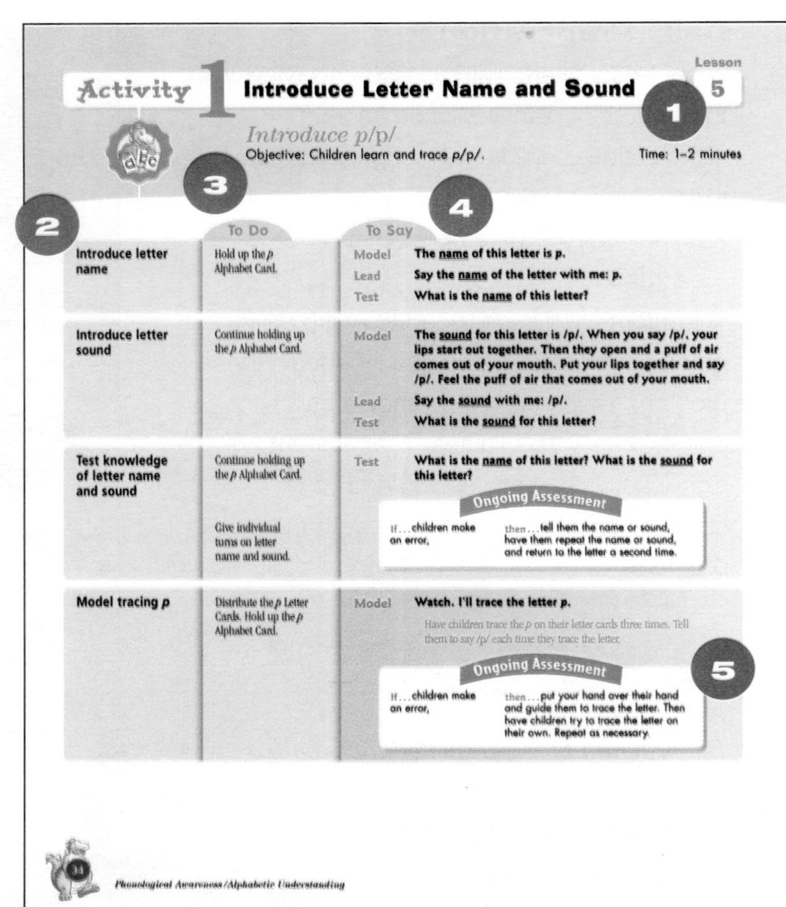

Lesson 5

Activity 1 **Introduce Letter Name and Sound**

Introduce p/p/

Objective: Children learn and trace *p*/p/.

Time: 1–2 minutes

	To Do		To Say
Introduce letter name	Hold up the *p* Alphabet Card.	Model	**The name of this letter is *p*.**
		Lead	**Say the name of the letter with me: *p*.**
		Test	**What is the name of this letter?**
Introduce letter sound	Continue holding up the *p* Alphabet Card.	Model	**The sound for this letter is /p/. When you say /p/, your lips start out together. Then they open and a puff of air comes out of your mouth. Put your lips together and say /p/. Feel the puff of air that comes out of your mouth.**
		Lead	**Say the sound with me: /p/.**
		Test	**What is the sound for this letter?**
Test knowledge of letter name and sound	Continue holding up the *p* Alphabet Card.	Test	**What is the name of this letter? What is the sound for this letter?**
	Give individual turns on letter name and sound.		Ongoing Assessment If...children make an error, then...tell them the name or sound, have them repeat the name or sound, and return to the letter a second time.
Model tracing *p*	Distribute the *p* Letter Cards. Hold up the *p* Alphabet Card.	Model	**Watch. I'll trace the letter *p*.** Have children trace the *p* on their letter cards three times. Tell them to say /p/ each time they trace the letter.
			Ongoing Assessment If...children make an error, then...put your hand over their hand and guide them to trace the letter. Then have children try to trace the letter on their own. Repeat as necessary.

14 *Phonological Awareness/Alphabetic Understanding*

Professional Development

Professional development is an important component of Scott Foresman Early Reading Intervention. We offer two professional development videos to help teachers get the best results from our program.

Research: A Message from the Authors

This 15-minute video introduces program authors Dr. Deborah Simmons and Dr. Edward Kame'enui. Dr. Simmons and Dr. Kame'enui discuss Project Optimize, the longitudinal research study that served as the basis for Scott Foresman Early Reading Intervention. You can use this video

- As an overview of early reading intervention
- To get background information on the design of the research study
- To learn the amazing results after the first year
- To assess prior knowledge and experience related to early reading intervention

Classroom Demonstration Lesson

This 30-minute demonstration shows teacher Amy Riepma teaching an Early Reading Intervention lesson with a group of her students. Use this video

- To see what 30 minutes of instruction looks like
- To get a feel for the pace and flow of a lesson
- As part of instructor training
- As a refresher for program training
- As a model for classroom-management methodology
- As a model for evaluating the program and determining its most effective use in your school

Scope and Sequence

Part 1 Learning Letters and Sounds

- Learning Letter Names and Sounds
- Identifying First and Last Sounds

Lesson	New Phonological Awareness Skill	New Phoneme	Review Phonological Awareness Skill
1	Identify initial sound	*m*/m/	
2		*m*/m/	
3		*m*/m/	
4		*p*/p/	
5		*p*/p/	
6		*p*/p/	
7	Identify initial sound	*f*/f/	Identify initial sound
8		*f*/f/	
9		*f*/f/	
10		*c*/k/	
11		*c*/k/	
12		*c*/k/	
13	Identify initial sound	*t*/t/	Identify initial sound
14		*t*/t/	
15		*t*/t/	
16		*s*/s/	
17		*s*/s/	
18		*s*/s/	
19	Identify initial sound	*d*/d/	Identify initial sound
20		*d*/d/	
21		*d*/d/	
22		*l*/l/	
23		*l*/l/	
24		*l*/l/	
25	Identify initial sound	*a*/a/	Identify initial sound
26		*a*/a/	
27		*a*/a/	
28		*a*/a/	
29		*a*/a/	
30		*a*/a/	
31	Identify final sound	*o*/o/	Identify initial sound
32	Initial and final sound discrimination	*o*/o/	
33		*o*/o/	
34		*o*/o/	
35		*o*/o/	
36		*o*/o/	
37	Identify final sound	*r*/r/	Identify initial sound and final sound
38		*r*/r/	
39		*r*/r/	
40		*r*/r/	
41		*r*/r/	
42		*r*/r/	

Part 2 Segmenting, Blending, and Integrating

- Segmenting and Blending Sounds in Words
- Integrating Sounds and Letters

Lesson	New Phonological Awareness Skill	New Phoneme	Review Phonological Awareness Skill
43	Segmenting	*b*/b/	Identify initial and final sound
44		*b*/b/	
45		*b*/b/	
46		*b*/b/	
47		*b*/b/	
48		*b*/b/	
49	Segmenting with letter tiles: initial sound	*i*/i/	Identify initial and final sound Segmenting
50		*i*/i/	
51		*i*/i/	
52		*i*/i/	
53		*i*/i/	
54		*i*/i/	
55	Segmenting with letter tiles: final sound	*n*/n/	Identify initial and final sound Segmenting with letter tiles: initial sound
56		*n*/n/	
57		*n*/n/	
58		*n*/n/	
59		*n*/n/	
60		*n*/n/	
61	Segmenting with letter tiles: initial and final sound	*g*/g/	Identify initial and final sound Segmenting with letter tiles: initial or final sound
62		*g*/g/	
63		*g*/g/	
64		*g*/g/	
65		*g*/g/	
66		*g*/g/	
67	Segmenting with letter tiles: initial, medial, and final sound Combined oral segmenting and blending	*u*/u/	Identify initial and final sound
68		*u*/u/	
69		*u*/u/	
70		*u*/u/	
71		*u*/u/	
72		*u*/u/	

Part 3 Reading Words

- Segmenting and Blending Sounds in Words
- Reading Simple Words

Lesson	Skill	New Phoneme	# of Words	Word Type	Continuous Sounds vs. Stop Sounds in the Words
73	Review combined oral segmenting and blending	*j*/j/	10	VC and CVC	All continuous sounds for L73–L75
74		*j*/j/			
75	Sounding out words	*j*/j/			Initial continuous sound for L76–L77
76		*w*/w/			
77		*w*/w/			A combination of the above for L78
78		*w*/w/			
79	Review combined oral segmenting and blending	*e*/e/	15	VC and CVC	Initial continuous sound
80		*e*/e/			
81	Sounding out words	*e*/e/			
82		*e*/e/			
83		*e*/e/			
84		*e*/e/			
85	Review combined oral segmenting and blending	*z*/z/	20	VC and CVC	Initial continuous sound
86		*z*/z/			
87	Sounding out words	*z*/z/			
88		*h*/h/			
89		*h*/h/			
90		*h*/h/			
91	Review combined oral segmenting and blending	*y*/y/	21	VC and CVC	Initial continuous sound or initial stop sound
92		*y*/y/			
93	Sounding out words	*y*/y/		Irregular	
94		*y*/y/			
95	Introduce one irregular word	*y*/y/			
96		*y*/y/			

Part 4 Reading Sentences and Storybooks

- Segmenting and Blending Sounds in Words
- Reading Sentences

Lesson	Skill	New Phoneme	# of Words	Word Type	Continuous Sounds vs. Stop Sounds
97	Sounding out words:	*k*/k/	25	VC and CVC	Initial continuous sound or initial stop sound
98	• Overtly sound out some words	*k*/k/	2–4 words per		
99	• Introduce sounding out "in your head"	*k*/k/	sentence	Irregular	
100	Read four irregular words	*v*/v/	(1 sentence at		
101	Sentence reading (overt sounding out)	*v*/v/	a time)		
102	Storybook reading	*v*/v/			
103	Sounding out words:	*x*/ks/	30	VC and CVC	Initial continuous sound or initial stop sound
104	• Overtly sound out some words	*x*/ks/	3–6 words per		
105	• Introduce "Big Kid Reading"	*x*/ks/	sentence	Irregular	
106	Read seven irregular words	*q*/kw/	(2 sentences at		
107	Sentence reading (sound out each word "in your head")	*q*/kw/	a time)		
108	Storybook reading	*q*/kw/			
109	Sounding out words:	none	37	VC and CVC	Initial continuous sound or initial stop sound
110	• Overtly sound out a few words	none	3–7 words per		
111	• "Big Kid Reading"	none	sentence	Irregular	
112	Read eight irregular words	none	(1–2 sentences		
113	Sentence reading ("Big Kid Reading")	none	at a time)		
114	Storybook reading	none			
115	Sounding out words:	none	36	VC and CVC	Initial continuous sound or initial stop sound
116	• Overtly sound out CVCC words	none	4–6 words per		
117	• "Big Kid Reading"	none	sentence	VCC and CVCC	Initial continuous sound
118	Read eight irregular words	none	(2 sentences at		
119	Sentence reading ("Big Kid Reading")	none	a time)		
120	Storybook reading	none		Irregular	
121	Sounding out words:	none	43	VC and CVC	Initial continuous sound or initial stop sound
122	• Overtly sound out CVCC words	none	4–8 words per		
123	• "Big Kid Reading"	none	sentence	VCC and CVCC	Initial continuous sound
124	Read eight irregular words	none	(3 sentences at		
125	Sentence reading("Big Kid Reading")	none	a time)		
126	Storybook reading	none		Irregular	

Contents

Part 3 Reading Words

- Segmenting and Blending Sounds in Words
- Reading Simple Words

New Sound /j/
Review Sounds /a/, /o/, /r/, /b/, /i/, /n/, /g/, /u/
Key Reading Skills Letter-Sound Correspondences; Word Reading

Phonological Awareness and Alphabetic Understanding

Activity	Materials	Time
1. Alphabetic Introduce *j*/j/	Alphabet Card: *j* Letter Card: *j* (one per child)	1–2 minutes
2. Phonologic Does It Begin with /j/?	Picture Cards: *jam, inch, jeep, jet, jump rope, up*	4–5 minutes
New **3. Alphabetic** Sounds	Sounds Teacher Resource Package 3	4–5 minutes
New **4. Phonologic/Reading** Say the Sounds/ Say the Word with Fingers; Regular Words	Regular Words Teacher Resource Package 3 Word Cards: *am, man* (Lessons 73–78)	4–5 minutes

Writing and Spelling

Activity	Materials	Time
5. Writer's Warm-Up Introduce *j*	Writer's Warm-Up (one per child) Student Activity Book 3, p. 4 or 5 Tracing Cards: *j, u, g, n, i, b, r, a*	2–3 minutes
6. Integrated Phonologic/Alphabetic Practice Session: Spelling	3-Square Strip Letter Tiles: *u, a, o, g, m, n, p, b*	2–3 minutes
7. Phonologic/Spelling Word Maze	Word Maze (one per child) Student Activity Book 3, p. 6	6–8 minutes

Activity 1 Introduce Letter Name and Sound

Introduce j/j/

Objective: Children learn and trace *j*/j/.

Time: 1–2 minutes

	To Do	To Say
Introduce letter name	Hold up the *j* Alphabet Card.	Model **The name of this letter is *j*.** Lead **Say the name with me: *j*.** Test **What is the name of this letter?**
Introduce letter sound	Continue holding up the *j* Alphabet Card.	Model **The sound for this letter is /j/. When you say /j/, your tongue is up and your lips are open. Watch, /j/.** Lead **Say the sound with me: /j/.** Test **What is the sound for this letter?**
Test knowledge of letter name and sound	Continue holding up the *j* Alphabet Card. Give individual turns on letter name and sound.	Test **What is the name of this letter? What is the sound for this letter?** **Ongoing Assessment** **If...** children make an error, **then...** tell them the name or sound, have them repeat the name or sound, and return to the letter a second time.
Model tracing *j*	Model how to trace *j* using your alphabet card.	Model **Watch. I'll trace the letter *j*.** Ask children to trace the letter *j* on their letter cards three times. Have them say /j/ each time they trace the letter. **Ongoing Assessment** **If...** children make an error, **then...** put your hand over their hand and guide them to trace the letter. Then have children try to trace the letter on their own. Repeat as necessary.

Activity 2 Isolate Initial Sound

Does It Begin with /j/?

Objective: Children isolate initial /j/.

Time: 4–5 minutes

	To Do	To Say
Model names of pictures	Gather the picture cards. Hold up each picture card.	**Model** **This is ____. What is this?** Model names of pictures selected for the game. Have children repeat them. Test children on the picture names: **What is this?**
Introduce the game Does It Begin with /j/?	Practice production of the target sound.	Tell children they will play a game. They will name pictures that have the first sound /j/. **When you say /j/, your tongue is up and your lips are open. Watch, /j/. Open your lips and say /j/.**
Model the game	Model two examples: *jam, inch.*	**Model** **It's my turn. I'll say the name of the picture and then tell if it has the first sound /j/: *jam*** (exaggerate the first sound). ***Jam* has the first sound /j/. My lips are open when I say /j/, *jam*. Next picture: *inch*** (exaggerate the first sound). ***Inch* does not have the first sound /j/.**
Play the game to test knowledge of initial /j/	Test children with *jeep, jet, jump rope,* and *up.* Give individual turns.	**Test** **What is this? Does *jeep* have the first sound /j/?** Exaggerate the first sound. Confirm correct responses and prompt sound production: **Yes, *jeep* has the first sound /j/. Let's say /j/. Remember, when you say /j/, your lips are open.** Continue with the remaining cards. **Ongoing Assessment** **If...** children make an error, **then...** model the correct answer. Review the sound production cue. Have children repeat the correct answer. Return to the example a second time.

Activity 3 Discriminate Letter Sounds

Sounds

Objective: Children discriminate letter sounds.

Time: 4–5 minutes

	To Do	To Say
Introduce the activity	Display the Sounds page.	**I will point to a letter. You will tell me the sound for the letter. Some of the sounds will be quick sounds. You should say a quick sound only for as long as I touch under the letter.** (Point to the letter briefly if it is a stop sound such as /b/. Hold your finger under the letter for about two seconds if it is a continuous sound such as /aaa/.)
Test knowledge of letter sounds	Continue to display the Sounds page. Point to *a*.	**Test** **What is the <u>sound</u> for this letter?** Hold your finger under the letter for about two seconds as children say the sound. Confirm correct responses: **Yes, /aaa/.** Continue with the remaining letters, moving from left to right across the page.
	Give individual turns.	**Ongoing Assessment** **If...** children make an error, **then...** tell them the sound, have them repeat the sound, and move back two letters on the page (or repeat the letter if it is at the beginning of the page). **If...** children miss more than two sounds on the page, **then...** repeat the test for all of the letters on the page.

Activity 4 Read Words

Say the Sounds/Say the Word with Fingers; Regular Words

Objective: Children segment, blend, and read words. Time: 4–5 minutes

	To Do	To Say
Introduce the activity		**It's time to play Say the Sounds/Say the Word with Fingers. I will say the sounds of a word slowly. You'll slowly repeat each sound as you touch a finger. Then you'll say the sounds quickly to say the word.**
Lead the activity	Segment and blend *map*.	**Lead** **Let's do a three-sound word together. Hold out three fingers.** Have children hold out three fingers pointed toward you. Have them use the pointer finger of the other hand to touch a finger for each sound, moving from left to right. **Listen to the sounds:** (pause) **/mmm/ /aaa/ /p/.** Touch a finger as you say each sound without stopping between the sounds. **Say the sounds slowly with me: /mmm/ /aaa/ /p/.** Touch a finger for each sound. **Now say the sounds quickly with me to say the word.** Clap with children as you and they say the word: ***map.***
Test knowledge of segmenting and blending	Test children on *fin*. Give individual turns.	**Test** **It's your turn to do a three-sound word. Hold out three fingers. Listen to the sounds:** (pause) **/fff/ /iii/ /nnn/.** Touch a finger as you say each sound. **Say the sounds slowly.** Touch a finger for each sound as children say the sounds slowly. **Now say the sounds quickly to say the word.** Clap with children as they say the word. Repeat the test with *am, sun, man,* and *up*. For *am* and *up*, have children hold out two fingers.

Ongoing Assessment

If... children do not touch the appropriate finger for each sound,	**then...** model how to do it. Have them try again. If necessary, guide their hands to touch the appropriate fingers.
If... children stop between the sounds,	**then...** model how to say the sounds without stopping between them. Have children say the sounds again.
If... children have trouble saying the sounds quickly,	**then...** tell them the word. Say the sounds slowly and quickly for them before having them try again.

Activity 4 Read Words (continued)

	To Do	To Say
Introduce the activity	Display the Regular Words page.	**Now it's time to read some words. First, we'll say the sounds in the word slowly. Then we'll say the sounds quickly to say the word.**
Model the activity	Model sounding out and reading *am*.	**Model** **It's my turn to read a word. First, I'll say the sounds in the word slowly. Then I'll say them quickly. When I touch a letter, I'll say its sound. I won't stop between the sounds.** Point to *am* on the word page: **/aaa/ /mmm/.** Move your finger under each square as you say the sounds. Touch beneath each square for one to two seconds, without pausing between the sounds. **Now I'll say the sounds quickly to say the word: *am*.** Move your finger quickly across the arrow. **The word is *am*.**
Lead the activity	Lead children in sounding out and reading *am*.	**Lead** **Now let's read this word together. First, we'll say the sounds slowly. Then we'll say them quickly. When I touch a letter, we'll say its sound. We'll keep saying the sound until I touch the next letter. Get ready: /aaa/ /mmm/. Now let's say the sounds quickly: *am*. What's the word? *Yes, am*.**
Test sounding out and reading	Test children on sounding out and reading *am*.	**Test** **Now it's your turn to read the word. First, you'll say the sounds slowly. Then you'll say them quickly. Say the sounds. Get ready.** Move your finger beneath the squares as children say the sounds without pausing. Touch under each square for one to two seconds. **Now say the sounds quickly.** Move your finger quickly across the arrow. **What's the word?** Model, lead, and test sounding out and reading *man*.

Ongoing Assessment

If... children pause between sounds,	**then...** model saying the sounds without stopping between them. Have children sound out the word again.
If... children say the wrong sound,	**then...** keep your finger on the missed sound. Model the correct sound and have children repeat it. Have children sound out the word again.
If... children say the wrong word when they say the sounds quickly,	**then...** model the correct word and have them repeat it. Have children say the sounds slowly and quickly again.

This activity is a modification of an activity from Carnine, Silbert, and Kame'enui (1977).

To Do	To Say
Give individual turns.	Give a child one of the word cards from the word page to sound out and read. Have the child touch under each square while slowly saying the sounds and then move a finger quickly across the arrow while quickly saying the sounds. Provide physical assistance as needed.

Ongoing Assessment

If... a child makes an error,	**then...** correct the error with the whole group. Have the child who made the error sound out and read the word again.
If... children make many errors during their individual turns,	**then...** model, lead, and test each word again with the whole group. When the whole group can successfully sound out and read each word, resume individual turns.

Activity 5 Writer's Warm-Up

Introduce j

Objective: Children trace and write *j* and review writing *a, g, u, b, n, i,* and *r.*

Time: 2–3 minutes

	To Do	To Say
Review letter name and sound	Hold up the *j* Tracing Card.	Review the letter name and sound.
Model tracing *j*	Distribute a Writer's Warm-Up to each child. Continue holding up the tracing card.	**Model** **Watch as I trace the letter *j* with my finger.** Have children trace the first two letters on their warm-up sheets. Then model tracing *j* again, and have children use their pencils to trace the next two letters on their sheets.
Model writing *j*	Model writing *j* on the lined side of the tracing card.	**Model** **Watch as I write the letter *j*. I start at the dot and write the letter.** Have children write the letter two times on their warm-up sheets. Remind them to write their letters carefully and correctly. **Ongoing Assessment** **If...** children make an error, **then...** put your hand over their hand and guide the writing of the letter. Then have children write the letter on their own. Repeat as necessary.
Test children on writing *j*	Model writing *j* again.	Have children cover the letters they traced and wrote. Have them write the letter two times from memory. Then have them uncover their papers and compare the letters. **Do your letters look the same? Circle the letter that is your best work.**
Review ***a, g, u, b, n, i, r***	Gather the tracing cards.	Have children trace and write each review letter one time. **Ongoing Assessment** **If...** children make an error, **then...** use the tracing card to model tracing the letter. If necessary, guide the writing of the letter. Then have children write the letter on their own. Repeat as necessary.

Connect Sound to Letter

Practice Session: Spelling

Objective: Children segment words and connect sounds to letters.

Time: 2–3 minutes

	To Do	To Say
Introduce the activity	Gather the 3-Square Strip and the letter tiles.	**Today we're going to practice spelling some words to get ready for a word maze. We're going to touch our fingers while we say the sounds in the words. Then we're going to choose the letters that go with the sounds.**
Lead the activity	Set out the 3-Square Strip and the letter tiles. Segment the word *gum.*	Lead **The first word is *gum.* What is the first word?** Have children hold out three fingers. **Say the sounds in *gum* and touch a finger for each sound.**
	Isolate the first sound in *gum.*	**What is the first sound in *gum?*** Point to your index finger. **That's right; /g/ is the first sound in *gum.***
	Lay out two letter tiles, *g* and one other. Identify the letter for the first sound in *gum.*	**Does everyone know what the first letter in *gum* is?** Call on a child to choose the correct letter tile and place it in the first square of the strip.
	Isolate the middle sound in *gum.*	**Say the sounds in *gum* again and touch a finger for each sound. Stop when you get to the next sound. What is the next sound in *gum?*** Point to your middle finger. **That's right; /uuu/ is the next sound in *gum.***
	Lay out two letter tiles, *u* and one other. Identify the letter for the middle sound in *gum.*	**Does everyone know what the next letter in *gum* is?** Call on a child to choose the correct letter tile and place it in the middle square.
	Isolate the last sound in *gum.*	**Say the sounds in *gum* again and touch a finger for each sound. Stop when you get to the last sound. What is the last sound in *gum?*** Point to your ring finger. **That's right; /mmm/ is the last sound in *gum.***

Connect Sound to Letter (continued)

To Do	To Say
Lay out two letter tiles, *m* and one other. Identify the letter for the last sound in *gum*.	**Does everyone know what the last letter in *gum* is?** Call on a child to choose the correct letter tile and place it in the last square.
Confirm the spelling of *gum*.	**Now say each sound in *gum* with me as I point to the letters: /g/ /uuu/ /mmm/. Now say the sounds quickly to say the word: *gum*. That's right; *g-u-m* spells *gum*. The sounds in *gum* are /g/ /uuu/ /mmm/.** Practice with *nob, pan, bug,* and *mop,* as time allows.

Ongoing Assessment

If... children make an error,	**then...** model the answer, have them repeat it, and return to the sound and letter a second time.

Activity 7 Connect Sound to Letter

Word Maze

Objective: Children connect sounds to letters to spell words. Time: 6–8 minutes

	To Do	To Say
Introduce the activity	Distribute a Word Maze to each child.	**The next activity is a word maze. I'm going to say a word. You are going to spell the word by writing the letters that go with the word's sounds. Let's see if we can get through the maze!**
Model the activity	Hold up a Word Maze. Point to the first word blank.	Model **The first word in the maze is *bun*. I will say the sounds in *bun* and touch a finger for each sound: /b/ /uuu/ /nnn/. The first sound in *bun* is /b/.** Point to your index finger. **I'm going to write the first letter in *bun*.** Write a *b* in the first box. **Now you write the first letter in *bun*.** Continue using this process to model the sounds /uuu/ and /nnn/ (use your middle and ring fingers) and write the letters *u* and *n* in the middle and last boxes. Have children write these letters in the boxes with you. Confirm the spelling: **Say each sound in *bun* with me and touch your letters as we say each sound: /b/ /uuu/ /nnn/. Say the sounds quickly. That's right; *b-u-n* spells *bun*.**
Test children on spelling *gum*, *pan*, and *bog*		Test **Find your way through the maze to the next word. The next word is *gum*. What is the word? Say the sounds in *gum* and touch a finger for each sound: /g/ /uuu/ /mmm/. What is the first sound in *gum*?** Point to your index finger. **That's right; /g/ is the first sound in *gum*. Everyone, write the first letter in *gum* in the first box.** Continue in this fashion until children have identified the other sounds and letters in *gum* and have written all three letters in the squares.
	Confirm the spelling.	**Now say each sound in *gum* with me and point to your letters as we say each sound: /g/ /uuu/ /mmm/. Say the sounds quickly. That's right; *g-u-m* spells *gum*.** Repeat the test for *pan* and *bog*. After each word, have children find their way through the maze to the next word.

Ongoing Assessment

If... children make an error,	**then...** model the letter name and sound and have children repeat them. Have children write the correct letter.

New Sound /j/
Review Sounds /s/, /a/, /o/, /i/, /n/, /g/, /u/
Key Reading Skills Letter-Sound Correspondences; Word Reading: VC, CVC

Phonological Awareness and Alphabetic Understanding

Activity	Materials	Time
1. Alphabetic Introduce *j*/j/	Alphabet Card: *j* Letter Card: *j* (one per child)	1–2 minutes
2. Phonologic Which Picture Begins with /j/?	Picture Choices: 74-1, 74-2, 74-3 Teacher Resource Package 3	4–5 minutes
3. Alphabetic Sounds	Sounds Teacher Resource Package 3	4–5 minutes
4. Phonologic/Reading Say the Sounds/ Say the Word with Fingers; Regular Words	Regular Words Teacher Resource Package 3 Word Cards: *on*, *Sam* (Lessons 73–78)	4–5 minutes

Writing and Spelling

Activity	Materials	Time
5. Writer's Warm-Up Introduce *j*	Writer's Warm-Up (one per child) Student Activity Book 3, p. 7 or 8 Tracing Cards: *j, u, a, g, d, n, i, b*	2–3 minutes
6. Integrated Phonologic/Alphabetic Practice Session: Spelling	3-Square Strip Letter Tiles: *u, o, i, r, l, d, s, t*	2–3 minutes
7. Phonologic/Spelling Monster Words	Write-On/Wipe-Off Cards (three) markers (one per child/not provided)	6–8 minutes

Activity 1 Introduce Letter Name and Sound

Introduce j/j/

Objective: Children learn and trace *j*/j/.

Time: 1–2 minutes

	To Do	To Say	
Introduce letter name	Hold up the *j* Alphabet Card.	**Model**	**The name of this letter is *j*.**
		Lead	**Say the name with me: *j*.**
		Test	**What is the name of this letter?**
Introduce letter sound	Continue holding up the *j* Alphabet Card.	**Model**	**The sound for this letter is /j/. When you say /j/, your tongue is up and your lips are open. Watch, /j/. Open your lips and say /j/.**
		Lead	**Say the sound with me: /j/.**
		Test	**What is the sound for this letter?**
Test knowledge of letter name and sound	Continue holding up the *j* Alphabet Card.	**Test**	**What is the name of this letter? What is the sound for this letter?**
	Give individual turns on letter name and sound.		**Ongoing Assessment** **If...** children make an error, **then...** tell them the name or sound, have them repeat the name or sound, and return to the letter a second time.
Model tracing *j*	Model tracing *j* on your alphabet card.	**Model**	**Watch. I'll trace the letter *j*.** Ask children to trace the letter *j* on their letter cards three times. Tell them to say /j/ each time they trace the letter.
			Ongoing Assessment **If...** children make an error, **then...** put your hand over their hand and guide them to trace the letter. Then have children try to trace the letter on their own. Repeat as necessary.

Activity 2 Isolate Initial Sound

Which Picture Begins with /j/?

Objective: Children isolate initial /j/.

Time: 4–5 minutes

	To Do	To Say
Model names of pictures	Gather the picture choices. Display Picture Choice 74-1. Point to *jet.*	**Model** **This is *jet*. What is this?** Continue with *gum, rake, rose, inch,* and *jeep*. Test children on the picture names by pointing to the pictures one at a time and asking: **What is this?** Repeat for Picture Choices 74-2 *(rain, jam, bike; juice, game, up)* and 74-3 *(goose, rug, jump; bone, juggle, goal post).*
Introduce the game Which Picture Begins with /j/?	 Practice production of the target sound.	**We're going to play another game with our new sound /j/. I'll show you three pictures. You'll tell which picture has the first sound /j/.** **Let's say /j/. Remember, when you say /j/, your tongue is up and your lips are open. Watch, /j/. Open your lips and say /j/.**
Model the game	Display Picture Choice 74-1. Cover the bottom row.	**Model** **My turn. I'll show you how to play the game. This is *jet, gum, rake*. I'll find the picture that has the first sound /j/: *jet*** (exaggerate the first sound). ***Jet* has the first sound /j/.** Exaggerate the first sound and say the word: **/j/, *jet*.** Model again with the bottom row of pictures: *rose, inch, jeep.*
Play the game to test knowledge of initial /j/	Display Picture Choice 74-2. Cover the bottom row. Give individual turns.	Have children name each picture. **Which picture has the first sound /j/?** Confirm correct responses and prompt sound production: **Yes, *jam* has the first sound /j/. Let's say /j/. Remember, when you say /j/, your lips are open.** Continue with the bottom row of pictures and Picture Choice 74-3. **Ongoing Assessment** **If . . .** children make incorrect responses, **then . . .** model the correct answer. Review the sound production cue. Have children repeat the correct answer. Go back to the example a second time.

Activity 3 Discriminate Letter Sounds

Sounds

Objective: Children discriminate letter sounds.

Time: 4–5 minutes

	To Do	To Say
Introduce the activity	Display the Sounds page.	**I will point to a letter. You will say the sound for that letter. Some of the sounds will be quick sounds. You should say a quick sound only for as long as I touch under the letter.** (Point to the letter briefly if it is a stop sound such as /b/. Hold your finger under the letter for about two seconds if it is a continuous sound such as /aaa/.)
Test children on the letter sounds	Continue to display the Sounds page. Point to *j*.	**Test** **What is the <u>sound</u> for this letter?** Tap your finger under the letter as children say the sound. **Yes, /j/.** Repeat the test with each letter. If children miss more than two sounds on the page, repeat the test for all of the letters on the page.
	Give individual turns.	**Ongoing Assessment** **If...** children make an error, **then...** tell them the sound, have them repeat the sound, and move back two letters on the page (or repeat the letter if it is at the beginning of the page).

Activity 4 Read Words

Say the Sounds/Say the Word with Fingers; Regular Words

Objective: Children segment, blend, and read words. Time: 4–5 minutes

	To Do	To Say
Introduce the activity		**It's time to play Say the Sounds/Say the Word with Fingers. I will say the sounds of a word slowly. You will slowly repeat each sound as you touch a finger. Then you'll say the sounds quickly to say the word.**
Lead the activity	Segment and blend *run*.	**Lead** **Let's do a word together. Hold out three fingers.** Have children hold out three fingers pointed toward you. Have them use the pointer finger of the other hand to touch a finger for each sound, moving from left to right. **Listen to the sounds:** (pause) **/rrr/ /uuu/ /nnn/.** Touch a finger as you say each sound. **Say the sounds slowly with me: /rrr/ /uuu/ /nnn/.** Touch a finger for each sound. **Now say the sounds quickly with me to say the word.** Clap with children as you and they say the word: ***run.***
Test knowledge of segmenting and blending	Test children on segmenting and blending *mad*. Give individual turns.	**Test** **It's your turn to do a three-sound word. Hold out three fingers. Listen to the sounds:** (pause) **/mmm/ /aaa/ /d/.** Touch a finger as you say each sound. **Say the sounds slowly.** Touch a finger for each sound as children say the sounds slowly. **Now say the sounds quickly to say the word.** Clap with children as they say the word *mad.* Repeat the test with *on, if, Sam,* and *sad*. For *on* and *if,* have children hold out two fingers.

Ongoing Assessment

If... children do not touch the appropriate finger for each sound,	**then...** model how to do it. Have children try again. If needed, guide their hands to touch the appropriate fingers.
If... children stop between the sounds,	**then...** model how to say the sounds without stopping between them. Have children say the sounds again.
If... children have difficulty saying the sounds quickly,	**then...** model how to say the sounds slowly and quickly. Have children segment and blend the word again.

Activity 4 Read Words (continued)

	To Do	To Say
Introduce the activity	Display the Regular Words page.	**Now it's time to read some words. First, we'll say the sounds in the word slowly. Then we'll say the sounds quickly to say the word.**
Model the activity	Continue to display the Regular Words page. Model sounding out and reading the word *on.*	**Model** **My turn to read a word. First, I'll say the sounds in the word slowly. Then I'll say the sounds quickly to say the word. Watch my finger. Each time I touch a letter, I'll say its sound. I won't stop between the sounds.** Point to *on:* **/ooo/ /nnn/.** Touch under each square for one to two seconds, without pausing between the sounds. **Now I'll say the sounds quickly to say the word: *on.*** Move your finger quickly across the arrow as you quickly say the sounds. **The word is *on.***
Lead the activity	Continue to display the Regular Words page. Lead sounding out and reading the word *on.*	**Lead** **Now let's read the word together. First, we'll say the sounds slowly. Then we'll say the sounds quickly to say the word. When I touch a letter, say its sound with me. We'll keep saying the sound until I touch the next letter. Watch my finger. Get ready.** Point to *on:* **/ooo/ /nnn/.** Touch under each square for one to two seconds as you and children say the sounds. Do not pause between the sounds. **Now let's say the sounds quickly to say the word: *on.*** Move your finger quickly across the arrow as you and children quickly say the sounds. **What's the word? *Yes, on.***
Test sounding out and reading *on*		**Test** **Now it's your turn to read the word. First, you'll say the sounds slowly. Then you'll say the sounds quickly to say the word. Say the sounds. Get ready.** Touch under each square for one to two seconds as children say the sounds. Do not pause between the sounds. **Now say the sounds quickly.** Move you finger quickly across the arrow as children quickly say the sounds. **What's the word?**

Model, lead, and test sounding out and reading the word *Sam*. Be sure to point out that *Sam* begins with a capital *S* because it is a name, and names always begin with a capital letter. You may want to point out an *Ss* displayed together in your classroom and review the letter sounds.

Ongoing Assessment

If...children pause between sounds,	**then**...model saying the sounds without stopping between them. Have children sound out the word again.
If...children say the wrong sound,	**then**...keep your finger on the missed sound. Model the correct sound and have children repeat it. Have children sound out the word again.
If...children say the wrong word when they say the sounds quickly,	**then**...model the correct word and have children repeat it. Have children say the sounds slowly and quickly again.

To Do	To Say
Give individual turns.	Give a child one of the word cards from the word page to sound out and read. Have the child touch under each square while slowly saying the sounds and then move a finger quickly across the arrow while quickly saying the sounds. Provide physical assistance as needed.

Ongoing Assessment

If... a child makes an error,	**then...** correct the error with the whole group. Have the child who made the error sound out and read the word again.
If... children make many errors during their individual turns,	**then...** model, lead, and test each word again with the whole group. When the whole group can successfully sound out and read each word, resume individual turns.

Activity 5 Writer's Warm-Up

Lesson 74

Introduce j

Objective: Children trace and write *j* and review writing *a, g, u, d, n, i,* and *b*.

Time: 2–3 minutes

	To Do	To Say
Review letter name and sound	Hold up the *j* Tracing Card.	Review the letter name and sound: **What is the name of this letter? What is the sound for this letter?**
Model tracing *j*	Give a Writer's Warm-Up to each child. Continue holding up the tracing card.	**Model** **Watch as I trace the letter *j* with my finger.** Have children trace the first two letters on their warm-up sheets. Then model tracing *j* again and have children use their pencils to trace the next two letters on their sheets.
Model writing *j*	Model writing *j* on the lined side of the tracing card.	**Model** **Watch as I write the letter *j*. I start at the dot and write the letter.** Have children write the letter two times on their warm-up sheets. Remind them to write their letters carefully and correctly. **Ongoing Assessment** **If...** children make an error, **then...** put your hand over their hand and guide the writing of the letter. Then have children write the letter on their own. Repeat as necessary.
Test writing *j*	Model writing *j* again.	Have children cover the letters they traced and wrote. Have them write the letter two times from memory. Then have them uncover their papers and compare the letters. **Do your letters look the same? Circle the letter that is your best work.**
 Review ***a, g, u, d, n, i, b***	Gather the tracing cards.	Have children trace and write each review letter one time. **Ongoing Assessment** **If...** children make an error, **then...** use the tracing card to model tracing the letter. If needed, guide the writing of the letter. Then have children write the letter on their own. Repeat as necessary.

Connect Sound to Letter

Practice Session: Spelling

Objective: Children segment words and connect sounds to letters.

Time: 2–3 minutes

	To Do	To Say
Introduce the activity	Gather the 3-Square Strip and the letter tiles.	**Today we're going to practice spelling some words to get ready for Monster Words. We're going to touch our fingers while we say the sounds in the words. Then we're going to choose the letters that go with the sounds.**
Lead the activity	Set out the 3-Square Strip and the letter tiles. Segment the word *rod.*	**Lead** **The first word is *rod*. What is the first word?** Have children hold out three fingers. **Say the sounds in *rod* and touch a finger for each sound.**
	Isolate the first sound in *rod.*	**What is the first sound in *rod?*** Point to your index finger. **That's right; /rrr/ is the first sound in *rod*.**
	Lay out two letter tiles, *r* and one other. Identify the letter for the first sound in *rod.*	**Does everyone know what the first letter in *rod* is?** Call on a child to choose the correct letter tile and place it in the first square of the strip.
	Isolate the middle sound in *rod.*	**Say the sounds in *rod* again and touch a finger for each sound. Stop when you get to the next sound. What is the next sound in *rod?*** Point to your middle finger. **That's right; /ooo/ is the next sound in *rod*.**
	Lay out two letter tiles, *o* and one other. Identify the letter for the middle sound in *rod.*	**Does everyone know what the next letter in *rod* is?** Call on a child to choose the correct letter tile and place it in the middle square.
	Isolate the last sound in *rod.*	**Say the sounds in *rod* again and touch a finger for each sound. Stop when you get to the last sound. What is the last sound in *rod?*** Point to your ring finger. **That's right; /d/ is the last sound in *rod*.**
	Lay out two letter tiles, *d* and one other. Identify the letter for the last sound in *rod.*	**Does everyone know what the last letter in *rod* is?** Call on a child to choose the correct letter tile and place it in the last square.

Activity 6 Connect Sound to Letter (continued)

To Do	To Say
Confirm the spelling of *rod*.	**Now say each sound in *rod* with me as I point to the letters: /rrr/ /ooo/ /d/. Now say the sounds quickly to say the word: *rod*. That's right; *r-o-d* spells *rod*. The sounds in *rod* are /rrr/ /ooo/ /d/.** Practice with *lit, sit, rut,* and *lid,* as time allows.

Ongoing Assessment

If... children make an error,	**then**... model the answer, have them repeat it, and return to the sound and letter a second time.

Activity 7 Connect Sound to Letter

Monster Words

Objective: Children spell words.

Time: 6–8 minutes

	To Do	To Say
Introduce the activity	Place three Write-On/ Wipe-Off Cards on the table, facing children.	**We are going to spell some monster words. I'm going to say a word. *You* are going to spell the word by writing big monster letters that go with the word's sounds on the white cards. Let's see how many monster words we can spell!**
Model the activity	Model identifying the sounds in *dot* and spelling the word.	Model **The first word is *dot*. Listen. I will say the sounds in *dot* and touch a finger for each sound: /d/ /ooo/ /t/. The first sound in *dot* is /d/.** Point to your index finger. **I'm going to write the first letter in *dot*.** Write the letter *d* on the first white card. Write it large enough to fill most of the card. Repeat this procedure for /o/ and /t/ (use your middle and ring fingers) and write the letters *o* and *t* on the middle and last white cards. Confirm the spelling: **Say each sound in *dot* with me while I point to the letters: /d/ /ooo/ /t/. Say the sounds quickly. That's right; *d-o-t* spells *dot*.**
Test spelling *sit, rat,* and *lid*	Confirm the spelling.	Test **The next word is *sit*. What is the word? Say the sounds in *sit* and touch a finger for each sound. What is the first sound in *sit*?** Point to your index finger. **That's right; /sss/ is the first sound in *sit*.** Choose a child to write the first letter in *sit* on the first white card. Continue until children have identified the other sounds and letters in *sit* and have written them on the cards. **Now say each sound in *sit* with me while I point to the letters: /sss/ /iii/ /t/. Say the sounds quickly. That's right; *s-i-t* spells *sit*.** Repeat with *rut* and *lid*. **Ongoing Assessment** **If...** children make an error, **then...** model the letter name and sound and have children repeat them. Have children write the correct letter.

New Sound /j/
Review Sounds /m/, /f/, /t/, /l/, /a/, /o/, /b/, /i/, /n/
Key Reading Skills Letter-Sound Correspondences; Word Reading

Phonological Awareness and Alphabetic Understanding

Activity	Materials		Time
1. Alphabetic Introduce *j*/j/	Alphabet Card: *j* Letter Card: *j* (one per child)		1–2 minutes
2. Integrated Phonologic/Alphabetic Which Picture Begins with /j/?	Alphabet Card: *j* Picture Choices: 75-1, 75-2, 75-3 Teacher Resource Package 3		4–5 minutes
New **3. Alphabetic** Sounds Dash	Sounds Dash Teacher Resource Package 3	timer (not provided)	4–5 minutes
4. Phonologic/Reading Say the Sounds/ Say the Word with Fingers; Regular Words	Regular Words Teacher Resource Package 3	Word Cards: *fin, an* (Lessons 73–78)	4–5 minutes

Writing and Spelling

Activity	Materials		Time
5. Writer's Warm-Up Memory Review: *a, i, o, m, l, b, p, r, n*	Write-On/Wipe-Off Cards (one per child) markers (one per child/ not provided)	Tracing Cards: *a, i, o, m, l, b, p, r, n*	2–3 minutes
6. Integrated Phonologic/Alphabetic Practice Session: Spelling	3-Square Strip	Letter Tiles: *u, i, a, c, p, f, g, n*	2–3 minutes
7. Phonologic/Spelling Word Race	Word Race (one per child) Student Activity Book 3, p. 9		6–8 minutes

Activity 1 Introduce Letter Name and Sound

Introduce j/j/

Objective: Children learn and trace *j*/j/.

Time: 1–2 minutes

	To Do	To Say
Introduce letter name	Hold up the *j* Alphabet Card.	**Model** **The name of this letter is *j*.** **Lead** **Say the name with me: *j*.** **Test** **What is the name of this letter?**
Introduce letter sound	Continue holding up the *j* Alphabet Card.	**Model** **The sound for this letter is /j/. When you say /j/, your tongue is up and your lips are open. Watch, /j/. Open your lips and say /j/.** **Lead** **Say the sound with me: /j/.** **Test** **What is the sound for this letter?**
Test knowledge of letter name and sound	Continue holding up the *j* Alphabet Card. Give individual turns on letter name and sound.	**Test** **What is the name of this letter? What is the sound for this letter?** **Ongoing Assessment** **If...** children make an error, **then...** tell them the name or sound, have them repeat the name or sound, and return to the letter a second time.
Model tracing *j*	Distribute the *j* Letter Cards. Model tracing *j* on your alphabet card.	**Model** **Watch. I'll trace the letter *j*.** Ask children to trace the letter *j* on their letter cards three times. Tell them to say /j/ each time they trace the letter. **Ongoing Assessment** **If...** children make an error, **then...** put your hand over their hand and guide them to trace the letter. Then have children try to trace the letter on their own. Repeat as necessary.

Isolate Initial Sound

Which Picture Begins with /j/?

Objective: Children isolate initial /j/ and connect to letter. Time: 4–5 minutes

	To Do	To Say
Model names of pictures	Gather the picture choices. Display Picture Choice 75-1. Point to *rake.*	Model **This is *rake.* What is this?** Continue with *jump, boat, jam, bed,* and *rain.* Test children on the picture names by pointing to the pictures one at a time and asking: **What is this?** Repeat for Picture Choices 75-2 *(juice, read, inch; ox, box, jeep)* and 75-3 *(bee, up, juggle; roof, jet, otter).*
Introduce the game Which Picture Begins with /j/?		**We're going to play another game with our new sound /j/. I'll show you a letter and three pictures. You'll find the picture that begins with the sound for the letter.**
Model the game	Hold up the *j* Alphabet Card.	Model **The <u>name</u> of this letter is *j.* The <u>sound</u> for this letter is /j/. Remember, when you say /j/, your lips are open.** Test **What is the <u>sound</u> for this letter?**
	Display Picture Choice 75-1. Cover the bottom row.	Model **My turn. I'll show you how to play the game. This is *rake, jump, boat.* I'll find the picture that has the first sound /j/.** Point to the *j* Alphabet Card. ***Jump*** (exaggerate the first sound) **has the first sound /j/.** Exaggerate the first sound and say the word: **/j/, *jump.*** Model again with the bottom row of pictures: *jam, bed, rain.*
Play the game to test knowledge of initial /j/	Display Picture Choice 75-2. Cover the bottom row.	Have children name each picture. Point to the *j* Alphabet Card: **Which picture has the first sound /j/?** Confirm correct responses and prompt sound production: ***Yes, juice* has the first sound /j/. Let's say /j/. Remember, when you say /j/, your lips are open.** Continue with the bottom row of pictures and Picture Choice 75-3.
	Give individual turns.	**Ongoing Assessment** **If...** children make incorrect responses, **then...** model the correct answer. Review the sound production cue. Have children repeat the correct answer. Go back to the example a second time.

Activity 3 Build Sounds Fluency

Sounds Dash

Objective: Children increase fluency in identifying letter sounds. Time: 4–5 minutes

	To Do	To Say
Introduce the game Sounds Dash	Display the Sounds Dash.	**Today we are going to play the game Sounds Dash. I will point to a letter. You will say the sound for the letter. Let's see how close we can get to the finish line in one minute! Be careful, though. If there is a mistake, you will have to go back three letters. Remember, too, that you will hold some of the sounds. Some of the sounds you will say only for as long as I touch under the letter.**
Model the game	Display the Sounds Dash.	**Model** **Let's get warmed up for our Sounds Dash game. We'll practice the sounds in the first row. Then we'll start the timer for our dash.** Point to *m*. **What is the <u>sound</u> for this letter?** Hold your finger under the letter for about two seconds as children say the sound. **Yes, /mmm/.** Practice the sound of each letter in the first row.
Play the game	Display the Sounds Dash. Set the timer for one minute.	**Lead** **Now you're ready for the Sounds Dash. Everyone, look at my finger. On your mark, get set, go!** Point to *m* in the first row. **What is the <u>sound</u> for this letter?** Repeat for each sound in the first row. Then go immediately to the second row, third row, and so on. Stop the group after exactly one minute. Praise children for how far they made it. Tell them that they will have a chance to beat their score in three days when they play again.

Ongoing Assessment (Model the game)

If... children make an error,	**then...** tell them the sound, have them repeat it, and move back three letters on the page (or repeat the letter if it is at the beginning of the row).
If... children miss more than two sounds,	**then...** do not proceed with the activity. Instead, provide additional practice on the nine sounds on the page, especially those sounds children are less sure of.

Ongoing Assessment (Play the game)

If... children make an error,	**then...** tell them the sound, have them repeat it, and move back three letters (or repeat the letter if it is at the beginning of the row).

Activity 4 Read Words

Say the Sounds/Say the Word with Fingers; Regular Words

Objective: Children segment, blend, and read words.

Time: 4–5 minutes

	To Do	To Say
Introduce the activity		**It's time to play Say the Sounds/Say the Word with Fingers. I'll say the sounds of a word slowly. You'll slowly repeat each sound as you touch a finger. Then you'll say the sounds quickly to say the word.**
Lead the activity	Segment and blend *mop*.	**Lead** **Let's do a three-sound word together. Hold out three fingers.** Have children hold out three fingers pointed toward you. Have them use the pointer finger of the other hand to touch a finger for each sound, moving from left to right. **Listen to the sounds:** (pause) **/mmm/ /ooo/ /p/.** Touch a finger as you say each sound. **Say the sounds slowly with me: /mmm/ /ooo/ /p/.** Touch a finger for each sound. **Now say the sounds quickly with me to say the word.** Clap with children as you and they say the word: ***mop*.**
Test knowledge of segmenting and blending	Test children on segmenting and blending *fin*. Give individual turns.	**Test** **It's your turn to do a three-sound word. Hold out three fingers. Listen to the sounds:** (pause) **/fff/ /iii/ /nnn/.** Touch a finger as you say each sound. **Say the sounds slowly.** Touch a finger for each sound as children say the sounds slowly. **Now say the sounds quickly to say the word.** Clap with children as they say the word *fin*. Repeat the test with *it, rat, an,* and *log*. For *an* and *it*, have children hold out two fingers.

Ongoing Assessment

If . . . children do not touch the appropriate finger for each sound,	**then . . .** model how to do it. Have children try again. If needed, guide their hands to touch the appropriate fingers.
If . . . children stop between the sounds,	**then . . .** model how to say the sounds without stopping between them. Have children say the sounds again.
If . . . children have difficulty saying the sounds quickly,	**then . . .** model how to say the sounds slowly and quickly. Have children segment and blend the word again.

Activity 4 Read Words (continued)

	To Do	To Say
Introduce the activity	Display the Regular Words page.	**Now it's time to read some words. First, we'll say the sounds in the word slowly. Then we'll say the sounds quickly to say the word.**
Model the activity	Continue to display the Regular Words. Model sounding out and reading the word *fin.*	**Model** **My turn to read a word. First, I'll say the sounds in the word slowly. Then I'll say the sounds quickly to say the word. Watch my finger. Each time I touch a letter, I'll say its sound. I won't stop between the sounds.** Point to *fin:* **/fff/ /iii/ /nnn/.** Touch under each square for one to two seconds, without pausing between the sounds. **Now I'll say the sounds quickly to say the word: *fin.*** Move your finger quickly across the arrow as you quickly say the sounds. **The word is *fin.***
Lead the activity	Continue to display the Regular Words. Lead children in sounding out and reading the word *fin.*	**Lead** **Now let's read the word together. First, we'll say the sounds slowly. Then we'll say the sounds quickly to say the word. When I touch a letter, say its sound with me. We'll keep saying the sound until I touch the next letter. Watch my finger. Get ready.** Point to *fin:* **/fff/ /iii/ /nnn/.** Touch under each square for one to two seconds as you and children say the sounds. Do not pause between the sounds. **Now let's say the sounds quickly to say the word: *fin.*** Move your finger quickly across the arrow as you and children quickly say the sounds. **What's the word? *Yes, fin.***
Test sounding out and reading *fin*		**Test** **Now it's your turn to read the word. First, you'll say the sounds slowly. Then you'll say the sounds quickly to say the word. Say the sounds. Get ready.** Touch under each square for one to two seconds as children say the sounds. Do not pause between the sounds. **Now say the sounds quickly.** Move your finger quickly across the arrow as children quickly say the sounds. **What's the word?** Model, lead, and test sounding out and reading the word *an.*

Ongoing Assessment

If... children pause between sounds,	**then...** model saying the sounds without stopping between them. Have children sound out the word again.
If... children say the wrong sound,	**then...** keep your finger on the missed sound. Model the correct sound and have children repeat it. Have children sound out the word again.
If... children say the wrong word when they say the sounds quickly,	**then...** model the correct word and have children repeat it. Have children say the sounds slowly and quickly again.

To Do	To Say
Give individual turns.	Give a child one of the word cards from the word page to sound out and read. Have the child touch under each square while slowly saying the sounds and then move a finger quickly across the arrow while quickly saying the sounds. Provide physical assistance as needed.

Ongoing Assessment

If . . . a child makes an error,	**then . . .** correct the error with the whole group. Have the child who made the error sound out and read the word again.
If . . . children make many errors during their individual turns,	**then . . .** model, lead, and test each word again with the whole group. When the whole group can successfully sound out and read each word, resume individual turns.

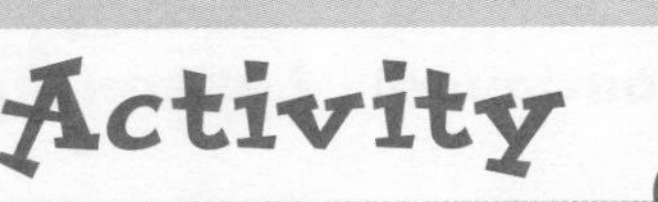

5 Writer's Warm-Up

Memory Review: a, i, o, m, l, b, p, r, n

Objective: Children write review letters from memory.

Time: 2–3 minutes

	To Do	To Say
Review letter names	Gather the tracing cards. Hold up each tracing card.	Test **What is the <u>name</u> of this letter?**
Introduce the activity	Distribute a Write-On/ Wipe-Off Card and a marker to each child.	**I will name a letter. You will write the letter on your Write-On/Wipe-Off Card.**
Model the activity	Hold up a Write-On/ Wipe-Off Card.	Model **I'll show you how this activity works. The first letter is *n*. Now I'll write the letter *n* on my Write-On/ Wipe-Off Card.** Write an *n* on your card.
Test the activity	Test children on writing *a, i, o, m, l, b, p, r,* and *n.*	Dictate a letter name and have children write the letter on their Write-On/ Wipe-Off Cards. Reinforce the group on the letter name: **Everyone, what's the name of the letter you wrote?** Between each turn, erase the cards.

Ongoing Assessment

If... children write the wrong letter or don't remember a letter, **then...** show them the tracing card of the correct letter. Model tracing the letter and say the letter name.

Activity 6 Connect Sound to Letter

Practice Session: Spelling

Objective: Children segment words and connect the sounds to letters.

Time: 2–3 minutes

	To Do	To Say
Introduce the activity	Gather the 3-Square Strip and the letter tiles.	**Today we're going to practice spelling some words to get ready for a word race. We're going to touch our fingers while we say the sounds in the words. Then we're going to choose the letters that go with the sounds.**
Lead the activity	Set out the 3-Square Strip and the letter tiles. Segment the word *pin*.	**Lead** **The first word is *pin*. What is the first word?** Have children hold out three fingers. **Say the sounds in *pin* and touch a finger for each sound.**
	Isolate the first sound in *pin*.	**What is the first sound in *pin?*** Point to your index finger. **That's right; /p/ is the first sound in *pin*.**
	Lay out two letter tiles, *p* and one other. Identify the letter for the first sound in *pin*.	**Does everyone know what the first letter in *pin* is?** Call on a child to choose the correct letter tile and place it in the first square of the strip.
	Isolate the middle sound in *pin*.	**Say the sounds in *pin* again and touch a finger for each sound. Stop when you get to the next sound. What is the next sound in *pin?*** Point to your middle finger. **That's right; /iii/ is the next sound in *pin*.**
	Lay out two letter tiles, *i* and one other. Identify the letter for the middle sound in *pin*.	**Does everyone know what the next letter in *pin* is?** Call on a child to choose the correct letter tile and place it in the middle square.
	Isolate the last sound in *pin*.	**Say the sounds in *pin* again and touch a finger for each sound. Stop when you get to the last sound. What is the last sound in *pin?*** Point to your ring finger. **That's right; /nnn/ is the last sound in *pin*.**
	Lay out two letter tiles, *n* and one other. Identify the letter for the last sound in *pin*.	**Does everyone know what the last letter in *pin* is?** Call on a child to choose the correct letter tile and place it in the last square.

Activity 6 Connect Sound to Letter (continued)

To Do	To Say
Confirm the spelling of *pin*.	**Now say each sound in pin with me as I point to the letters: /p/ /iii/ /nnn/. Now say the sounds quickly to say the word: *pin*. That's right; *p-i-n* spells *pin*. The sounds in *pin* are /p/ /iii/ /nnn/.** Practice with *fun, pig, can,* and *cup,* as time allows.

Ongoing Assessment

If...	then...
If... children make an error,	**then...** model the answer, have them repeat it, and return to the sound and letter a second time.

Activity 7 Connect Sound to Letter

Word Race

Objective: Children connect sounds to letters to spell words. Time: 6–8 minutes

	To Do	To Say
Introduce the activity	Distribute a Word Race to each child.	**We're going to have a word race. I'm going to say a word. You're going to spell the word by listening to the word's sounds. Let's see who wins the race!**
Model the activity	Hold up a Word Race. Model identifying the letter for the first sound in *bus*.	**Model** **The first word is for the frog: *bus*. Listen. I'll say the sounds in *bus* and touch a finger for each sound: /b/ /uuu/ /sss/. The first sound in *bus* is /b/.** Point to your index finger. **I'm going to write the first letter in *bus*.** Write a *b* in the first box. **Now you write the first letter in *bus*.**
	Model identifying the letter for the middle sound in *bus*.	**I'll say the sounds in *bus* again and touch a finger for each sound. I'll stop when I get to the next sound: /b/ /uuu/. The next sound in *bus* is /uuu/.** Point to your middle finger. **I'm going to write the next letter in *bus*.** Write a *u* in the middle box. **Now you write the next letter in *bus*.**
	Model identifying the letter for the last sound in *bus*.	**I'll say the sounds in *bus* again and touch a finger for each sound. I'll stop when I get to the last sound: /b/ /uuu/ /sss/. The last sound in *bus* is /sss/.** Point to your ring finger. **I'm going to write the last letter in *bus*.** Write an *s* in the last box. **Now you write the last letter in *bus*.**
	Confirm the spelling of *bus*.	**Now say each sound in *bus* with me and point to your letters as we say each sound: /b/ /uuu/ /sss/. Say the sounds quickly to say the word: *bus*. That's right; *b-u-s* spells *bus*.**

	To Do	To Say
Test children on spelling *job, rat, jut,* and *sat*		Test **The next word is for the turtle. This word is *job*. What is the word? Say the sounds in *job* and touch a finger for each sound. What is the first sound in *job?*** Point to your index finger. **That's right; /j/ is the first sound in *job*. Everyone, write the first letter in *job* in the first box.** Continue in this fashion until children have identified the other sounds and letters in *job*. Then confirm the spelling: **Now say each sound in *job* with me and point to your letters as we say each sound: /j/ /ooo/ /b/. Say the sounds quickly: *job*. That's right; *j-o-b* spells *job*.** Continue with *rat, jut,* and *sat.*

Ongoing Assessment

If... children make an error,	**then...** model the letter name and sound and have children repeat them. Have children write the correct letter.

New Sound /w/
Review Sounds /t/, /a/, /o/, /r/, /i/, /n/, /u/, /j/
Key Reading Skills Letter-Sound Correspondences; Word Reading

Phonological Awareness and Alphabetic Understanding

Activity	Materials		Time
1. Alphabetic Introduce *w*/w/	Alphabet Card: *w*	Letter Card: *w* (one per child)	1–2 minutes
2. Phonologic Does It Begin with /w/?	Picture Cards: *watermelon, gate, web, well, wave, jet*		4–5 minutes
3. Alphabetic Sounds	Sounds Teacher Resource Package 3		4–5 minutes
4. Phonologic/Reading Say the Sounds/ Say the Word with Fingers; Regular Words	Regular Words Teacher Resource Package 3 Word Cards: *sat, lid* (Lessons 73–78)		4–5 minutes

Writing and Spelling

Activity	Materials		Time
5. Writer's Warm-Up Introduce *w*	Writer's Warm Up (one per child) Student Activity Book 3, p. 10 or 11 Tracing Cards: *w, a, g, u, b, n, i, j*		2–3 minutes
6. Integrated Phonologic/Alphabetic Practice Session: Spelling	3-Square Strip	Letter Tiles: *u, a, o, j, b, r, t, s*	2–3 minutes
7. Phonologic/Spelling Word Dictation	Write-On/Wipe-Off Cards (one per child)	markers (one per child/not provided)	6–8 minutes

Activity 1 Introduce Letter Name and Sound

Introduce w/w/

Objective: Children learn and trace w/w/.

Time: 1–2 minutes

	To Do	To Say	
Introduce letter name	Hold up the *w* Alphabet Card.	Model	**The name of this letter is *w*.**
		Lead	**Say the name with me: *w*.**
		Test	**What is the name of this letter?**
Introduce letter sound	Continue holding up the *w* Alphabet Card.	Model	**The sound for this letter is /www/. When you say /www/, your lips make a circle. Say /www/ and feel your lips make a circle.**
		Lead	**Say the sound with me: /www/.**
		Test	**What is the sound for this letter?**
Test knowledge of letter name and sound	Continue holding up the *w* Alphabet Card.	Test	**What is the name of this letter? What is the sound for this letter?**
	Give individual turns.		**Ongoing Assessment** — If... children make an error, then... tell them the name or sound, have them repeat the name or sound, and return to the letter a second time.
Model tracing *w*	Distribute the *w* Letter Cards. Model tracing *w* on your alphabet card.	Model	**Watch. I'll trace the letter *w*.** Ask children to trace the letter *w* on their letter cards three times. Tell them to say /www/ each time they trace the letter.
			Ongoing Assessment — If... children make an error, then... put your hand over their hand and guide them to trace the letter. Then have children try to trace the letter on their own. Repeat as necessary.

Isolate Initial Sound

Does It Begin with /w/?

Objective: Children isolate initial /w/.

Time: 4–5 minutes

	To Do	To Say
Model names of pictures	Gather the picture cards. Hold up each picture card.	**Model** **This is ____. What is this?** Model names of pictures selected for the game. Have children repeat them. Test children on the picture names: **What is this?**
Introduce the game Does It Begin with /w/?	Practice production of the target sound.	Tell children they will play a game. They will find the pictures with the first sound /www/. **When you say /www/, your lips make a circle. Say /www/ and feel your lips make a circle.**
Model the game	Display the *watermelon* Picture Card. Display the *gate* Picture Card.	**Model** **It's my turn. I'll say the name of the picture and then tell if it has the first sound /www/: *watermelon*** (exaggerate the first sound). ***Watermelon* has the first sound /www/. My lips make a circle, *watermelon*.** **Next picture: *gate*** (exaggerate the first sound). ***Gate* does not have the first sound /www/.**
Play the game to test knowledge of initial /w/	Display the *web* Picture Card. Give individual turns.	**Test** **What is this? Does *web*** (exaggerate the first sound) **have the first sound /www/?** Confirm correct responses and prompt sound production: **Yes, *web* has the first sound /www/. Let's say /www/. Remember, when you say /www/, your lips make a circle.** Repeat the test with *well, wave,* and *jet.* **Ongoing Assessment** **If...** children make incorrect responses, **then...** model the correct answer. Review the sound production cue. Have children repeat the correct answer. Return to the example a second time.

Activity 3 Discriminate Letter Sounds

Sounds

Objective: Children discriminate letter sounds.

Time: 4–5 minutes

	To Do	To Say
Introduce the activity	Display the Sounds page.	**I will point to a letter, and you will say the sound for that letter. Remember that some of the sounds are quick sounds. You should say a quick sound only for as long as I touch under the letter.** (Point to the letter briefly if it is a stop sound such as /b/. Hold your finger under the letter for about two seconds if it is a continuous sound such as /aaa/.)
Test children on the letter sounds	Continue to display the Sounds page. Point to *o*.	**Test** **What is the <u>sound</u> for this letter?** Hold your finger under the letter for about two seconds as children say the sound. **Yes, /ooo/.** Repeat the test for each letter. If children miss more than two sounds on the page, repeat the test for all of the letters.
	Give individual turns.	**Ongoing Assessment** **If...** children make an error, **then...** tell them the sound, have them repeat it, and move back two letters (or repeat the letter if it is at the beginning of the page).

Activity 4 Read Words

Say the Sounds/Say the Word with Fingers; Regular Words

Objective: Children segment, blend, and read words. Time: 4–5 minutes

	To Do	To Say
Introduce the activity		**It's time to play Say the Sounds/Say the Word with Fingers. I'll say the sounds of a word slowly. You'll slowly repeat each sound as you touch a finger. Then you'll say the sounds quickly to say the word.**
Lead the activity	Segment and blend the word *on*.	**Lead** **Let's do a two-sound word together. Hold out two fingers.** Have children hold out two fingers pointed toward you. Have them use the pointer finger of the other hand to touch a finger for each sound, moving from left to right. **Listen to the sounds:** (pause) **/ooo/ /nnn/.** Touch a finger as you say each sound. **Say the sounds slowly with me: /ooo/ /nnn/.** Touch a finger for each sound. **Now say the sounds quickly with me to say the word.** Clap with children as you and they say the word: ***on.***
Test knowledge of segmenting and blending	Test children on segmenting and blending *sat*. Give individual turns.	**Test** **It's your turn to do a three-sound word. Hold out three fingers. Listen to the sounds:** (pause) **/sss/ /aaa/ /t/.** Touch a finger as you say each sound. **Say the sounds slowly.** Touch a finger for each sound as children slowly say the sounds. **Now say the sounds quickly to say the word.** Clap with children as they say the word *sat*. Repeat the test for *lid, rag, fan,* and *in*. For *in*, have children hold out two fingers.

Ongoing Assessment

If... children do not touch the appropriate finger for each sound,	**then...** model how to do it. Have children try again. If needed, guide their hands to touch the appropriate fingers.
If... children stop between the sounds,	**then...** model how to say the sounds without stopping between them. Have children say the sounds again.
If... children have difficulty saying the sounds quickly,	**then...** model how to say the sounds slowly and quickly. Have children segment and blend the word again.

Activity 4 Read Words (continued)

	To Do	To Say
Introduce the activity	Display the Regular Words page.	**Now it's time to read some words. First, we'll say the sounds in the word slowly. Then we'll say the sounds quickly to say the word. Some of the words end with quick sounds, so you'll need to watch my finger carefully.**
Model the activity	Continue to display the Regular Words page. Model sounding out and reading the word *sat.*	**Model** **My turn to read a word. First, I'll say the sounds in the word slowly. Then I'll say the sounds quickly to say the word. Watch my finger. Each time I touch a letter, I'll say its sound. I won't stop between the sounds.** Point to *sat:* **/sss/ /aaa/ /t/.** Touch under the first two squares for one to two seconds. Tap your finger under the third square. Do not pause between the sounds. **Now I'll say the sounds quickly to say the word: *sat.*** Move your finger quickly across the arrow as you quickly say the sounds. **The word is *sat.***
Lead the activity	Continue to display the Regular Words page. Lead children in sounding out and reading the word *sat.*	**Lead** **Now let's read the word together. First, we'll say the sounds slowly. Then we'll say the sounds quickly to say the word. When I touch a letter, say its sound with me. We'll keep saying the sound until I touch the next letter. Watch my finger because this word ends with a quick sound. Get ready.** Point to *sat:* **/sss/ /aaa/ /t/.** Touch under the first two squares for one to two seconds. Tap your finger under the third square. Do not pause between the sounds. **Now let's say the sounds quickly to say the word: *sat.*** Move your finger quickly across the arrow as you and children quickly say the sounds. **What's the word? *Yes, sat.***

	To Do	To Say
Test sounding out and reading *sat*		**Test** **Now it's your turn to read the word. First, you'll say the sounds slowly. Then you'll say the sounds quickly to say the word. Say the sounds. Get ready.** Touch under the first two squares for one to two seconds. Tap your finger under the third square. Do not pause between the sounds. **Now say the sounds quickly.** Move you finger quickly across the arrow as children quickly say the sounds. **What's the word?** Model, lead, and test sounding out and reading the word *lid.*

Ongoing Assessment

If... children pause between sounds,	**then...** model saying the sounds without stopping between them. Have children sound out the word again.
If... children say the wrong sound,	**then...** keep your finger on the missed sound. Model the correct sound and have children repeat it. Have children sound out the word again.
If... children say the wrong word when they say the sounds quickly,	**then...** model the correct word and have children repeat it. Have children say the sounds slowly and quickly again.

	To Do	To Say
	Give individual turns.	Give a child one of the word cards from the word page to sound out and read. Have the child touch under each square while slowly saying the sounds and then move a finger quickly across the arrow while quickly saying the sounds. Provide physical assistance as needed.

Ongoing Assessment

If... a child makes an error,	**then...** correct the error with the whole group. Have the child who made the error sound out and read the word again.
If... children make many errors during their individual turns,	**then...** model, lead, and test each word again with the whole group. When the whole group can successfully sound out and read each word, resume individual turns.

Activity  Writer's Warm-Up

Introduce w

Objective: Children trace and write *w* and review writing *a, g, u, b, n, i,* and *j*.

Time: 2–3 minutes

	To Do	To Say
Review letter name and sound	Hold up the *w* Tracing Card.	**What is the <u>name</u> of this letter? What is the <u>sound</u> for this letter?**
Model tracing *w*	Distribute a Writer's Warm-Up to each child. Continue holding up the *w* Tracing Card.	Model **Watch as I trace the letter *w* with my finger.** Have children trace the first two *w*'s on their Writer's Warm-Up. Then model tracing *w* again, and have children use their pencils to trace the next two letters on their warm-up sheet.
Model writing *w*	Model writing *w* on the lined side of the tracing card.	Model **Watch as I write the letter *w*. I start at the dot and write the letter.** Have children write the letter two times on their Writer's Warm-Up. Remind them to write their letters carefully and correctly. **Ongoing Assessment** — **If...** children make an error, **then...** have them write the letter again. If needed, place your hand over their hand and guide them to write the letter. Then have them write the letter on their own. Repeat as necessary.
Test writing *w*	Model writing *w* again.	Have children cover the letters they traced and wrote. Have them write the letter *w* two times from memory. Then have them uncover their papers and compare the letters. **Do your letters look the same? Circle your best letter.**
 ***a, g, u, b, n, i, j***		Have children trace and write each review letter. **Ongoing Assessment** — **If...** children make an error, **then...** use the tracing card to model tracing the letter and ask them to write the letter again. If needed, guide the writing of the letter. Then have children try to write the letter on their own. Repeat as necessary.

Connect Sound to Letter

Practice Session: Spelling

Objective: Children segment words and connect sounds to letters.

Time: 2–3 minutes

	To Do		To Say
Introduce the activity	Gather the 3-Square Strip and the letter tiles.		**Today we're going to practice spelling some words to get ready for a word dictation. We're going to touch our fingers while we say the sounds in the words. Then we're going to choose the letters that go with the sounds.**
Lead the activity	Set out the 3-Square Strip and the letter tiles. Segment the word *job.*	**Lead**	**The first word is *job*. What is the first word?** Have children hold out three fingers. **Say the sounds in *job* and touch a finger for each sound.**
	Isolate the first sound in *job.*		**What is the first sound in *job?*** Point to your index finger. **That's right; /j/ is the first sound in *job*.**
	Lay out two letter tiles, *j* and one other. Identify the letter for the first sound in *job.*		**Does everyone know what the first letter in *job* is?** Call on a child to choose the correct letter tile and place it in the first square of the strip.
	Isolate the middle sound in *job.*		**Say the sounds in *job* again and touch a finger for each sound. Stop when you get to the next sound. What is the next sound in *job?*** Point to your middle finger. **That's right; /ooo/ is the next sound in *job*.**
	Lay out two letter tiles, *o* and one other. Identify the letter for the middle sound in *job.*		**Does everyone know what the next letter in *job* is?** Call on a child to choose the correct letter tile and place it in the middle square.
	Isolate the last sound in *job.*		**Say the sounds in *job* again and touch a finger for each sound. Stop when you get to the last sound. What is the last sound in *job?*** Point to your ring finger. **That's right; /b/ is the last sound in *job*.**
	Lay out two letter tiles, *b* and one other. Identify the letter for the last sound in *job.*		**Does everyone know what the last letter in *job* is?** Call on a child to choose the correct letter tile and place it in the last square.

To Do	To Say
Confirm the spelling of *job*.	**Now say each sound in *job* with me as I point to the letters: /j/ /ooo/ /b/. Now say the sounds quickly to say the word: *job*. That's right; *j-o-b* spells *job*. The sounds in *job* are /j/ /ooo/ /b/.** Practice with *rub, bus, jut,* and *bat,* as time allows.

Ongoing Assessment

If...	then...
If... children make an error,	**then...** model the answer, have them repeat it, and return to the sound and letter a second time.

7 Connect Sound to Letter

Lesson **76**

Word Dictation

Objective: Children connect sounds to letters to spell words. Time: 6–8 minutes

	To Do	To Say
Introduce the activity	Distribute a Write-On/ Wipe-Off Card and a marker to each child.	**I'm going to say a word. You are going to spell the word by writing the letters that go with the word's sounds. Let's see how many words we can spell!**
Lead the activity	Identify the letter for the first sound in *rat*.	**Lead** **The first word is *rat*. Listen. I will say the sounds in *rat* and touch a finger for each sound: /rrr/ /aaa/ /t/. The first sound in *rat* is /rrr/.** Point to your index finger. **I'm going to write the first letter in *rat*.** Write the letter *r* on your card. **Now you write the first letter in *rat*.**
	Identify the letter for the middle sound in *rat*.	**Listen. I will say the sounds in *rat* and touch a finger for each sound. I'll stop when I get to the next sound: /rrr/ /aaa/. The middle sound in *rat* is /aaa/.** Point to your middle finger. **I'm going to write the middle letter in *rat*.** Write the letter *a* on your card. **Now you write the middle letter in *rat*.**
	Identify the letter for the last sound in *rat*.	**Listen. I will say the sounds in *rat* and touch a finger for each sound. I'll stop when I get to the last sound: /rrr/ /aaa/ /t/. The last sound in *rat* is /t/.** Point to your ring finger. **I'm going to write the last letter in *rat*.** Write the letter *t* on your card. **Now you write the last letter in *rat*.**
	Confirm the spelling of *rat*.	**Say each sound in *rat* with me and point to your letters as we say each sound: /rrr/ /aaa/ /t/. Say the sounds quickly. That's right; *r-a-t* spells *rat*.**

Connect Sound to Letter (continued)

	To Do	To Say
Test children on spelling *cob*, *jab*, *bus*, *sat*, *tub*, and *rot*		Test **The next word is *cob*. What is the word? Say the sounds in *cob* and touch a finger for each sound. What is the first sound in *cob*?** Point to your index finger. **That's right; /k/ is the first sound in *cob*. Everyone, write the first letter in *cob* on your card.** Continue in this fashion until children have identified the other sounds and letters in *cob*.
	Confirm the spelling.	**Now say each sound in *cob* with me and point to your letters as we say each sound: /k/ /ooo/ /b/. Say the sounds quickly. That's right; *c-o-b* spells *cob*.**
		Continue with *jab, bus, sat, tub,* and *rot.*

Ongoing Assessment

If... children make an error, **then...** model the letter name and sound and have children repeat them. Have children write the correct letter.

New Sound /w/
Review Sounds /l/, /o/, /b/, /i/, /g/, /u/, /j/
Key Reading Skills Letter-Sound Correspondences; Word Reading: VC, CVC

Phonological Awareness and Alphabetic Understanding

Activity	Materials		Time
1. Alphabetic Introduce *w*/w/	Alphabet Card: *w*	Letter Card: *w* (one per child)	1–2 minutes
2. Phonologic Which Picture Begins with /w/?	Picture Choices: 77-1, 77-2, 77-3 Teacher Resource Package 3		4–5 minutes
3. Alphabetic Sounds	Sounds Teacher Resource Package 3		4–5 minutes
4. Phonologic/Reading Say the Sounds/ Say the Word with Fingers; Regular Words	Regular Words Teacher Resource Package 3	Word Cards: *not, in* (Lessons 73–78)	4–5 minutes

Writing and Spelling

Activity	Materials	Time
5. Writer's Warm-Up Introduce *w*	Writer's Warm-Up (one per child) Student Activity Book 3, p. 12 or 13 Tracing Cards: *w, a, g, u, j, n i, d*	2–3 minutes
6. Integrated Phonologic/Alphabetic Practice Session: Spelling	3-Square Strip Letter Tiles: *u, o, i, j, f, n, g, d*	2–3 minutes
7. Phonological/Spelling Jack and the Beanstalk	Jack and the Beanstalk (one per child) Student Activity Book 3, p. 14	6–8 minutes

Activity 1 Introduce Letter Name and Sound

Introduce w/w/

Objective: Children learn and trace w/w/.

Time: 1–2 minutes

	To Do	To Say	
Introduce letter name	Hold up the *w* Alphabet Card.	Model	**The <u>name</u> of this letter is *w*.**
		Lead	**Say the <u>name</u> with me: *w*.**
		Test	**What is the <u>name</u> of this letter?**
Introduce letter sound	Continue holding up the *w* Alphabet Card.	Model	**The <u>sound</u> for this letter is /www/. When you say /www/, your lips make a circle. Say /www/ and feel your lips make a circle.**
		Lead	**Say the <u>sound</u> with me: /www/.**
		Test	**What is the <u>sound</u> for this letter?**
Test knowledge of letter name and sound	Continue holding up the *w* Alphabet Card.	Test	**What is the <u>name</u> of this letter? What is the <u>sound</u> for this letter?**
	Give individual turns.		**Ongoing Assessment** **If**...children make an error, **then**...tell them the name or sound, have them repeat the name or sound, and return to the letter a second time.
Model tracing *w*	Distribute the *w* Letter Cards. Model how to trace *w* using your alphabet card.	Model	**Watch. I'll trace the letter *w*.** Have children trace the *w* on their letter cards three times. Tell them to say /www/ each time they trace the letter.
			Ongoing Assessment **If**...children make an error, **then**...put your hand over their hand and guide the tracing of the letter. Then have children try to trace the letter on their own. Repeat as necessary.

Activity 2 Isolate Initial Sound

Which Picture Begins with /w/?

Objective: Children isolate initial /w/.

Time: 4–5 minutes

	To Do	To Say
Model names of pictures	Gather the picture choices. Display Picture Choice 77-1. Point to *gum*.	**Model** **This is *gum*. What is this?** Continue with *net, web, wood, goalpost,* and *nail*. Test children on the picture names by pointing to the pictures one at a time and asking: **What is this?** Repeat for Picture Choices 77-2 *(alligator, wave, nut; nest, ant, wall)* and 77-3 *(wheel, nose, inch; goose, well, apple)*.
Introduce the game Which Picture Begins with /w/?	Practice production of the target sound.	**We're going to play another game with our new sound /www/. I'll show you three pictures. You'll find the picture that has the first sound /www/.** **Let's say /www/. When you say /www/, your lips make a circle. Say /www/ and feel your lips make a circle.**
Model the game	Display Picture Choice 77-1. Cover the bottom row.	**Model** **It's my turn. I'll show you how to play the game. This is *gum, net, web*. I'll find the picture that has the first sound /www/: *web*. *Web* has the first sound /www/.** Exaggerate the first sound and say the word: **/www/, *web*.** Model again with the bottom row of pictures: *wood, goalpost, nail*.
Play the game to test knowledge of initial /w/	Display Picture Choice 77-2. Cover the bottom row. Give individual turns.	Have children name each picture. **Which picture has the first sound /www/?** Confirm correct responses and prompt sound production: **Yes, *wave* has the first sound /www/. Let's say /www/. Remember, when you say /www/, your lips make a circle.** Continue with the bottom row of pictures and Picture Choice 77-3. **Ongoing Assessment** **If**... children make incorrect responses, **then**... model the correct answer. Review the sound production cue. Have children repeat the correct answer. Go back to the example a second time.

Activity 3 Discriminate Letter Sounds

Sounds

Objective: Children identify letter sounds.

Time: 4–5 minutes

	To Do	To Say
Introduce the activity	Display the Sounds page.	Tell children that you will point to a letter. They will say the sound for the letter. Remind them that some of the sounds will be quick sounds. They should say these sounds only for as long as you touch under the letter.
Test children on the letter sounds	Continue to display the Sounds page. Point to *o*.	**Test** **What is the sound for this letter?** Hold your finger under the letter for about two seconds as children say the sound. ***Yes, /ooo/.*** Continue with the remaining letters. If children miss more than two sounds on the page, repeat the test for all of the letters on the page.
	Give individual turns.	**Ongoing Assessment** **If...** children make an error, **then...** tell them the sound, have them repeat it, and move back two letters on the page (or repeat the letter if it is at the beginning of the page).

Activity 4 Read Words

Say the Sounds/Say the Word with Fingers; Regular Words

Objective: Children segment, blend, and read words. Time: 4–5 minutes

	To Do	To Say
Introduce the activity		**It's time to play Say the Sounds/Say the Word with Fingers. I will say the sounds of a word slowly. You will slowly repeat each sound as you touch a finger. Then you will say the sounds quickly to say the word.**
Lead the activity	Lead children in segmenting and blending *not*.	Lead **Let's do a three-sound word together. Hold out three fingers.** Have children hold out three fingers pointed toward you. Have them use the pointer finger of the other hand to touch a finger for each sound, moving from left to right. **Listen to the sounds:** (pause) **/nnn/ /ooo/ /t/.** Touch a finger as you say each sound, without stopping between the sounds. **Say the sounds slowly with me: /nnn/ /ooo/ /t/.** Touch a finger for each sound. **Now say the sounds quickly with me to say the word.** Clap with children as you and they say the word: ***not.***
Test knowledge of segmenting and blending	Test children on segmenting and blending *sad*. Give individual turns.	Test **It's your turn to do a three-sound word. Hold out three fingers. Listen to the sounds:** (pause) **/sss/ /aaa/ /d/.** Touch a finger for each sound, without stopping between the sounds. **Say the sounds slowly.** Touch a finger for each sound as children say the sounds slowly. **Now say the sounds quickly to say the word.** Clap with children as they say the word *sad.* Repeat the test with *mom, in, mud,* and *fat*. For *in*, have children hold out two fingers.

Ongoing Assessment

If... children do not touch the appropriate finger for each sound,	**then...** model how to do it. Have them try again. If necessary, guide children's hands to touch the appropriate fingers.
If... children stop between the sounds,	**then...** model how to say the sounds without stopping between them. Have children say the sounds again.
If... children have trouble saying the sounds quickly,	**then...** tell them the word. Say the sounds slowly and quickly again before having them try again.

Activity 4 Read Words (continued)

	To Do	To Say
Introduce the activity	Display the Regular Words page.	**Now it's time to read some words. First, we'll say the sounds in the word slowly. Then we'll say the sounds quickly to say the word. Some of the words end with quick sounds, so you'll need to watch my finger carefully.**
Model the activity	Continue to display the Regular Words page. Model sounding out and reading the word *not.*	**Model** **It's my turn to read a word. First, I'll say the sounds in the word slowly. Then I'll say the sounds quickly to say the word. Watch my finger. Each time I touch a letter, I'll say its sound. I won't stop between the sounds.** Point to *not:* **/nnn/ /ooo/ /t/.** Touch under the first two squares for one to two seconds. Tap your finger under the third square. Do not pause between the sounds. **Now I'll say the sounds quickly to say the word: *not.*** Move your finger quickly across the arrow as you quickly say the sounds. **The word is *not.***
Lead the activity	Continue to display the Regular Words. Lead children in sounding out and reading the word *not.*	**Lead** **Now let's read the word together. First, we'll say the sounds slowly. Then we'll say the sounds quickly to say the word. When I touch a letter, say its sound with me. We'll keep saying the sound until I touch the next letter. Watch my finger because this word ends with a quick sound. Get ready.** Point to *not:* **/nnn/ /ooo/ /t/.** Touch under the first two squares for one to two seconds. Tap your finger under the third square. Do not pause between the sounds. **Now let's say the sounds quickly to say the word: *not.*** Move your finger quickly across the arrow as you and children quickly say the sounds. **What's the word? *Yes, not.***

	To Do	To Say
Test sounding out and reading *not*		**Test** **Now it's your turn to read the word. First, you'll say the sounds slowly. Then you'll say the sounds quickly to say the word. Say the sounds. Get ready.** Touch under the first two squares for one to two seconds. Tap your finger under the third square. Do not pause between the sounds. **Now say the sounds quickly.** Move your finger quickly across the arrow as children quickly say the sounds. **What's the word?** Model, lead, and test sounding out and reading the word *in*.

Ongoing Assessment

If . . . children pause between sounds,	**then . . .** model saying the sounds without stopping between them. Have children sound out the word again.
If . . . children say the wrong sound,	**then . . .** keep your finger on the missed sound. Model the correct sound and have children repeat it. Have children sound out the word again.
If . . . children say the wrong word when they say the sounds quickly,	**then . . .** model the correct word and have children repeat it. Have children say the sounds slowly and quickly again.

	To Do	To Say
	Give individual turns.	Give a child one of the word cards from the word page to sound out and read. Have the child touch under each square while slowly saying the sounds and then move a finger quickly across the arrow while quickly saying the sounds. Provide physical assistance as needed.

Ongoing Assessment

If . . . a child makes an error,	**then . . .** correct the error with the whole group. Have the child who made the error sound out and read the word again.
If . . . children make many errors during their individual turns,	**then . . .** model, lead, and test each word again with the whole group. When the whole group can successfully sound out and read each word, resume individual turns.

Activity  Writer's Warm-Up

Introduce w

Objective: Children trace and write *w* and review writing *a, g, u, j, n, i,* and *d*.

Time: 2–3 minutes

	To Do	To Say
Review letter name and sound	Hold up the *w* Tracing Card.	**What is the name of this letter? What is the sound for this letter?**
Model tracing *w*	Distribute a Writer's Warm-Up to each child. Hold up the *w* Tracing Card. Model tracing *w* with your finger.	Model **Watch as I trace the letter *w*. Now you trace the first two letter *w*'s on your warm-up sheet with your finger.**
	Model tracing *w* again.	**Use your pencil to trace the next two *w*'s.**
Model writing *w*	Hold up the lined side of the *w* Tracing Card.	Model **Watch as I write the letter *w*. I start at the dot and write the letter.** **Now you write two letter *w*'s. Start at the dot like I did. Write carefully.** **Ongoing Assessment** **If**... children make an error, **then**... have them write the letter again. If needed, place your hand over their hand and guide them to write the letter. Then have them write the letter on their own. Repeat as necessary.
Test writing *w*	Model writing *w* again.	Have children cover the letters they traced and wrote. Have them write the letter *w* two times from memory. Then have them uncover their papers and compare the letters. **Do your letters look the same? Circle your best letter.**
 Review ***a, g, u, j, n, i, d***	Gather the tracing cards.	**Trace *a*. Now write *a* with your pencil.** Continue this procedure for the remaining letters. **Ongoing Assessment** **If**... children make an error, **then**... use the tracing card to model tracing the letter and ask them to write the letter again. If needed, guide the writing of the letter. Then have children try to write the letter on their own. Repeat as necessary.

Connect Sound to Letter

Practice Session: Spelling

Objective: Children segment words and connect sounds to letters.

Time: 2–3 minutes

	To Do	To Say
Introduce the activity	Gather the 3-Square Strip and the letter tiles.	**Today we're going to practice spelling some words to get ready for Jack and the Beanstalk. We're going to touch our fingers while we say the sounds in the words. Then we're going to choose the letters that go with the sounds.**
Lead the activity	Set out the 3-Square Strip and the letter tiles. Segment the word *fun.*	**Lead** **The first word is *fun*. What is the first word?** Have children hold out three fingers. **Say the sounds in *fun* and touch a finger for each sound.**
	Isolate the first sound in *fun.*	**What is the first sound in *fun?*** Point to your index finger. **That's right; /fff/ is the first sound in *fun.***
	Lay out two letter tiles, *f* and one other. Identify the letter for the first sound in *fun.*	**Does everyone know what the first letter in *fun* is?** Call on a child to choose the correct letter tile and place it in the first square of the strip.
	Isolate the middle sound in *fun.*	**Say the sounds in *fun* again and touch a finger for each sound. Stop when you get to the next sound. What is the next sound in *fun?*** Point to your middle finger. **That's right; /uuu/ is the next sound in *fun.***
	Lay out two letter tiles, *u* and one other. Identify the letter for the middle sound in *fun.*	**Does everyone know what the next letter in *fun* is?** Call on a child to choose the correct letter tile and place it in the middle square.
	Isolate the last sound in *fun.*	**Say the sounds in *fun* again and touch a finger for each sound. Stop when you get to the last sound. What is the last sound in *fun?*** Point to your ring finger. **That's right; /nnn/ is the last sound in *fun.***
	Lay out two letter tiles, *n* and one other. Identify the letter for the last sound in *fun.*	**Does everyone know what the last letter in *fun* is?** Call on a child to choose the correct letter tile and place it in the last square.

 Connect Sound to Letter (continued)

To Do	To Say
Confirm the spelling of *fun.*	**Now say each sound in *fun* with me as I point to the letters: /fff/ /uuu/ /nnn/. Now say the sounds quickly to say the word: *fun.* That's right; *f-u-n* spells *fun.* The sounds in *fun* are /fff/ /uuu/ /nnn/.** Practice with *jog, dog, nod,* and *fin,* as time allows.

Ongoing Assessment

If... children make an error,	**then...** model the answer, have them repeat it, and return to the sound and letter a second time.

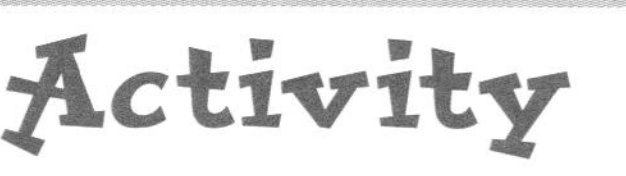 

Connect Sound to Letter

Jack and the Beanstalk

Objective: Children connect sounds to letters to spell words. Time: 6–8 minutes

	To Do	To Say	
Introduce the activity	Distribute a Jack and the Beanstalk sheet to each child.	**I'm going to say a word. You are going to spell the word by writing the letters that go with the word's sounds. Let's see if we can climb the beanstalk to reach the castle!**	
Lead the activity	Hold up a Jack and the Beanstalk sheet. Point to the word space at the bottom of the beanstalk.	**Lead**	**The first word is at the bottom of the beanstalk: *dug*. Listen. I will say the sounds in *dug* and touch a finger for each sound: /d/ /uuu/ /g/. The first sound in *dug* is /d/.** Point to your index finger. **I'm going to write the first letter in *dug*.** Write the letter *d* in the first box. **Now you write the first letter in *dug*.**
	Identify the letter for the middle sound in *dug*.		**Listen. I will say the sounds in *dug* and touch a finger for each sound. I'll stop when I get to the next sound: /d/ /uuu/. The next sound in *dug* is /uuu/.** Point to your middle finger. **I'm going to write the middle letter in *dug*.** Write the letter in the middle box. **Now you write the middle letter in *dug*.**
	Identify the letter for the last sound in *dug*.		**Listen. I will say the sounds in *dug* and touch a finger for each sound: /d/ /uuu/ /g/. The last sound in *dug* is /g/.** Point to your ring finger. **I'm going to write the last letter in *dug*.** Write the letter in the last box. **Now you write the last letter in *dug*.**
	Confirm the spelling of *dug*.		**Say each sound in *dug* with me and point to your letters as we say each sound: /d/ /uuu/ /g/. Say the sounds quickly. That's right; *d-u-g* spells *dug*.**

Connect Sound to Letter (continued)

	To Do	To Say	
Test children on spelling *fin, fog, jug,* and *nod*		**Test**	**Find your way up the beanstalk to the next word. This word is *fin*. What is the word? Say the sounds in *fin* and touch a finger for each sound: /fff/ /iii/ /nnn/. What is the first sound in *fin*?** Point to your index finger. **That's right; /fff/ is the first sound in *fin*. Everyone, write the first letter in *fin* in the first box.** Continue in this fashion until children have identified the other sounds and letters in *fin*.
	Confirm the spelling.		**Now say each sound in *fin* with me and point to your letters as we say each sound: /fff/ /iii/ /nnn/. Say the sounds quickly. That's right; *f-i-n* spells *fin*.** Continue with *fog, jug,* and *nod*.

Ongoing Assessment

If... children make an error,	**then...** model the letter name and sound and have children repeat them. Have children write the correct letter.

New Sound /w/
Review Sounds /p/, /k/, /s/, /d/, /r/, /a/, /o/, /i/, /n/
Key Reading Skills Letter-Sound Correspondences; Word Reading: VC, CVC

Phonological Awareness and Alphabetic Understanding

Activity	Materials		Time
1. **Alphabetic** Introduce *w*/w/	Alphabet Card: *w*	Letter Card: *w* (one per child)	1–2 minutes
2. **Integrated Phonologic Alphabetic** Which Picture Begins with /w/?	Alphabet Card: *w* Picture Choices: 78-1, 78-2, 78-3 Teacher Resource Package 3		4–5 minutes
3. **Alphabetic** Sounds Dash	Sounds Dash Teacher Resource Package 3	timer (not provided)	4–5 minutes
New 4. **Reading** Word Reading Game	Game Board 3 game markers (one per child/ not provided) number cube (not provided)	Word Cards: *am, man, on, Sam, fin, an, sat, lid, not, in* (Lessons 73–78)	4–5 minutes

Writing and Spelling

Activity	Materials		Time
5. **Writer's Warm-Up** Treasure Hunt	Treasure Hunt (one per child) Student Activity Book 3, p. 15 Tracing Cards: *j, w, n, u, r, b, g, a*		2–3 minutes
6. **Integrated Phonologic/Alphabetic** Practice Session: Spelling	3-Square Strip	Letter Tiles: *u, i, o, j, p, m, g, l*	2–3 minutes
7. **Phonologic/Spelling** Word Page	Word Page (one per child) Student Activity Book 3, p. 16		6–8 minutes

Activity 1 Introduce Letter Name and Sound

Introduce w/w/

Objective: Children learn and trace w/w/.

Time: 1–2 minutes

	To Do	To Say	
Introduce letter name	Hold up the *w* Alphabet Card.	Model	**The <u>name</u> of this letter is *w*.**
		Lead	**Say the <u>name</u> with me: *w*.**
		Test	**What is the <u>name</u> of this letter?**
Introduce letter sound	Continue holding up the *w* Alphabet Card.	Model	**The <u>sound</u> for this letter is /www/. When you say /www/, your lips make a circle. Say /www/ and feel your lips make a circle.**
		Lead	**Say the <u>sound</u> with me: /www/.**
		Test	**What is the <u>sound</u> for this letter?**
Test knowledge of letter name and sound	Continue holding up the *w* Alphabet Card.	Test	**What is the <u>name</u> of this letter? What is the <u>sound</u> for this letter?**
	Give individual turns.		**Ongoing Assessment** If . . . children make an error, then . . . tell them the name or sound, have them repeat the name or sound, and return to the letter a second time.
Model tracing *w*	Distribute the *w* Letter Cards. Model tracing *w* on your Alphabet Card.	Model	**Watch. I'll trace the letter *w*.** Ask children to trace the letter *w* on their letter cards three times. Tell them to say /www/ each time they trace the letter.
			Ongoing Assessment If . . . children make an error, then . . . put your hand over their hand and guide the tracing of the letter. Then have children try to trace the letter on their own. Repeat as necessary.

Activity 2 Isolate Initial Sound

Which Picture Begins with /w/?

Objective: Children isolate initial /w/ and connect to letter. Time: 4–5 minutes

	To Do	To Say
Model names of pictures	Gather the picture choices. Display Picture Choice 78-1. Point to *rose*.	**Model** **This is *rose.* What is this?** Continue with *wood, boat, run, bat,* and *web*. Test children on the picture names by pointing to the pictures one at a time and asking: **What is this?** Repeat for Picture Choices 78-2 *(bag, jam, wave; wheel, rug, juice)* and 78-3 *(wall, jump, bed; jeep, well, read)*.
Introduce the game Which Picture Begins with /w/?		**We are going to play a game. I will show you a letter and three pictures. You will find the picture that begins with the sound for the letter.**
Model the game	Hold up the *w* Alphabet Card.	**Model** **I'll show you how to play the game. The name of this letter is *w*. The sound for this letter is /www/. Remember, when you say /www/, your lips make a circle.**
		Test **What is the sound for this letter?**
	Display Picture Choice 78-1. Cover the bottom row.	**Model** **This is *rose, wood, boat.* Now I'll find the picture that has the first sound /www/.** Point to the letter *w*. ***Wood*** (exaggerate the first sound). ***Wood* has the first sound /www/.** Exaggerate the first sound of the correct picture and say the word: **/www/, *wood*.** Model another example with *run, bat,* and *web*.
Play the game to test knowledge of /w/	Hold up the *w* Alphabet Card.	**Test** **What is the sound for this letter?**
	Display Picture Choice 78-2. Cover the bottom row.	Have children name each picture: **What is this?** Point to *w*. **Which picture has the first sound /www/?** Confirm correct responses and prompt sound production: **Yes, *wave* has the first sound /www/. Let's say /www/. When you say /www/, your lips make a circle.** Continue with the bottom row of pictures and Picture Choice 78-3.
	Give individual turns.	**Ongoing Assessment** — **If . . .** children make incorrect responses, **then . . .** model the correct answer. Review the sound production cue. Have children repeat the correct answer. Go back to the example a second time.

Activity 3 Build Sounds Fluency

Sounds Dash

Objective: Children increase fluency in identifying letter sounds.

Time: 4–5 minutes

	To Do	To Say
Introduce the activity	Display the Sounds Dash.	**I will point to a letter and you will say the sound for that letter. Be careful, though. If I hear a mistake, the group will have to go back three letters. Remember to say a sound only for as long as I touch under the letter. Some of the sounds will be quick sounds.**
Model the activity	Review the sounds in the first row of the Sounds Dash.	**Model** **Let's get warmed up for our Sounds Dash. We'll practice the sounds in the first row. Then we'll start the timer for our dash.** Point to *a*. **What is the <u>sound</u> for this letter?** Hold your finger under the letter for about two seconds. **Yes, /aaa/.** Practice the sound of each letter in the first row. **Ongoing Assessment** **If...** children make an error, **then...** tell them the sound, have them repeat it, and move back three letters on the page (or repeat the letter if it is at the beginning of the row). **If...** children miss more than two sounds in the first row, **then...** do not proceed with the activity. Instead, provide additional practice on the nine sounds on the page, especially those sounds children are less sure of.
Lead the activity	Continue to display the Sounds Dash. Set a timer for one minute.	**Test** **Now you're ready for the Sounds Dash. Let's see how far we can get in one minute! Everybody, eyes on my finger. On your mark, get set, go!** Point to *a* in the first row. **What is the <u>sound</u> for this letter?** Repeat for each letter in the first row. Then go immediately to the second row, and so on, until one minute is up. Reinforce children's progress in the Sounds Dash. Tell them that they will have a chance to beat their score when they play the game again in three days. **Ongoing Assessment** **If...** children make an error, **then...** tell them the sound, have them repeat it, and move back three letters (or repeat the letter if it is at the beginning of the row).

Activity 4 Read Words

Word Reading Game

Objective: Children segment, blend, and read words. Time: 4–5 minutes

	To Do	To Say
Introduce the Word Reading Game	Gather Game Board 3, a marker for each child, a number cube, and the word cards. Place the word cards face down in a pile on the table.	**We're going to play a new game. Each of you will have a turn to roll the number cube, pick the top card from the pile, and sound out and read the word on the card. If you correctly sound out and read the word, you will move your marker the number of spaces shown on the number cube. Then you will place the word card at the bottom of the pile, and someone else will have a turn.**
Play the game	Have children take turns playing the game.	After a child rolls the number cube and picks up the top card, ask him or her to sound out and read the word: **Say the sounds. Get ready. Now say the sounds quickly to say the word. What's the word?** Play the game until one player makes it to the finish line or time runs out.

Ongoing Assessment

If... children pause between sounds,	**then...** model saying the sounds without stopping between them. Have children sound out the word again.
If... children say the wrong sound,	**then...** keep your finger on the missed sound. Model the correct sound and have children repeat it. Have children sound out the word again.
If... children say the wrong word when they say the sounds quickly,	**then...** model the correct word and have children repeat it. Have children say the sounds slowly and quickly again.

5 Writer's Warm-Up

Treasure Hunt

Objective: Children write letters.

Time: 2–3 minutes

	To Do	To Say
Introduce the activity	Distribute a Treasure Hunt to each child.	**We are going to go on a treasure hunt. I'm going to tell you the name of a letter, and you are going to write it. Let's see if we can get past the monsters and find the hidden treasure!**
Model the activity	Hold up a Treasure Hunt. Point to the first letter space.	**Model** **Let's do one together. The first letter is *j*. Watch as I write the letter *j*.** Write the letter *j* on your sheet. **Now you write the letter *j*.**
Lead the activity		Say the name of each remaining letter: *w, n, u, r, b, g, a.* Have children write the letter. Reinforce the group on each letter name: **Everyone, what's the <u>name</u> of the letter you wrote?**

Ongoing Assessment

If...children write the wrong letter or don't remember a letter, **then**...show them the tracing card of the correct letter and model tracing the letter.

Connect Sound to Letter

Practice Session: Spelling

Objective: Children segment words and connect sounds to letters.

Time: 2–3 minutes

	To Do	To Say
Introduce the activity	Gather the 3-Square Strip and the letter tiles.	**Today we're going to practice spelling some words to get ready for a Word Page. We're going to touch our fingers while we say the sounds in the words. Then we're going to choose the letters that go with the sounds.**
Lead the activity	Set out the 3-Square Strip and the letter tiles. Segment the word *lip*.	**Lead** **The first word is *lip*. What is the first word?** Have children hold out three fingers. **Say the sounds in *lip* and touch a finger for each sound.**
	Isolate the first sound in *lip*.	**What is the first sound in *lip?*** Point to your index finger. **That's right; /lll/ is the first sound in *lip*.**
	Lay out two letter tiles, *l* and one other. Identify the letter for the first sound in *lip*.	**Does everyone know what the first letter in *lip* is?** Call on a child to choose the correct letter tile and place it in the first square of the strip.
	Isolate the middle sound in *lip*.	**Say the sounds in *lip* again and touch a finger for each sound. Stop when you get to the next sound. What is the next sound in *lip?*** Point to your middle finger. **That's right; /iii/ is the next sound in *lip*.**
	Lay out two letter tiles, *i* and one other. Identify the letter for the middle sound in *lip*.	**Does everyone know what the next letter in *lip* is?** Call on a child to choose the correct letter tile and place it in the middle square.
	Isolate the last sound in *lip*.	**Say the sounds in *lip* again and touch a finger for each sound. Stop when you get to the last sound. What is the last sound in *lip?*** Point to your ring finger. **That's right; /p/ is the last sound in *lip*.**
	Lay out two letter tiles, *p* and one other. Identify the letter for the last sound in *lip*.	**Does everyone know what the last letter in *lip* is?** Call on a child to choose the correct letter tile and place it in the last square.

To Do	To Say
Confirm the spelling of *lip*.	**Now say each sound in *lip* with me as I point to the letters: /lll/ /iii/ /p/. Now say the sounds quickly to say the word: *lip*. That's right; *l-i-p* spells *lip*. The sounds in *lip* are /lll/ /iii/ /p/.** Practice with *jug, gum, mop,* and *jig,* as time allows.

Ongoing Assessment

If... children make an error,	**then...** model the answer, have them repeat it, and return to the sound and letter a second time.

Activity 7 Connect Sound to Letter

Word Page

Objective: Children connect sounds to letters to spell words. Time: 6–8 minutes

	To Do	To Say	
Introduce the activity	Distribute a Word Page to each child.		**We're going to spell words that go with each picture. Let's spell words for all of the pictures on this page!**
Lead the activity	Identify the letter for the first sound in *mop*.	**Lead**	**The first picture is *mop*. Listen. I will say the sounds in *mop* and touch a finger for each sound: /mmm/ /ooo/ /p/. The first sound in *mop* is /mmm/.** Point to your index finger. **I'm going to write the first letter in *mop*.** Write an *m* in the first letter space. **Now you write the first letter in *mop*.**
	Identify the letter for the middle sound in *mop*.		**Listen. I will say the sounds in *mop* and touch a finger for each sound. I'll stop when I get to the next sound: /mmm/ /ooo/. The middle sound in *mop* is /ooo/.** Point to your middle finger. **I'm going to write the middle letter in *mop*.** Write an *o* in the middle letter space. **Now you write the middle letter in *mop*.**
	Identify the letter for the last sound in *mop*.		**Listen. I will say the sounds in *mop* and touch a finger for each sound. I'll stop when I get to the last sound: /mmm/ /ooo/ /p/. The last sound in *mop* is /p/.** Point to your ring finger. **I'm going to write the last letter in *mop*.** Write a *p* in the last letter space. **Now you write the last letter in *mop*.**
	Confirm the spelling.		**Say each sound in *mop* with me and point to your letters as we say each sound: /mmm/ /ooo/ /p/. Say the sounds quickly. That's right; *m-o-p* spells *mop*.**

	To Do	To Say
Test children on spelling *pig, lip, gum,* and *jam*		Test **Look at the next picture. This is *pig*. What is this? Say the sounds in *pig* and touch a finger for each sound. What is the first sound in *pig*?** Point to your index finger. **That's right; /p/ is the first sound in *pig*. Everyone, write the first letter in *pig* in the first letter space.** Continue until children have identified the other sounds and letters in *pig*.
	Confirm the spelling.	**Now say each sound in *pig* with me and point to your letters as we say each sound: /p/ /iii/ /g/. Say the sounds quickly. That's right; *p-i-g* spells *pig*.**
		Repeat the test with *lip, gum,* and *jam*.

Ongoing Assessment

If... children make an error,	**then...** model the letter name and sound and have children repeat them. Have children write the correct letter.

New Sound /e/
Review Sounds /m/, /p/, /a/, /o/, /g/, /u/, /j/, /w/
Key Reading Skills Letter-Sound Correspondence; Word Reading: VC, CVC

Phonological Awareness and Alphabetic Understanding

Activity	Materials	Time
1. Alphabetic Introduce *e*/e/	Alphabet Card: *e* Letter Card: *e* (one per child)	1–2 minutes
2. Phonologic Does It Begin with /e/?	Picture Cards: *egg, elephant, escalator, elbow, jam, game*	4–5 minutes
3. Alphabetic Sounds	Sounds Teacher Resource Package 3	4–5 minutes
4. Phonologic/Reading Say the Sounds/ Say the Word with Fingers; Regular Words	Regular Words Teacher Resource Package 3 Word Cards: *us, fun, sad* (Lessons 79–84)	4–5 minutes

Writing and Spelling

Activity	Materials	Time
5. Writer's Warm-Up Introduce *e*	Writer's Warm-Up (one per child) Student Activity Book 3, p. 17 or 18 Tracing Cards: *e, w, g, u, b, n, i, j*	2–3 minutes
6. Integrated Phonologic/Alphabetic Practice Session: Spelling	3-Square Strip Letter Tiles: *j, o, g, a, i, m, n, p*	2–3 minutes
7. Phonologic/Spelling Word Dictation	Write-On/Wipe-Off Cards (one per child) marker (one per child/not provided)	6–8 minutes

Activity 1 Introduce Letter Name and Sound

Introduce e/e/

Objective: Children identify letter name and sound: *e*/e/.

Time: 1–2 minutes

	To Do	To Say	
Introduce letter name	Hold up the *e* Alphabet Card.	Model	**The name of this letter is *e*.**
		Lead	**Say the name with me: *e*.**
		Test	**What is the name of this letter?**
Introduce letter sound	Continue holding up the *e* Alphabet Card.	Model	**The sound for this letter is /eee/. When you say /eee/, your mouth is open, and your tongue is behind your bottom teeth. Say /eee/. Did your mouth open? Yes, your mouth is open, and your tongue is behind your bottom teeth. Say /eee/.**
		Lead	**Say the sound with me: /eee/.**
		Test	**What is the sound for this letter?**
Test letter name and sound	Continue holding up the *e* Alphabet Card.	Test	**What is the name of this letter? What is the sound for this letter?**
	Give individual turns.		**Ongoing Assessment** **If...** children make an error, **then...** tell them the name or sound, have them repeat the name or sound, and return to the letter a second time.
Model tracing *e*	Distribute an *e* Letter Card to each child. Model how to trace *e* using your alphabet card.	Model	**Watch. I'll trace the letter *e*. Now you try. Trace the letter *e* on your letter card three times. Say /eee/ each time you trace the letter.**
			Ongoing Assessment **If...** children make an error, **then...** put your hand over their hand and guide the tracing of the letter. Then have children try to trace the letter on their own. Repeat as necessary.

2 Isolate Initial Sound

Does It Begin with /e/?

Objective: Children isolate initial /e/.

Time: 4–5 minutes

	To Do	To Say
Model names of pictures	Gather the picture cards. Place the *egg* Picture Card on the table.	**Model** **This is *egg*. What is this?** Continue with *elephant, escalator, elbow, jam,* and *game.*
	Have children identify each picture again.	**Test** **What is this?**
Introduce the game Does It Begin with /e/?	Practice production of the target sound.	**We're going to play a game. You'll need to find the pictures that begin with /eee/. Let's say /eee/. When you say /eee/, your mouth is open, and your tongue is behind your bottom teeth. Say /eee/. Did your mouth open? *Yes*, your mouth is open, and your tongue is behind your bottom teeth. Say /eee/.**
Model the game	Gather the *egg* and *jam* Picture Cards. Place *egg* on the table.	**Model** **My turn. I'll say the name of the picture and then tell if it begins with /eee/: *egg*** (exaggerate the first sound). ***Egg* begins with /eee/. My mouth is open and my tongue is behind my bottom teeth when I say /eee/, *egg*. Next picture: *jam*** (exaggerate the first sound). ***Jam* does not begin with /eee/.**
Test knowledge of initial /e/	Place the *elephant* Picture Card on the table.	**Test** **Your turn. What is this? Does *elephant* begin with /eee/?** Confirm correct responses and prompt sound production: **Yes, *elephant* begins with /eee/. Let's say /eee/. When you say /eee/, your mouth is open and your tongue is behind your bottom teeth; /eee/.** Continue the test with three other examples: *escalator, game, elbow.*
	Give individual turns.	**Ongoing Assessment** **If . . .** children make incorrect responses, **then . . .** model the correct answer. Review the sound production cue. Have children repeat the correct answer. Go back to the example a second time.

Activity 3 Discriminate Letter Sounds

Sounds

Objective: Children connect sound to letter.

Time: 4–5 minutes

	To Do	To Say
Introduce the activity	Display the Sounds page.	**I'll point to a letter and you'll say the sound for the letter. Some of the sounds will be quick sounds and some of the sounds you'll hold. *You'll* need to say each sound only for as long as I touch the letter.**
Test children on the sounds	Point to the first letter on the Sounds page. Note: If the letter has a stop sound, such as /b/, point to the letter briefly. If the letter has a continuous sound, such as /aaa/, hold your finger under the sound for about two seconds.	**Test** **What is the <u>sound</u> for this letter? *Yes,* /www/.** Repeat this test for each letter. If children miss more than two sounds on the page, repeat the test for all the letters on the page. Then give individual turns.

Ongoing Assessment

If... children make an error,	**then...** tell them the sound, have them repeat it, and move back two letters on the page or repeat the letter if it's at the beginning of the page.

Activity 4 Read Words

Say the Sounds/Say the Word with Fingers; Regular Words

Objective: Children segment, blend, and read words. Time: 4–5 minutes

	To Do	To Say
Introduce the activity		**It's time to play Say the Sounds/Say the Word with Fingers. I'll say the sounds of a word slowly. *You'll* slowly repeat each sound as you touch a finger. Then you'll say the sounds quickly to say the word.**
Lead the activity	Lead children in segmenting and blending *rip.*	Lead **Let's do a three-sound word together. Hold out three fingers.** Have children hold out three fingers pointed toward you. Have them use the pointer finger of the other hand to touch a finger for each sound, moving from left to right. **Listen to the sounds:** (pause) **/rrr/ /iii/ /p/.** Touch a finger as you say each sound. **Say the sounds slowly with me: /rrr/ /iii/ /p/.** Touch a finger for each sound. **Now say the sounds quickly with me to say the word.** Clap with children as you and they say the word: ***rip.***
Test knowledge of segmenting and blending	Test children on segmenting *mad.*	Test **It's your turn to do a three-sound word. Hold out three fingers. Listen to the sounds:** (pause) **/mmm/ /aaa/ /d/.** Touch a finger as you say each sound. **Say the sounds slowly.** Only children say the sounds, but you and they touch a finger for each sound.

Ongoing Assessment

If...	then...
If... children do not touch the appropriate finger for each sound,	**then...** model how to do it. Have children try again. If needed, guide their hands to touch the appropriate fingers.
If... children stop between the sounds,	**then...** model how to say the sounds without stopping between them. Have children say the sounds again.

	To Do	To Say
	Test children on blending *mad.*	Test **Now say the sounds quickly to say the word.** Clap with children as they say the word *mad.*

Ongoing Assessment

If...	then...
If... children have difficulty saying the sounds quickly,	**then...** model how to say the sounds slowly and quickly. Have children segment and blend the word again.

Repeat the test with *us, fun, at,* and *sad.* For *us* and *at,* have children hold out two fingers. Then give individual turns.

	To Do	To Say
Introduce the activity	Gather the word cards. Display the Regular Words card.	**Now it's time to read some words. First, we'll say the sounds in the word slowly. Then we'll say the sounds quickly to say the word. Some of the words end with quick sounds, so you'll need to watch my finger carefully.**
Lead children in sounding out and reading the word *us*	Continue to display the Regular Words card. Point to *us*.	Lead **Let's read this word together. First, we'll say the sounds slowly. Then we'll say the sounds quickly to say the word. When I touch a letter, say its sound with me. We'll keep saying the sound until I touch the next letter. Watch my finger. Get ready.** Point to *us*: **/uuu/ /sss/.** Touch under each square for one to two seconds as you and children say the sounds. Do not pause between the sounds. **Now let's say the sounds quickly to say the word: *us*.** Move your finger quickly across the arrow as you and children quickly say the sounds. **What's the word? *Yes, us*.**
Test children on sounding out and reading the word *us*		Test **Now it's your turn to read the word. First, you'll say the sounds slowly. Then you'll say the sounds quickly to say the word. Say the sounds. Get ready.** Touch under each square for one to two seconds as children say the sounds. Do not pause between the sounds. **Now say the sounds quickly.** Move your finger quickly across the arrow as children quickly say the sounds. **What's the word? *Yes, us*.**

Ongoing Assessment

If...	then...
If... children pause between sounds,	**then...** model saying the sounds without stopping between them. Have children sound out the word again.
If... children say the wrong sound,	**then...** keep your finger on the missed sound. Model the correct sound and have children repeat it. Have children sound out the word again.
If... children say the wrong word when they say the sounds quickly,	**then...** model the correct word and have children repeat it. Have children say the sounds slowly and quickly again.

Lead and test children on sounding out and reading the words *fun* and *sad*. For *sad*, tap your finger under the final stop sound /d/.

To Do	To Say
Test the group.	Point to the words in random order. Have the group say the sounds slowly and then quickly.
Give individual turns.	Give a child one of the word cards to sound out and read. Have the child touch under each square while slowly saying the sounds and then move a finger quickly across the arrow while quickly saying the sounds. Provide physical assistance as needed.

Ongoing Assessment

If... a child makes an error,	**then...** correct the error with the whole group. Have the child who made the error sound out and read the word again.
If... children make many errors during their individual turns,	**then...** model, lead, and test each word again with the whole group. When the whole group can successfully sound out and read each word, resume individual turns.

Activity 5 Writer's Warm-Up

Introduce *e*

Objective: Children trace and write *e* and review writing *w, g, u, b, n, i,* and *j*.

Time: 2–3 minutes

	To Do	To Say
Review letter name and sound	Hold up the *e* Tracing Card.	**What is the name of this letter? What is the sound for this letter?**
Model tracing *e*	Distribute a Writer's Warm-Up to each child. Hold up the *e* Tracing Card.	Model **Watch as I trace the letter *e* with my finger.** Lead **Now you trace the first two letter *e*'s on your warm-up sheet with your finger.** Model tracing *e* again. Then have children use their pencils to trace the next two *e*'s.
Model writing *e*	Hold up the lined side of the *e* Tracing Card.	Model **Watch as I write the letter *e*. I start at the dot and write the letter.** Lead **Now you write two letter e's. Start at the dot like I did. Write carefully.** **Ongoing Assessment** **If...** children make an error, **then...** place your hand over their hand and guide them to write the letter. Then have them write the letter on their own. Repeat as necessary.
Test children on writing *e*	Hold up the lined side of the *e* Tracing Card. Model writing *e* again.	Have children cover the letters they traced and wrote. Have them write the letter *e* two times from memory. Then have them uncover their papers and compare the letters. **Do your letters look the same? Circle your best letter.**
Review ***w, g, u, b, n, i, j***	Gather the tracing cards.	**Trace *w*. Now write *w* with your pencil.** Continue this procedure for the remaining letters. **Ongoing Assessment** **If...** children make an error, **then...** use the tracing card to model tracing the letter. If necessary, guide children to write the letter. Then have them write the letter on their own. Repeat as necessary.

Connect Sound to Letter

Practice Session: Spelling

Objective: Children segment words and connect sounds to letters.

Time: 2–3 minutes

	To Do	To Say
Introduce the activity	Gather the 3-Square Strip and the letter tiles.	**Today we are going to practice spelling for Word Dictation. We are going to touch our fingers while we say the sounds in some words. Then we are going to choose the letters that go with the sounds.**
Lead the activity	Set out the 3-Square Strip. Lead children in segmenting the word *jog*.	**Lead** **The first word is *jog*. What is the word?** Have children hold out three fingers. **Say the sounds in *jog* and touch a finger for each sound.**
	Lay out two letter tiles, *j* and one other. Identify the initial letter in *jog*.	Point to the first square on the strip. **Does everyone know what the first letter in *jog* is?** Call on a child to identify the *j* and place it in the first square.
	Isolate the middle sound in *jog*.	**Say the sounds in *jog* again and touch a finger for each sound. Stop when you get to the next sound.**
	Lay out two letter tiles, *o* and one other. Identify the letter for the middle sound in *jog*.	**Does everyone know what the next letter in *jog* is?** Call on a child to choose the correct letter tile and place it in the middle square of the 3-Square Strip.
	Isolate the final sound in *jog*.	**Say the sounds in *jog* again and touch a finger for each sound. Stop when you get to the last sound.**
	Lay out two letter tiles, *g* and one other. Identify the letter for the final sound in *jog*.	**Does everyone know what the last letter in *jog* is?** Call on a child to choose the correct letter tile and place it in the last square of the 3-Square Strip.
	Confirm the spelling of *jog*.	**Say each sound in *jog* with me as I point to the letters: /j/ /ooo/ /g/. Now say the word. That's right; *j-o-g* spells *jog*.** Practice with two to four more words as time allows: *man, nap, pig, jam.*

Ongoing Assessment

If...	then...
children make an error,	model the answer, have them repeat it, and return to the sound and letter a second time.

Activity 7 Connect Sound to Letter

Word Dictation

Objective: Children connect sounds to letters to spell words. Time: 6–8 minutes

	To Do	To Say
Introduce the activity	Distribute the Write-On/ Wipe-Off Cards and markers.	**I'm going to say a word, and you are going to spell it. Let's see how many words we can spell!**
Model the activity	Model identifying the letter for the initial sound in *mop*.	Model **The first word is *mop*. Listen. I will say the sounds in *mop* and touch a finger for each sound: /mmm/ /ooo/ /p/.** Point to your index finger and say: **I'm going to write the first letter in *mop*.** Write an *m* on your card and show children. **Now you write the first letter in *mop*.**
	Model identifying the letter for the middle sound in *mop*.	**I'll say the sounds in *mop* again and touch a finger for each sound. I'll stop when I get to the next sound: /mmm/ /ooo/.** Point to your middle finger and say: **I'm going to write the next letter in *mop*.** Write an *o* on your card and show children. **Now you write the next letter in *mop*.**
	Model identifying the letter for the final sound in *mop*.	**I will say the sounds in *mop* again and touch a finger for each sound. I'll stop when I get to the last sound: /mmm/ /ooo/ /p/.** Point to your ring finger and say: **I'm going to write the last letter in *mop*.** Write a *p* on your card and show children. **Now you write the last letter in *mop*.**
	Confirm the spelling of the word.	Lead **Now say each sound in *mop* with me and point to your letters as we say each sound: /mmm/ /ooo/ /p/. Say the word: *mop*. That's right; *m-o-p* spells *mop*.**
Test the activity	Repeat the Word Dictation routine.	Have children spell and write each of the words. Have children erase their cards after each word. Continue with *pan, jog, gap, nip,* and *jam.*

Ongoing Assessment

If... children make an error, **then...** model the letter name and sound. Have children repeat the letter name and sound and write the correct letter.

New Sound /e/
Review Sounds /f/, /a/, /o/, /b/, /u/, /j/, /w/
Key Reading Skills Letter-Sound Correspondence; Word Reading: VC, CVC

Phonological Awareness and Alphabetic Understanding

Activity	Materials	Time
1. Alphabetic Introduce *e*/e/	Alphabet Card: *e* Letter Card: *e* (one per child)	1–2 minutes
2. Phonologic Does It Begin with /e/?	Picture Choices: 80-1, 80-2, 80-3 Teacher Resource Package 3	4–5 minutes
3. Alphabetic Sounds	Sounds Teacher Resource Package 3	4–5 minutes
4. Phonologic/Reading Say the Sounds/Say the Word with Fingers; Regular Words	Regular Words Teacher Resource Package 3 Word Cards: *rug, fan, up* (Lessons 79–84)	4–5 minutes

Writing and Spelling

Activity	Materials	Time
5. Writer's Warm-Up Introduce *e*	Writer's Warm-Up (one per child) Student Activity Book 3, p. 19 or 20 Tracing Cards: *e, w, g, u, j, n, b, d*	2–3 minutes
6. Integrated Phonologic/Alphabetic Practice Session: Spelling	3-Square Strip Letter Tiles: *c, o, t, j, b, i, r, u*	2–3 minutes
7. Phonologic/Spelling Word Writing Game	Word Writing Game (one per child) Student Activity Book 3, p. 21 Game Board 3 number cube (not provided) game markers (not provided)	6–8 minutes

Activity 1 Introduce Letter Name and Sound

Introduce e/e/

Objective: Children identify letter name and sound: *e*/e/. Time: 1–2 minutes

	To Do	To Say	
Introduce letter name	Hold up the *e* Alphabet Card.	**Model**	**The name of this letter is *e*.**
		Lead	**Say the name with me: *e*.**
		Test	**What is the name of this letter?**
Introduce letter sound	Continue holding up the *e* Alphabet Card.	**Model**	**The sound for this letter is /eee/. When you say /eee/, your mouth is open, and your tongue is behind your bottom teeth. Say /eee/. Did your mouth open? Yes, your mouth is open, and your tongue is behind your bottom teeth. Say /eee/.**
		Lead	**Say the sound with me: /eee/.**
		Test	**What is the sound for this letter?**
Test letter name and sound	Continue holding up the *e* Alphabet Card.	**Test**	**What is the name of this letter? What is the sound for this letter?**
	Give individual turns.		**Ongoing Assessment** — **If . . .** children make an error, **then . . .** tell them the letter name or sound, have them repeat the name or sound, and return to the letter a second time.
Model tracing e	Distribute an *e* Letter Card to each child. Model how to trace *e* using your alphabet card.	**Model**	**Watch. I'll trace the letter *e*. Now you try. Trace the letter *e* on your letter card three times. Say /eee/ each time you trace the letter.**
			Ongoing Assessment — **If . . .** children make an error, **then . . .** put your hand over their hand and guide the tracing of the letter. Then have children try to trace the letter on their own. Repeat as necessary.

2 Isolate Initial Sound

Does It Begin with /e/?

Objective: Children isolate initial /e/.

Time: 4–5 minutes

	To Do	To Say
Model names of pictures	Gather the picture choices. Place Picture Choice 80-1 on the table. Point to the first picture.	**Model** **This is *egg*. What is this?** Continue with the remaining pictures: *gum, jam; goose, elbow, juice.* Then test children on all the picture names. For each picture, ask: **What is this?**
Introduce the game Does It Begin with /e/?	Practice production of the target sound.	**We're going to play a game. I'll show you three pictures, and you'll find the one that has the first sound /eee/.** **Let's say /eee/. When you say /eee/, your mouth is open, and your tongue is behind your bottom teeth. Say /eee/.**
Model the game	Display Picture Choice 80-1. Cover the bottom row of pictures.	**Model** **My turn. I'll show you how to play the game.** Point to each picture in the top row and name it: **This is *egg, gum, jam.* I'll find the picture that has the first sound /eee/: *egg*. *Egg* has the first sound /eee/.** Exaggerate the first sound of the correct picture and say the word: **/eee/, *egg*.** Cover the top row of pictures and model one more example with *goose, elbow,* and *juice.*
Play the game to test knowledge of /e/	Cover up the bottom row of Picture Choice 80-2. Point to each picture in the top row: *goal post, dot, elephant.*	**Test** **What is this?** Have children tell the name of each picture. **Which picture has the first sound /eee/?** Confirm correct responses and prompt sound production: **Yes, *elephant* has the first sound /eee/. Let's say /eee/. When you say /eee/, your mouth is open, and your tongue is behind your bottom teeth.** Continue this routine with the remaining examples on Picture Choices 80-2 and 80-3: *envelope, jeep, doll; dog, elbow, glue; jump, deer, egg.* Then give individual turns.

Ongoing Assessment

If . . . children make an error,

then . . . model the correct answer. Review the sound production cue. Have children repeat the correct answer. Go back to the example a second time.

Activity 3 Discriminate Letter Sounds

Sounds

Objective: Children connect sound to letter.

Time: 4–5 minutes

	To Do	To Say
Introduce the activity	Display the Sounds page.	**I'll point to a letter and you'll say the sound for the letter. Some of the sounds will be quick sounds. You'll need to say each sound only for as long as I touch the letter.**
Test children on the sounds	Point to the first letter on the Sounds page. Note: If the letter has a stop sound, such as /b/, point to the letter briefly. If the letter has a continuous sound, such as /aaa/, hold your finger under the sound for about two seconds.	**Test** **What is the sound for this letter? Yes, /fff/.** Repeat this test for each letter. If children miss more than two sounds on the page, repeat the test for all the letters on the page. Then give individual turns. **Ongoing Assessment** **If...** children make an error, **then...** tell them the sound, have them repeat it, and move back two letters on the page or repeat the letter if it's at the beginning of the page.

Activity  Read Words

Lesson **80**

Say the Sounds/Say the Word with Fingers; Regular Words

Objective: Children segment, blend, and read words. Time: 4–5 minutes

	To Do	To Say
Introduce the activity		**It's time to play Say the Sounds/Say the Word with Fingers. I'll say the sounds of a word slowly. You'll slowly repeat each sound as you touch a finger. Then you'll say the sounds quickly to say the word.**
Lead the activity	Lead children in segmenting and blending *rug*.	**Lead** **Let's do a three-sound word together. Hold out three fingers.** Have children hold out three fingers pointed toward you. Have them use the pointer finger of the other hand to touch a finger for each sound, moving from left to right. **Listen to the sounds:** (pause) **/rrr/ /uuu/ /g/.** Touch a finger as you say each sound, without stopping between the sounds. **Say the sounds slowly with me: /rrr/ /uuu/ /g/.** Touch a finger for each sound. **Now say the sounds quickly with me to say the word.** Clap with children as you and they say the word: ***rug.***
Test knowledge of segmenting and blending	Test children on segmenting *fan*.	**Test** **It's your turn to do a three-sound word. Hold out three fingers. Listen to the sounds:** (pause) **/fff/ /aaa/ /nnn/.** Touch a finger as you say each sound, without stopping between the sounds. **Say the sounds slowly.** You and children touch a finger for each sound, but only children say the sounds.

Ongoing Assessment

If...	then...
If... children do not touch the appropriate finger for each sound,	**then...** model how to do it. Have children try again. If needed, guide their hands to touch the appropriate fingers.
If... children stop between the sounds,	**then...** model how to say the sounds without stopping between them. Have children say the sounds again.

	To Do	To Say
	Test children on blending *fan*.	**Test** **Now say the sounds quickly to say the word.** Clap with children as they say the word *fan*.

Ongoing Assessment

If...	then...
If... children have difficulty saying the sounds quickly,	**then...** model how to say the sounds slowly and quickly. Have children segment and blend the word again.

Repeat the test with *if, sit, lit,* and *up.* For *if* and *up,* have children hold out two fingers. Then give individual turns.

Activity 4 Read Words (continued)

	To Do	To Say
Introduce the activity	Gather the word cards. Display the Regular Words.	**Now it's time to read some words. First, we'll say the sounds in the word slowly. Then we'll say the sounds quickly to say the word. Some of the words end with quick sounds, so you'll need to watch my finger carefully.**
Lead children in sounding out and reading the word *rug*	Continue to display the Regular Words. Point to *rug*.	**Lead** **Let's read this word together. First, we'll say the sounds slowly. Then we'll say the sounds quickly to say the word. When I touch a letter, say its sound with me. We'll keep saying the sound until I touch the next letter. Watch my finger because this word ends with a quick sound. Get ready.** Point to *rug*: **/rrr/ /uuu/ /g/.** Touch under each of the first two squares for one to two seconds. Tap your finger under the third square. Do not pause between the sounds. **Now let's say the sounds quickly to say the word: *rug*.** Move your finger quickly across the arrow as you and children quickly say the sounds. **What's the word? *Yes, rug*.**

	To Do	To Say
Test children on sounding out and reading the word *rug*		Test **Now it's your turn to read the word. First, you'll say the sounds slowly. Then you'll say the sounds quickly to say the word. Say the sounds. Get ready.** Touch under each of the first two squares for one to two seconds. Tap your finger under the third square. Do not pause between the sounds. **Now say the sounds quickly.** Move your finger quickly across the arrow as children quickly say the sounds. **What's the word? *Yes, rug.***

Ongoing Assessment

If...	then...
If... children pause between sounds,	**then...** model saying the sounds without stopping between them. Have children sound out the word again.
If... children say the wrong sound,	**then...** keep your finger on the missed sound. Model the correct sound and have children repeat it. Have children sound out the word again.
If... children say the wrong word when they say the sounds quickly,	**then...** model the correct word and have children repeat it. Have children say the sounds slowly and quickly again.

Lead and test children on sounding out and reading the words *fan* and *up*. For *up*, tap your finger under the final stop sound /p/.

To Do	To Say
Test the group.	Point to the words in random order. Have the group say the sounds slowly and then quickly.
Give individual turns.	Give a child one of the word cards to sound out and read. Have the child touch under each square while slowly saying the sounds and then move a finger quickly across the arrow while quickly saying the sounds. Provide physical assistance as needed.

Ongoing Assessment

If...	then...
If... a child makes an error,	**then...** correct the error with the whole group. Have the child who made the error sound out and read the word again.
If... children make many errors during their individual turns,	**then...** model, lead, and test each word again with the whole group. When the whole group can successfully sound out and read each word, resume individual turns.

Activity 5 Writer's Warm-Up

Introduce e

Objective: Children trace and write *e* and review writing *w, g, u, j, n, b,* and *d*.

Time: 2–3 minutes

	To Do	To Say
Review letter name and sound	Hold up the *e* Tracing Card.	**What is the name of this letter? What is the sound for this letter?**
Model tracing *e*	Distribute a Writer's Warm-Up to each child. Hold up the *e* Tracing Card. Model tracing *e* with your finger.	Model **Watch as I trace the letter *e* with my finger.** Lead **Now you trace the first two letter *e's* on your warm-up sheet with your finger.** Model tracing *e* again. Then have children use their pencils to trace the next two *e's*.
Model writing *e*	Hold up the lined side of the *e* Tracing Card.	Model **Watch as I write the letter *e*. I start at the dot and write the letter.** Lead **Now you write two letter *e's*. Start at the dot like I did. Write carefully.** **Ongoing Assessment** **If...** children make an error, **then...** place your hand over their hand and guide them to write the letter. Then have them write the letter on their own. Repeat as necessary.
Test children on writing *e*	Hold up the lined side of the *e* Tracing Card. Model writing *e* again.	Have children cover the letters they traced and wrote. Have them write the letter *e* two times from memory. Then have them uncover their papers and compare the letters. **Do your letters look the same? Circle your best letter.**
Review ***w, g, u, j, n, b, d***	Gather the tracing cards.	**Trace *w*. Now write *w* with your pencil.** Continue this procedure for the remaining letters. **Ongoing Assessment** **If...** children make an error, **then...** use the tracing card to model tracing the letter. If needed, guide children to write the letter. Then have them write the letter on their own. Repeat as necessary.

Lesson 80

Activity 6 Connect Sound to Letter

Practice Session: Spelling

Objective: Children segment three-phoneme words and connect sounds to letters.

Time: 2–3 minutes

	To Do	To Say
Introduce the activity	Gather a 3-Square Strip and the letter tiles.	**Today we are going to practice spelling some words to get ready for the Word Writing game.**
Lead the activity	Set out the 3-Square Strip and the letter tiles. Segment the word *cot*.	**Lead** **The first word is *cot*. What is the first word?** Have children hold out three fingers. **Say the sounds in *cot* and touch a finger for each sound.**
	Lay out two letter tiles, *c* and one other. Identify the letter for the first sound in *cot*.	**Does everyone know what the first letter in *cot* is?** Call on a child to choose the correct letter tile and place it in the first square of the strip.
	Isolate the middle sound in *cot*.	**Say the sounds in *cot* again and touch a finger for each sound. Stop when you get to the next sound.**
	Lay out two letter tiles, *o* and one other. Identify the letter for the middle sound in *cot*.	**Does everyone know what the next letter in *cot* is?** Call on a child to choose the correct letter tile and place it in the middle square.
	Isolate the last sound in *cot*.	**Say the sounds in *cot* again and touch a finger for each sound. Stop when you get to the last sound.**
	Lay out two letter tiles, *t* and one other. Identify the letter for the last sound in *cot*.	**Does everyone know what the last letter in *cot* is?** Call on a child to choose the correct letter tile and place it in the last square.
	Confirm the spelling of *cot*.	**Now say each sound in *cot* with me as I point to the letters: /k/ /ooo/ /t/. Now say the sounds quickly to say the word: *cot*. That's right; *c-o-t* spells *cot*. The sounds in *cot* are /k/ /ooo/ /t/.** Practice with *job, bit, rub,* and *cut*, as time allows.

Ongoing Assessment

If . . . children make an error,

then . . . model the answer, have them repeat it, and return to the sound or letter a second time.

Activity  7 Connect Sound to Letter

Word Writing Game

Objective: Children connect sounds to letters to spell words. Time: 6–8 minutes

	To Do	To Say
Introduce the activity	Gather the game board, game markers, and number cube. Distribute a Word Writing Game to each child.	**Today we're going to play a word writing game. I'm going to say a word. You're going to spell the word by listening to the word's sounds. Every time we write a word, someone will roll the number cube and move his or her marker on the game board.**
Model the activity	Display a Word Writing Game. Point to the first word space. Model identifying the letter for the first sound.	**Model** **The first word is *rot*. Listen. I will say the sounds in *rot* and touch a finger for each sound: /rrr/ /ooo/ /t/.** Point to your index finger. **I'm going to write the first letter in *rot*.** Write an *r* in the first letter space and show children. **Now you write the first letter in *rot*.**
	Model identifying the letter for the middle sound.	**I'll say the sounds in *rot* again and touch a finger for each sound. I'll stop when I get to the next sound: /rrr/ /ooo/.** Point to your middle finger. **I'm going to write the next letter in *rot*.** Write an *o* in the middle letter space and show children. **Now you write the next letter in *rot*.**
	Model identifying the letter for the last sound.	**I'll say the sounds in *rot* again and touch a finger for each sound. I'll stop when I get to the last sound: /rrr/ /ooo/ /t/.** Point to your ring finger. **I'm going to write the last letter in *rot*.** Write a *t* in the last letter space and show children. **Now you write the last letter in *rot*.**
	Confirm the spelling.	**Lead** **Now say each sound in *rot* with me and point to your letters as we say each sound: /rrr/ /ooo/ /t/. Now say the sounds quickly to say the word: *rot*. That's right; *r-o-t* spells *rot*.**

	To Do		To Say
Test children on spelling *rub, job, bit, cut,* and *cot*	Test children on identifying the letter for the first sound.	**Test**	**The next word is *rub*. What is the word? Say the sounds in *rub* and touch a finger for each sound. Now write the first letter in *rub*.** Point to your index finger.
	Test children on identifying the letter for the middle sound.		**Say the sounds in *rub* again and touch a finger for each sound. Stop when you get to the next sound. Now write the next letter in *rub*.** Point to your middle finger.
	Test children on identifying the letter for the last sound.		**Say the sounds in *rub* again and touch a finger for each sound. Stop when you get to the last sound. Now write the last letter in *rub*.** Point to your ring finger.
	Confirm the spelling.	**Lead**	**Now say each sound in *rub* with me and point to your letters as we say each sound: /rrr/ /uuu/ /b/. Say the sounds quickly to say the word. That's right; *r-u-b* spells *rub*.** Have a child roll the number cube and move his or her marker on the game board.
			Continue the test with *job, bit, cut,* and *cot*.

Ongoing Assessment

If... children make an error,	**then...** model the letter name and sound and have children repeat them and write the correct letter.

New Sound /e/
Review Sounds /l/, /a/, /o/, /b/, /m/, /f/, /t/, /i/, /g/
Key Reading Skills Letter-Sound Correspondence; Word Reading: VC, CVC

Phonological Awareness and Alphabetic Understanding

Activity	Materials		Time
1. **Alphabetic** Introduce *e*/e/	Alphabet Card: *e*	Letter Card: *e* (one per child)	1–2 minutes
2. **Integrated Phonologic/Alphabetic** Which Picture Has the First Letter *e?*	Picture Choices: 81-1, 81-2, 81-3 Teacher Resource Package 3	Alphabet Card: *e*	4–5 minutes
3. **Alphabetic** Sounds Dash	Sounds Dash Teacher Resource Package 3	timer (not provided)	4–5 minutes
4. **Phonologic/Reading** Say the Sounds/Say the Word with Fingers; Regular Words	Regular Words Teacher Resource Package 3 Word Cards: *nap, on, sun* (Lessons 79–84)		4–5 minutes

Writing and Spelling

Activity	Materials	Time
5. **Writer's Warm-Up** Memory Review: *l, i, u, a, j, s, g, b, e, w*	Tracing Cards: *l, i, u, a, j, s, g, b, e, w* Write-On/Wipe-Off Cards (one per child) markers (one per child/not provided)	2–3 minutes
6. **Integrated Phonologic/Alphabetic** Practice Session: Spelling	3-Square Strip Letter Tiles: *g, a, b, i, u, j, s, l*	2–3 minutes
7. **Phonologic/Spelling** Guess What I Am	Guess What I Am (one per child) Student Activity Book 3, p. 22	6–8 minutes

Activity 1 Introduce Letter Name and Sound

Introduce e/e/

Objective: Children identify letter name and sound: *e*/e/.

Time: 1–2 minutes

	To Do	To Say	
Introduce letter name	Hold up the *e* Alphabet Card.	Model	**The name of this letter is *e*.**
		Lead	**Say the name with me: *e*.**
		Test	**What is the name of this letter?**
Introduce letter sound	Continue holding up the *e* Alphabet Card.	Model	**The sound for this letter is /eee/. When you say /eee/, your mouth is open, and your tongue is behind your bottom teeth. Say /eee/. Did your mouth open? Yes, your mouth is open, and your tongue is behind your bottom teeth. Say /eee/.**
		Lead	**Say the sound with me: /eee/.**
		Test	**What is the sound for this letter?**
Test letter name and sound	Continue holding up the *e* Alphabet Card.	Test	**What is the name of this letter? What is the sound for this letter?**
	Give individual turns.		**Ongoing Assessment** **If...** children make an error, **then...** tell them the letter name or sound, have them repeat the name or sound, and return to the letter a second time.
Model tracing e	Distribute an *e* Letter Card to each child. Model how to trace *e* on your alphabet card.	Model	**Watch. I'll trace the letter *e*. Now you try. Trace the letter *e* on your letter card three times. Say /eee/ each time you trace the letter.**
			Ongoing Assessment **If...** children make an error, **then...** put your hand over their hand and guide the tracing of the letter. Then have children try to trace the letter on their own. Repeat as necessary.

Activity 2 Isolate Initial Sound

Which Picture Has the First Letter e?

Objective: Children isolate initial /e/.

Time: 4–5 minutes

	To Do	To Say
Model names of pictures	Gather the picture choices. Place Picture Choice 81-1 on the table. Point to the first picture.	**Model** **This is *wheel.* What is this?** Continue with the remaining pictures: *elbow, moon; egg, wood, bag.* Then test children on all the picture names. For each picture, ask: **What is this?**
Introduce the game Which Picture Has the First Letter *e?*	Practice production of the target sound.	**We're going to play a game. I'll show you a letter and three pictures. You'll find the picture that begins with the sound for the letter.** **Let's say /eee/. When you say /eee/, your mouth is open, and your tongue is behind your bottom teeth. Say /eee/.**
Model the game	Hold up the *e* Alphabet Card. Display Picture Choice 81-1. Cover the bottom row of pictures.	**Model** **The <u>name</u> of this letter is *e.* The <u>sound</u> for this letter is /eee/. Remember, when you say /eee/, your mouth is open and your tongue is behind your bottom teeth.** **Test** **What is the <u>sound</u> for this letter?** **Model** **My turn. I'll show you how to play the game. This is *wheel, elbow, moon.* I'll find the picture that has the first sound /eee/.** Point to the letter *e.* ***Elbow* has the first sound /eee/.** Exaggerate the first sound and say the word: ***/eee/, elbow.*** Cover the top row and model again with *egg, wood, bag.*
Play the game to test knowledge of /e/	Hold up the *e* Alphabet Card. Cover up the bottom row of Picture Choice 81-2. Point to each picture in the top row: *man, bat, elephant.* Give individual turns.	**Test** **What is the <u>sound</u> for this letter?** **What is this?** Have children name each picture. Point to the letter *e.* **Which picture has the first sound /eee/?** Confirm correct responses and prompt sound production: **Yes, *elephant* has the first sound /eee/. Let's say /eee/. When you say /eee/, your mouth is open, and your tongue is behind your bottom teeth.** Continue this routine with the remaining examples on Picture Choices 81-2 *(envelope, wave, bike)* and 81-3 *(up, envelope, mop; bone, wall, elephant).* **Ongoing Assessment** **If...** children make an error, **then...** model the correct answer. Review the sound production cue. Have children repeat the correct answer. Go back to the example a second time.

Activity 3 Build Sounds Fluency

Sounds Dash

Objective: Children increase fluency in identifying letter sounds.

Time: 4–5 minutes

	To Do	To Say
Introduce the activity	Hold up the Sounds Dash.	**We're going to do a Sounds Dash today. I'll point to a letter and you'll say the sound for the letter. Let's see how close you can get to the finish line in one minute. You'll need to be careful because if I hear a mistake, the whole group will go back three letters.**
Model the activity	Review the sounds in the first row of the Sounds Dash. Note: Point to the letter briefly if it has a stop sound. Point to the letter for about two seconds if it has a continuous sound.	**Model** **Let's get warmed up for our Sounds Dash. We'll practice the sounds in the first row. Then we can start the timer for our dash. Remember, some of the sounds you'll have to hold and some will be quick. Say each sound only for as long as I touch the letter.** Point to *l*. **What is the <u>sound</u> for this letter?** Hold your finger under the letter for about two seconds. **Yes, /lll/.** Finish the row.
Lead the activity	Hold up the Sounds Dash. Set the timer for one minute.	**Lead** **Now you're ready for the Sounds Dash. Everybody, eyes on my finger. On your mark, get set, go!** Point to *l* in the first row. **What is the <u>sound</u> for this letter?** Repeat with each letter in the first row. Then go immediately to the second row, third row, and so on. Stop the activity after exactly one minute. Reinforce children for how far they made it. Tell them that they will have a chance to beat their score in three days when they play again.

Ongoing Assessment (Model the activity)

If . . . children make an error,	**then . . .** tell them the sound, have them repeat it, and move back three letters on the page or repeat the letter if it is at the beginning of the row.
If . . . children miss more than two sounds in the first row,	**then . . .** do not proceed with the activity. Instead, provide additional practice on the nine sounds on the page, focusing on the ones children aren't firm on.

Ongoing Assessment (Lead the activity)

If . . . children make an error,	**then . . .** tell them the sound, have them repeat it, and move back three letters on the page or repeat the letter if it is at the beginning of the row.

Activity 4 Read Words

Say the Sounds/Say the Word with Fingers; Regular Words

Objective: Children segment, blend, and read words. Time: 4–5 minutes

	To Do	To Say
Introduce the activity		**It's time to play Say the Sounds/Say the Word with Fingers. I'll say the sounds of a word slowly. You'll slowly repeat each sound as you touch a finger. Then you'll say the sounds quickly to say the word.**
Lead the activity	Segment and blend *fin.*	**Lead** **Let's do a three-sound word together. Hold out three fingers.** Have children hold out three fingers pointed toward you. Have them use the pointer finger of the other hand to touch a finger for each sound, moving from left to right. **Listen to the sounds:** (pause) **/fff/ /iii/ /nnn/.** Touch a finger as you say each sound, without stopping between the sounds. **Say the sounds slowly with me: /fff/ /iii/ /nnn/.** Touch a finger for each sound. **Now say the sounds quickly with me to say the word.** Clap with children as you and they say the word: ***fin.***
Test knowledge of segmenting and blending	Test children on segmenting *nap.*	**Test** **It's your turn to do a three-sound word. Hold out three fingers. Listen to the sounds:** (pause) **/nnn/ /aaa/ /p/.** Touch a finger as you say each sound, without stopping between the sounds. **Say the sounds slowly.** You and children touch a finger for each sound, but only children say the sounds. **Ongoing Assessment** **If...** children do not touch the appropriate finger for each sound, **then...** model how to do it. Have children try again. If needed, guide their hands to touch the appropriate fingers. **If...** children stop between the sounds, **then...** model how to say the sounds without stopping between them. Have children say the sounds again.
	Test children on blending *nap.*	**Test** **Now say the sounds quickly to say the word.** Clap with children as they say the word *nap.* **Ongoing Assessment** **If...** children have difficulty saying the sounds quickly, **then...** model how to say the sounds slowly and quickly. Have children segment and blend the word again. Repeat the test with *on, in, sun,* and *win*. For *on* and *in*, have children hold out two fingers. Then give individual turns.

Activity 4 Read Words (continued)

	To Do	To Say
Introduce the activity	Gather the word cards. Display the Regular Words.	**Now it's time to read some words. First, we'll say the sounds in the word slowly. Then we'll say the sounds quickly to say the word. Some of the words end with quick sounds, so you'll need to watch my finger carefully.**
Lead children in sounding out and reading the word *nap*	Continue to display the Regular Words. Point to *nap*.	**Lead** **Let's read this word together. First, we'll say the sounds slowly. Then we'll say the sounds quickly to say the word. When I touch a letter, say its sound with me. We'll keep saying the sound until I touch the next letter. Watch my finger because this word ends with a quick sound. Get ready.** Point to *nap*: **/nnn/ /aaa/ /p/.** Touch under each of the first two squares for one to two seconds. Tap your finger under the third square. Do not pause between the sounds. **Now let's say the sounds quickly to say the word: *nap*.** Move your finger quickly across the arrow as you and children quickly say the sounds. **What's the word? *Yes, nap.***

	To Do	To Say
Test children on sounding out and reading the word *nap*		Test **Now it's your turn to read the word. First, you'll say the sounds slowly. Then you'll say the sounds quickly to say the word. Say the sounds. Get ready.** Touch under each of the first two squares for one to two seconds. Tap your finger under the third square. Do not pause between the sounds. **Now say the sounds quickly.** Move your finger quickly across the arrow as children say the sounds. **What's the word? Yes, *nap*.**

Ongoing Assessment

If . . . children pause between sounds,	**then . . .** model saying the sounds without stopping between them. Have children sound out the word again.
If . . . children say the wrong sound,	**then . . .** keep your finger on the missed sound. Model the correct sound and have children repeat it. Have children sound out the word again.
If . . . children say the wrong word when they say the sounds quickly,	**then . . .** model the correct word and have children repeat it. Have children say the sounds slowly and quickly again.

Lead and test children on sounding out and reading the words *on* and *sun*.

To Do	To Say
Test the group.	Point to the words in random order. Have the group say the sounds slowly and then quickly.
Give individual turns.	Give a child one of the word cards to sound out and read. Have the child touch under each square while slowly saying the sounds and then move a finger quickly across the arrow while quickly saying the sounds. Provide physical assistance as needed.

Ongoing Assessment

If . . . a child makes an error,	**then . . .** correct the error with the whole group. Have the child who made the error sound out and read the word again.
If . . . children make many errors during their individual turns,	**then . . .** model, lead, and test each word again with the whole group. When the whole group can successfully sound out and read each word, resume individual turns.

Activity 5 Writer's Warm-Up

Memory Review: l, i, u, a, j, s, g, b, e, w

Objective: Children write review letters from memory. Time: 2–3 minutes

	To Do	To Say
Review letter names	Gather the tracing cards. Hold up the *l* Tracing Card.	**What is the <u>name</u> of this letter?** Continue with *i, u, a, j, s, g, b, e,* and *w.*
Model the review	Distribute the Write-On/Wipe-Off Cards and markers.	Model **I'll say a letter name, and you'll write the letter on your card. I'll show you. The first letter is *l*. Now I'll write the letter *l* on my card.**
Test children on writing the review letters		Test **The next letter is *i*. Write the letter *i* on your card.** Reinforce the group on the letter name: **Everyone, what's the <u>name</u> of the letter you wrote? Good. Erase your cards.** Continue with *u, a, j, s, g, b, e, w,* and *l.*

Ongoing Assessment

If... children write the wrong letter or don't remember a letter, **then...** show them the tracing card of the correct letter. Model tracing the letter and say the letter name.

Activity 6 Connect Sound to Letter

Practice Session: Spelling

Objective: Children segment three-phoneme words and connect sounds to letters.

Time: 2–3 minutes

	To Do	To Say
Introduce the activity	Gather the 3-Square Strip and letter tiles.	**Today we are going to practice spelling some words to get ready for Guess What I Am.**
Lead the activity	Set out the 3-Square Strip and the letter tiles. Segment the word *gab*.	**Lead** **The first word is *gab*. What is the first word?** Have children hold out three fingers. **Say the sounds in *gab* and touch a finger for each sound.**
	Lay out two letter tiles, *g* and one other. Identify the letter for the first sound in *gab*.	**Does everyone know what the first letter in *gab* is?** Call on a child to choose the correct letter tile and place it in the first square of the strip.
	Isolate the middle sound in *gab*.	**Say the sounds in *gab* again and touch a finger for each sound. Stop when you get to the next sound.**
	Lay out two letter tiles, *a* and one other. Identify the letter for the middle sound in *gab*.	**Does everyone know what the next letter in *gab* is?** Call on a child to choose the correct letter tile and place it in the middle square.
	Isolate the last sound in *gab*.	**Say the sounds in *gab* again and touch a finger for each sound. Stop when you get to the last sound.**
	Lay out two letter tiles, *b* and one other. Identify the letter for the last sound in *gab*.	**Does everyone know what the last letter in *gab* is?** Call on a child to choose the correct letter tile and place it in the last square.
	Confirm the spelling of *gab*.	**Now say each sound in *gab* with me as I point to the letters: /g/ /aaa/ /b/. Now say the sounds quickly to say the word: *gab*. That's right; *g-a-b* spells *gab*. The sounds in *gab* are /g/ /aaa/ /b/.** Practice with *sub, lag, jab,* and *big*, as time allows.

Ongoing Assessment

If...	then...
If... children make an error,	**then...** model the answer, have them repeat it, and return to the sound or letter a second time.

Activity 7 Connect Sound to Letter

Guess What I Am

Objective: Children connect sounds to letters to spell words. Time: 6–8 minutes

	To Do	To Say
Introduce the game Guess What I Am	Distribute a Guess What I Am sheet to each child.	**We are going to play a guessing game. I'm going to give you a clue about something, and you will guess what it is. Then we will spell the word. Let's see if we can spell all of the words!**
Model the activity	Model identifying the letter for the first sound in *pig.*	**Model** **Here's the first clue: I'm a pink animal. I like to wallow in the mud. I oink. Guess what I am! That's right; the word is *pig*. Listen. I will say the sounds in *pig* and touch a finger for each sound: /p/ /iii/ /g/.** Point to your index finger. **I'm going to write the first letter in *pig*.** Write a *p* in the first letter space and show children. **Now you write the first letter in *pig*.**
	Model identifying the letter for the middle sound in *pig.*	**I'll say the sounds in *pig* again and touch a finger for each sound. I'll stop when I get to the next sound: /p/ /iii/.** Point to your middle finger. **I'm going to write the next letter in *pig*.** Write an *i* in the middle letter space and show children. **Now you write the next letter in *pig*.**
	Model identifying the letter for the last sound in *pig.*	**I'll say the sounds in *pig* again and touch a finger for each sound. I'll stop when I get to the last sound: /p/ /iii/ /g/.** Point to your ring finger. **I'm going to write the last letter in *pig*.** Write a *g* in the last letter space and show children. **Now you write the last letter in *pig*.**
	Confirm the spelling of *pig.*	**Lead** **Now say each sound in *pig* with me and point to your letters as we say each sound: /p/ /iii/ /g/. Say the sounds quickly to say the word. That's right; *p-i-g* spells *pig*.**

	To Do		To Say
Test children on five more words	Test children on identifying the letter for the first sound in *big*.	**Test**	**Here's the next clue: I'm not small, or tiny. Instead, I'm very, very ___. Guess what I am! That's right; the word is *big*. What is the word? Say the sounds in *big* and touch a finger for each sound. Now, everyone, write the first letter in *big*.** Point to your index finger.
	Test children on identifying the letter for the middle sound in *big*.		**Say the sounds in *big* again and touch a finger for each sound. Stop when you get to the next sound. Now, everyone, write the next letter in *big*.** Point to your middle finger.
	Test children on identifying the letter for the last sound in *big*.		**Say the sounds in *big* again and touch a finger for each sound. Stop when you get to the last sound. Now, everyone, write the last letter in *big*.** Point to your ring finger.
	Confirm the spelling of *big*.	**Lead**	**Now say each sound in *big* with me and point to your letters as we say each sound: /b/ /iii/ /g/. Say the sounds quickly to say the word: *big*. That's right, *b-i-g* spells *big*.**

Clue Bank

Test children on spelling the words that answer the following clues.

1. My cat likes to jump and sit in my _____. Guess what I am! *(lap)*
2. I'm another word for an insect, such as an ant or a fly. Guess what I am! *(bug)*
3. I'm a part of your face and can give you a big kiss. Guess what I am! *(lip)*
4. I want some water. I won't take a big gulp, just a little _____. Guess what I am! *(sip)*

Review Sounds /a/, /b/, /i/, /g/, /u/, /j/, /w/, /e/
Key Reading Skills Letter-Sound Correspondence; Word Reading: VC, CVC

Phonological Awareness and Alphabetic Understanding

Activity	Materials	Time
1. Alphabetic Review *e*/e/	Alphabet Card: *e*	1–2 minutes
2. Phonologic First Sound Song with /e/	Picture Cards: *elephant, elbow, egg*	4–5 minutes
3. Alphabetic Sounds	Sounds Teacher Resource Package 3	4–5 minutes
4. Phonologic/Reading Say the Sounds/ Say the Word with Fingers; Regular Words	Regular Words Teacher Resource Package 3 Word Cards: *at, mom, nut* (Lessons 79–84)	4–5 minutes

Writing and Spelling

Activity	Materials	Time
5. Writer's Warm-Up Review Letters	Tracing Cards: *g, w, j, i, r, n, a, d, e, u* Writer's Warm-Up (one per child) Student Activity Book 3, p. 23 or 24	2–3 minutes
6. Integrated Phonologic/Alphabetic Practice Session: Spelling	3-Square Strip Letter Tiles: *n, o, t, a, c, u, j*	2–3 minutes
7. Phonologic/Spelling Monster Words	Write-On/Wipe-Off Cards (three) marker (not provided)	6–8 minutes

Activity 1 Introduce Letter Name and Sound

Review e/e/

Objective: Children identify *e*/e/.

Time: 1–2 minutes

	To Do	To Say
Test letter name and sound	Hold up the *e* Alphabet Card.	Test **What is the name of this letter? What is the sound for this letter?**
	Give individual turns.	**Ongoing Assessment** **If...** children make an error, **then...** tell them the letter name or sound, have them repeat the name or sound, and return to the letter a second time.

2 Isolate Initial Sound

First Sound Song with /e/

Objective: Children isolate initial /e/.

Time: 4–5 minutes

	To Do	To Say
Introduce the song	Gather the *elephant, elbow,* and *egg* Picture Cards.	**I'm going to teach you a song. I'll show you three pictures that begin with /eee/. These pictures will be in the song.** **Model** **This is *elephant, elbow, egg.*** Point to the pictures as you say the words. **Lead** **Say the names of the pictures with me: *elephant, elbow, egg.***
Review /e/	Practice /e/ sound production.	Point to the pictures as you name them: ***elephant, elbow,* and *egg* all begin with /eee/. Say the sound /eee/ with me. Remember, when you say /eee/, your mouth is open and your tongue is behind your bottom teeth. Say /eee/. Did your mouth open? Yes, your mouth is open and your tongue is behind your bottom teeth. Say /eee/.**
Model the song	Sing the following lyrics to the tune of "Old MacDonald Had a Farm." Point to each picture as you sing its name.	**Model** **Listen as I sing. What is the sound that begins these words: *elephant, elbow, egg?* /eee/ is the sound that begins these words: *elephant, elbow, egg.* With an /eee/ /eee/ here and an /eee/ /eee/ there, here an /eee/, there an /eee/, everywhere an /eee/ /eee/. /eee/ is the sound that begins these words: *elephant, elbow, egg.*** Lead children through the song several times, pointing to the pictures as they sing.
Test knowledge of initial sound	Test children on the first sound of each picture from the song.	**Test** **Your turn. Say the first sound in *elephant.*** Confirm correct responses and prompt sound production cue. Repeat for *elbow* and *egg.* Then give individual turns. **Ongoing Assessment** **If...** children make an error, **then...** model the answer, have children repeat it, and return to the example a second time.

Activity 3 Discriminate Letter Sounds

Sounds

Objective: Children connect sound to letter.

Time: 4–5 minutes

	To Do	To Say
Introduce the activity	Display the Sounds page	**I'll point to a letter and you'll say the sound for the letter. Some of the sounds will be quick sounds and some of the sounds you'll hold. You'll need to say each sound only for as long as I touch the letter.**
Test children on the sounds	Point to the first letter on the Sounds page. Note: If the letter has a stop sound, such as /b/, point to the letter briefly. If the letter has a continuous sound, such as /aaa/, hold your finger under the letter for about two seconds.	**Test** **What is the <u>sound</u> for this letter? *Yes,* /uuu/.** Repeat this test for each letter. If children miss more than two sounds on the page, repeat the test for all the letters on the page. Then give individual turns. **Ongoing Assessment** **If...** children make an error, **then...** tell them the sound, have them repeat it, and move back two letters on the page or repeat the letter if it's at the beginning of the page.

Activity 4 Read Words

Say the Sounds/Say the Word with Fingers; Regular Words

Objective: Children segment, blend, and read words. Time: 4–5 minutes

	To Do	To Say
Introduce the activity		**It's time to play Say the Sounds/Say the Word with Fingers. I'll say the sounds of a word slowly. You'll slowly repeat each sound as you touch a finger. Then you'll say the sounds quickly to say the word.**
Lead the activity	Lead children in segmenting and blending *lip*.	**Lead** **Let's do a three-sound word together. Hold out three fingers.** Have children hold out three fingers pointed toward you. Have them use the pointer finger of the other hand to touch a finger for each sound, moving from left to right. **Listen to the sounds:** (pause) **/lll/ /iii/ /p/.** Touch a finger as you say each sound, without stopping between the sounds. **Say the sounds slowly with me: /lll/ /iii/ /p/.** Touch a finger for each sound. **Now say the sounds quickly with me to say the word.** Clap with children as you and they say the word: ***lip.***
Test knowledge of segmenting and blending	Test children on segmenting *at*.	**Test** **It's your turn to do a two-sound word. Hold out two fingers. Listen to the sounds:** (pause) **/aaa/ /t/.** Touch a finger as you say each sound, without stopping between the sounds. **Say the sounds slowly.** You and children touch a finger for each sound, but only children say the sounds.
		Ongoing Assessment **If...** children do not touch the appropriate finger for each sound, **then...** model how to do it. Have children try again. If needed, guide their hands to touch the appropriate fingers. **If...** children stop between the sounds, **then...** model how to say the sounds without stopping between them. Have children say the sounds again.
	Test children on blending *at*.	**Test** **Now say the sounds quickly to say the word.** Clap with children as they say the word *at*.
		Ongoing Assessment **If...** children have difficulty saying the sounds quickly, **then...** model how to say the sounds slowly and quickly. Have children segment and blend the word again.
		Repeat the test with *ran, mom, nut,* and *it.* Then give individual turns.

	To Do	To Say
Introduce the activity	Gather the word cards. Display the Regular Words card.	**Now it's time to read some words. First, we'll say the sounds in the word slowly. Then we'll say the sounds quickly to say the word. Some of the words end with quick sounds, so you'll need to watch my finger carefully.**
Lead children in sounding out and reading the word *at*	Continue to display the Regular Words card. Point to *at*.	**Lead** **Let's read this word together. First, we'll say the sounds slowly. Then we'll say the sounds quickly to say the word. When I touch a letter, say its sound with me. We'll keep saying the sound until I touch the next letter. Watch my finger because this word ends with a quick sound. Get ready.** Point to *at*: **/aaa/ /t/.** Touch under the first square for one to two seconds. Tap your finger under the second square. Do not pause between the sounds. **Now let's say the sounds quickly to say the word: *at*.** Move your finger quickly across the arrow as you and children say the sounds. **What's the word? *Yes, at*.**

	To Do	To Say
Test children on sounding out and reading the word *at*		Test **Now it's your turn to read the word. First, you'll say the sounds slowly. Then you'll say the sounds quickly to say the word. Say the sounds. Get ready.** Touch under the first square for one to two seconds. Tap your finger under the second square. Do not pause between the sounds. **Now say the sounds quickly.** Move your finger quickly across the arrow as children quickly say the sounds. **What's the word? *Yes, at*.**

Ongoing Assessment

If... children pause between sounds,	**then...** model saying the sounds without stopping between them. Have children sound out the word again.
If... children say the wrong sound,	**then...** keep your finger on the missed sound. Model the correct sound and have children repeat it. Have children sound out the word again.
If... children say the wrong word when they say the sounds quickly,	**then...** model the correct word and have children repeat it. Have children say the sounds slowly and quickly again.

Lead and test children on sounding out and reading the words *mom* and *nut*. For *nut*, tap your finger under the final stop sound /t/.

To Do	To Say
Test the group.	Point to the words in random order. Have the group say the sounds slowly and then quickly.
Give individual turns.	Give a child one of the word cards to sound out and read. Have the child touch under each square while slowly saying the sounds and then move a finger quickly across the arrow while quickly saying the sounds. Provide physical assistance as needed.

Ongoing Assessment

If... a child makes an error,	**then...** correct the error with the whole group. Have the child who made the error sound out and read the word again.
If... children make many errors during their individual turns,	**then...** model, lead, and test each word again with the whole group. When the whole group can successfully sound out and read each word, resume individual turns.

Activity 5 Writer's Warm-Up

Review Letters

Objective: Children trace and write review letters.

Time: 2–3 minutes

	To Do	To Say
Review letter names	Give each child a Writer's Warm-Up.	Review the letters on the sheet. Point to each letter, have children identify it, and then say the letter name together.
Test children on writing *g, w, j, i, r, n, a, d, e,* and *u*	Gather the tracing cards.	Have children trace and write each review letter. When children have finished, have them circle their best letters.

Ongoing Assessment

If... children make an error,	**then...** use the tracing card to model tracing the letter and have them write the letter again. If needed, place your hand over their hand and guide them to write the letter. Then have them write the letter on their own. Repeat as necessary.

Activity 6 Connect Sound to Letter

Practice Session: Spelling

Objective: Children segment three-phoneme words and connect sounds to letters.

Time: 2–3 minutes

	To Do	To Say
Introduce the activity	Gather the 3-Square Strip and the letter tiles.	**Today we are going to practice spelling some words to get ready for Monster Words.**
Lead the activity	Set out the 3-Square Strip and the letter tiles. Segment the word *not*.	**Lead** **The first word is *not*. What is the first word?** Have children hold out three fingers. **Say the sounds in *not* and touch a finger for each sound.**
	Lay out two letter tiles, *n* and one other. Identify the letter for the first sound in *not*.	**Does everyone know what the first letter in *not* is?** Call on a child to choose the correct letter tile and place it in the first square of the strip.
	Isolate the middle sound in *not*.	**Say the sounds in *not* again and touch a finger for each sound. Stop when you get to the next sound.**
	Lay out two letter tiles, *o* and one other. Identify the letter for the middle sound in *not*.	**Does everyone know what the next letter in *not* is?** Call on a child to choose the correct letter tile and place it in the middle square.
	Isolate the last sound in *not*.	**Say the sounds in *not* again and touch a finger for each sound. Stop when you get to the last sound.**
	Lay out two letter tiles, *t* and one other. Identify the letter for the last sound in *not*.	**Does everyone know what the last letter in *not* is?** Call on a child to choose the correct letter tile and place it in the last square.
	Confirm the spelling of *not*.	**Now say each sound in *not* with me as I point to the letters: /nnn/ /ooo/ /t/. Now say the sounds quickly to say the word. That's right; *n-o-t* spells *not*. The sounds in *not* are /nnn/ /ooo/ /t/.** Practice with *tan, cut, jot,* and *can*, as time allows.

Ongoing Assessment

If . . . children make an error, **then . . .** model the answer, have them repeat it, and return to the sound or letter a second time.

Activity  7 Connect Sound to Letter

Monster Words

Objective: Children connect sounds to letters to spell words. Time: 6–8 minutes

	To Do	To Say	
Introduce the activity	Set out three Write-On/ Wipe-Off Cards in a row on the table.		**We are going to spell some monster words. I will say a word, and you will spell the word by writing big monster letters that go with the sounds on the cards. Let's see how many monster words we can spell!**
Model the activity	Identify and write the letter for the initial sound in *nut.*	**Model**	**The first word is *nut.* Listen. I will say the sounds in *nut* and touch a finger for each sound: /nnn/ /uuu/ /t/.** Point to your index finger and say: **I am going to write the first letter in *nut.*** Write an *n* on the first card, big enough to fill most of the card.
	Identify and write the letter for the middle sound in *nut.*		**I'll say the sounds in *nut* again and touch a finger for each sound. I'll stop when I get to the next sound: /nnn/ /uuu/.** Point to your middle finger and say: **I am going to write the next letter in *nut.*** Write a big *u* on the next card.
	Identify and write the letter for the final sound in *nut.*		**I will say the sounds in *nut* again and touch a finger for each sound. I'll stop when I get to the last sound: /nnn/ /uuu/ /t/.** Point to your ring finger and say: **I am going to write the last letter in *nut.*** Write a big *t* on the last card.
	Confirm the spelling of the word *nut.*	**Lead**	**Now say each sound in *nut* with me as I point to the letters: /nnn/ /uuu/ /t/. Say the sounds quickly to say the word. That's right; /nnn/ /uuu/ /t/ are the sounds in *nut* and *n-u-t* spells *nut.*** Erase the cards.

	To Do		To Say
Test children on spelling *got, wag, not, jug,* and *tan*	Identify and write the letter for the initial sound in *got.*	**Test**	**The next word is *got*. What is the word? Say the sounds in *got* and touch a finger for each sound.** Choose a student to write the letter on the first card. **Write the first letter in *got* on the first card.** Point to your index finger.
	Identify and write the letter for the middle sound in *got.*		**Say the sounds in *got* again and touch a finger for each sound. Stop when you get to the next sound.** Choose a student to write the letter on the second card. **Write the next letter in *got* on the second card.** Point to your middle finger.
	Identify and write the letter for the final sound in *got.*		**Say the sounds in *got* again and touch a finger for each sound. Stop when you get to the last sound.** Choose a student to write the letter on the last card. **Write the last letter in *got* on the last card.** Point to your ring finger.
	Confirm the spelling of the word *got.*	**Lead**	**Now say each sound in *got* with me as I point to each letter: /g/ /ooo/ /t/. Say the sounds quickly to say the word: *got*. That's right; /g/ /ooo/ /t/ are the sounds in *got* and *g-o-t* spells *got*.** Continue the test procedure for the following words: *wag, not, jug, tan.*

Ongoing Assessment

If... children make an error,	**then**... model the letter name and sound and have children repeat them and write the correct letter.

Review Sounds /l/, /o/, /r/, /i/, /u/, /j/, /w/, /e/
Key Reading Skills Letter-Sound Correspondence; Word Reading: VC, CVC

Phonological Awareness and Alphabetic Understanding

Activity	Materials	Time
1. Alphabetic Review *e*/e/	Alphabet Card: *e*	1–2 minutes
2. Integrated Phonologic/Alphabetic First Sound Mix-Up Game with /e/ and /o/	Letter Cards: *e, o* Picture Cards: *otter, escalator, egg, olive, elbow, ox, elephant, octopus* Sound Production Cue Card	4–5 minutes
3. Alphabetic Sounds	Sounds Teacher Resource Package 3	4–5 minutes
4. Phonologic/Reading Say the Sounds/ Say the Word with Fingers; Regular Words	Regular Words Teacher Resource Package 3 Word Cards: *map, run, if* (Lessons 79–84)	4–5 minutes

Writing and Spelling

Activity	Materials	Time
5. Writer's Warm-Up Ready, Set, Go!	Tracing Cards: *j, b, p, e, u, w, n, f, d, i, o, a* Writer's Warm-Up (one per child) Student Activity Book 3, p. 25 or 26	2–3 minutes
6. Integrated Phonologic/Alphabetic Practice Session: Spelling	3-Square Strip Letter Tiles: *f, a, n, w, i, d, u*	2–3 minutes
New **7. Phonologic/Spelling** Where's the Letter?	3-Square Strip Letter Tiles: *f, i, t, w, n, u, a, j*	6–8 minutes

Activity 1 Introduce Letter Name and Sound

Review e/e/

Objective: Children identify *e*/e/.

Time: 1–2 minutes

	To Do	To Say
Test letter name and sound	Hold up the *e* Alphabet Card.	Test **What is the <u>name</u> of this letter? What is the <u>sound</u> for this letter?**
	Give individual turns.	**Ongoing Assessment** **If...** children make an error, **then...** tell them the letter name or sound, have them repeat the name or sound, and return to the letter a second time.

Activity 2 Isolate Initial Sound

Lesson **83**

First Sound Mix-Up Game with /e/ and /o/

Objective: Children isolate initial /e/ and initial /o/. Time: 4–5 minutes

	To Do	To Say
Review names of pictures	Gather the picture cards. Hold up each picture card.	Ask: **What is this?**
Introduce the game First Sound Mix-Up	Mix up the picture cards. Place the *e* and *o* Letter Cards on the table.	**We're going to play First Sound Mix-Up. I'll hold up a picture. You'll say the name of the picture and tell me its first sound. You'll have to be careful because the pictures are all mixed up. Some of the pictures begin with /eee/ and some begin with /ooo/.**
Model the game	Display *otter*.	**Model** **I'll show you how to play. This is *otter*. I'll say the first sound in *otter:* /ooo/. Now I'll place *otter* next to the letter for the sound /ooo/. Remember, the <u>name</u> of this letter is *o; o* is the letter for the <u>sound</u> /ooo/.**
	Display *escalator*.	**I'll do one more. This is *escalator*. I'll say the first sound in *escalator:* /eee/. Now I'll place *escalator* next to the letter for the sound /eee/. Remember, the <u>name</u> of this letter is *e; e* is the letter for the <u>sound</u> /eee/.**
Play the game to test knowledge of initial sounds	Test children with the remaining pictures.	**Test** **What is this? Say the first sound in ______.** Confirm correct responses and prompt sound production for /e/ or /o/. (Use the Sound Production Cue Card.) Have children place each picture next to the letter for its first sound.
	Give individual turns	**Ongoing Assessment** — **If...** children make incorrect responses, **then...** tell them the answer and have them repeat it. Put the picture back in the pile so you can return to it a second time.

Activity 3 Discriminate Letter Sounds

Sounds

Objective: Children connect sound to letter.

Time: 4–5 minutes

	To Do	To Say
Introduce the activity	Display the Sounds page.	**I'll point to a letter and you'll say the sound for the letter. Some of the sounds will be quick sounds and some of the sounds you'll hold. You'll need to say each sound only for as long as I touch the letter.**
Test children on the sounds	Point to the first letter on the Sounds page. Note: If the letter has a stop sound, such as /j/, point to the letter briefly. If the letter has a continuous sound, such as /rrr/, hold your finger under the sound for about two seconds.	**Test** **What is the <u>sound</u> for this letter? *Yes*, /rrr/.** Repeat the test for each letter. If children miss more than two sounds on the page, repeat the test for all the letters on the page. Then give individual turns.

Ongoing Assessment

If... children make an error, **then...** tell them the sound, have them repeat it, and move back two letters on the page or repeat the letter if it's at the beginning of the page.

Activity 4 Read Words

Say the Sounds/Say the Word with Fingers; Regular Words

Objective: Children segment, blend, and read words. Time: 4–5 minutes

	To Do	To Say
Introduce the activity		**It's time to play Say the Sounds/Say the Word with Fingers. I'll say the sounds of a word slowly. You'll slowly repeat each sound as you touch a finger. Then you'll say the sounds quickly to say the word.**
Lead the activity	Segment and blend *map.*	**Lead** **Let's do a three-sound word together. Hold out three fingers.** Have children hold out three fingers pointed toward you. Have them use the pointer finger of the other hand to touch a finger for each sound, moving from left to right. **Listen to the sounds:** (pause) **/mmm/ /aaa/ /p/.** Touch a finger as you say each sound, without stopping between the sounds. **Say the sounds slowly with me: /mmm/ /aaa/ /p/.** You and children touch a finger for each sound. **Now say the sounds quickly with me to say the word.** Clap with children as you and they say the word: ***map.***
Test knowledge of segmenting and blending	Test children on segmenting *run.*	**Test** **It's your turn to do a three-sound word. Hold out three fingers. Listen to the sounds:** (pause) **/rrr/ /uuu/ /nnn/.** Touch a finger as you say each sound, without stopping between the sounds. **Say the sounds slowly.** You and children touch a finger for each sound, but only children say the sounds. **Ongoing Assessment** **If...** children do not touch the appropriate finger for each sound, **then...** model how to do it. Have children try again. If needed, guide their hands to touch the appropriate fingers. **If...** children stop between the sounds, **then...** model how to say the sounds without stopping between them. Have children say the sounds again.
	Test children on blending *run.*	**Test** **Now say the sounds quickly to say the word.** Clap with children as they say the word *run.* **Ongoing Assessment** **If...** children have difficulty saying the sounds quickly, **then...** model how to say the sounds slowly and quickly. Have children segment and blend the word again. Repeat the test with *fit, lap, if,* and *sit.* Then give individual turns.

	To Do	To Say
Introduce the activity	Display the Regular Words card.	**Now it's time to read some words. First, we'll say the sounds in the word slowly. Then we'll say the sounds quickly to say the word. Some of the words end with quick sounds, so you'll have to watch my finger carefully.**
Lead children in sounding out and reading the word *map*	Continue to display the Regular Words card. Point to *map*.	**Lead** **Let's read this word together. First, we'll say the sounds slowly. Then we'll say the sounds quickly to say the word. When I touch a letter, say its sound with me. Keep saying the sound until I touch the next letter. Watch my finger because this word ends with a quick sound. Get ready.** Point to *map*: **/mmm/ /aaa/ /p/.** Touch under the first two squares for one to two seconds. Tap your finger under the third square. Do not pause between the sounds. **Now let's say the sounds quickly to say the word: *map*.** Move your finger quickly across the arrow as you and children quickly say the sounds. **What's the word? *Yes, map*.**

	To Do	To Say
Test children on sounding out and reading the word *map*		Test **Now it's your turn to read the word. First, you'll say the sounds slowly. Then you'll say the sounds quickly to say the word. Say the sounds. Get ready.** Touch under the first two squares for one to two seconds. Tap your finger under the third square. Do not pause between the sounds. **Now say the sounds quickly.** Move your finger quickly across the arrow as children quickly say the sounds. **What's the word? *Yes, map.***

Ongoing Assessment

If... children pause between sounds,	**then...** model saying the sounds without stopping between them. Have children sound out the word again.
If... children say the wrong sound,	**then...** keep your finger on the missed sound. Model the correct sound and have children repeat it. Have children sound out the word again.
If... children say the wrong word when they say the sounds quickly,	**then...** model the correct word and have children repeat it. Have children say the sounds slowly and quickly again.

Lead and test children on sounding out and reading the words *run* and *if*.

To Do	To Say
Test the group.	Point to the words in random order. Have the group say the sounds slowly and then quickly.
Give individual turns.	Give a child one of the word cards to sound out and read. Have the child touch under each square while slowly saying the sounds and then move a finger quickly across the arrow while quickly saying the sounds. Provide physical assistance as needed.

Ongoing Assessment

If... a child makes an error,	**then...** correct the error with the whole group. Have the child who made the error sound out and read the word again.
If... children make many errors during their individual turns,	**then...** model, lead, and test each word again with the whole group. When the whole group can successfully sound out and read each word, resume individual turns.

Writer's Warm-Up

Ready, Set, Go!

Objective: Children trace and write letters.

Time: 2–3 minutes

	To Do	To Say
Introduce the activity	Distribute a Writer's Warm-Up to each child.	Tell children they are going to write their best letters as quickly as they can.
Model the activity	Hold up a Writer's Warm-Up.	**Model** **I'll show you how this activity works. The letters in the first row are *j, b, p,* and *e.* Watch as I trace each of the letters.** Trace the first row on the teacher sheet. **Lead** **It's your turn to trace the letters in the first row on your sheet.** Wait until children finish. **Model** **After I say "Ready, set, go!" I'll write my best *j, b, p,* and *e* as quickly as I can on the second row. Watch me try. Ready, set, go!** Write the letters on the second row. When you have finished, put your pencil down. **Lead** **Now it's your turn to write your best *j, b, p,* and *e* as quickly as you can. Ready, set, go!** Have children put their pencils down when they have finished.
Test children on writing *u, w, n, f, d, i, o,* and *a*	Continue to hold up a Writer's Warm-Up. Point to the next row of letters.	**Test** **The letters in the next group are *u, w, n,* and *f.* For warm-up, trace each of the letters. Put your pencil down when you have finished.** **Now it's your turn to write your best *u, w, n,* and *f* as quickly as you can. Ready, set, go!** Remind children to put their pencils down when they have finished. Repeat for the last row of letters. Then have children look over their papers and circle their best letters: **Look over your paper and circle your best letters.**

Ongoing Assessment

If... children write the wrong letter or don't remember how to write a letter, **then...** show them the tracing card of the correct letter. Trace the letter and say its name.

Connect Sound to Letter

Practice Session: Spelling

Objective: Children segment three-phoneme words and connect sounds to letters.

Time: 2–3 minutes

	To Do	To Say
Introduce the activity	Gather the 3-Square Strip and the Letter Tiles.	**Today we are going to practice spelling some words to get ready for Where's the Letter?**
Lead the activity	Set out the 3-Square Strip and the letter tiles. Segment the word *fan*.	Lead **The first word is *fan*. What is the first word?** Have children hold out three fingers. **Say the sounds in *fan* and touch a finger for each sound.**
	Lay out two letter tiles, *f* and one other. Identify the letter for the first sound in *fan*.	**Does everyone know what the first letter in *fan* is?** Call on a child to choose the correct letter tile and place it in the first square of the strip.
	Isolate the middle sound in *fan*.	**Say the sounds in *fan* again and touch a finger for each sound. Stop when you get to the next sound.**
	Lay out two letter tiles, *a* and one other. Identify the letter for the middle sound in *fan*.	**Does everyone know what the next letter in *fan* is?** Call on a child to choose the correct letter tile and place it in the middle square.
	Isolate the last sound in *fan*.	**Say the sounds in *fan* again and touch a finger for each sound. Stop when you get to the last sound.**
	Lay out two letter tiles, *n* and one other. Identify the letter for the last sound in *fan*.	**Does everyone know what the last letter in *fan* is?** Call on a child to choose the correct letter tile and place it in the last square.
	Confirm the spelling of *fan*.	**Now say each sound in *fan* with me as I point to the letters: /fff/ /aaa/ /nnn/. Now say the sounds quickly to say the word: *fan*. That's right; *f-a-n* spells *fan*. The sounds in *fan* are /fff/ /aaa/ /nnn/.** Practice with *win, fin, fad,* and *fun*, as time allows.

Ongoing Assessment

If... children make an error, **then...** model the answer, have them repeat it, and return to the sound or letter a second time.

Activity 7 Connect Sound to Letter

Where's the Letter?

Objective: Children connect sounds to letters to spell words. Time: 6–8 minutes

	To Do	To Say
Introduce the activity	Gather the 3-Square Strip and the letter tiles. Distribute a different set of letter tiles to each child. (Children may not have the same number of tiles.)	**We are going to spell some words together. I will say a word, and you will look at your letter tiles to see if you have a letter that will help spell the word. Let's see how many words we can spell together!**
Model the activity	Identify the letter for the initial sound in *fit*.	Model **The first word is *fit*. Listen. I'll say the sounds in *fit* and touch a finger for each sound: /fff/ /iii/ /t/. I'm going to look for the first letter in *fit*.** Take the *f* Letter Tile from a child's set of letters and place it in the first square of the 3-Square Strip.
	Identify the letter for the middle sound in *fit*.	**I'll say the sounds in *fit* again and touch a finger for each sound. I'll stop when I get to the next sound: /fff/ /iii/. I'm going to look for the next letter in *fit*.** Take the *i* Letter Tile from a child's set of letters and place it in the next square of the 3-Square Strip.
	Identify the letter for the final sound in *fit*.	**I'll say the sounds in *fit* again and touch a finger for each sound. I'll stop when I get to the last sound: /fff/ /iii/ /t/. I'm going to look for the last letter in *fit*.** Take the *t* Letter Tile from a child's set of letters and place it in the last square of the 3-Square Strip.
	Confirm the spelling of *fit*.	**Now say each sound in *fit* with me as I point to the letters: /fff/ /iii/ /t/. Say the sounds quickly. That's right; /fff/ /iii/ /t/ are the sounds in *fit*. The letters *f-i-t* spell *fit*.**

	To Do	To Say	
Test children on spelling *win, nut, fan, jut,* and *tin*	Test children on identifying the letter for the initial sound in *win.*	**Test**	**The next word is *win*. What is the word? Say the sounds in *win* and touch a finger for each sound. Who has the first letter in *win?*** Have the child place the letter on the 3-Square Strip.
	Test children on identifying the letter for the middle sound in *win.*		**Say the sounds in *win* again and touch a finger for each sound. Stop when you get to the next sound. Who has the next letter in *win?*** Have the child place the letter on the 3-Square Strip.
	Test children on identifying the letter for the final sound in *win.*		**Say the sounds in *win* again and touch a finger for each sound. Stop when you get to the last sound. Who has the last letter in *win?*** Have the child place the letter on the 3-Square Strip.
	Confirm the spelling of *win.*	**Lead**	**Now say each sound in *win* with me as I point to the letters: /www/ /iii/ /nnn/. Say the sounds quickly: *win*. That's right; /www/ /iii/ /nnn/ are the sounds in *win*. The letters *w-i-n* spell *win*.** Continue this test procedure for the following words: *nut, fan, jut, tin.*

Ongoing Assessment

If... children don't know the correct letter name and sound,	**then...** tell them the correct letter name and sound and have children repeat them. Have the child with the letter place it on the 3-Square Strip in the correct box.
If... a child doesn't know in which box to place the letter on the 3-Square Strip,	**then...** place the letter in the correct position yourself. Take out the letter, and have the child place the letter in the correct position.

Review Sounds /a/, /r/, /p/, /k/, /g/, /i/, /n/, /s/, /d/
Key Reading Skills Letter-Sound Correspondence; Word Reading: VC, CVC

Phonological Awareness and Alphabetic Understanding

Activity	Materials		Time
1. Alphabetic Review *e*/e/	Alphabet Card: *e*		1–2 minutes
2. Integrated Phonologic/Alphabetic Hold the Pictures Game with /e/, /o/, and /a/	Letter Cards: *e, o, a* Picture Cards: *ant, apple, alligator, astronaut, egg, elbow, escalator, elephant, ox, otter, olive, octopus*		4–5 minutes
3. Alphabetic Sounds Dash	Sounds Dash Teacher Resource Package 3	timer (not provided)	4–5 minutes
4. Reading Word Reading Game	Word Cards: *us, fun, sad, rug, fan, up, nap, on, sun, at, mom, nut, map, run, if* (Lessons 79–84) Game Board 3	game markers (one per child/ not provided) number cube (not provided)	4–5 minutes

Writing and Spelling

Activity	Materials		Time
5. Writer's Warm-Up Treasure Hunt	Treasure Hunt (one per child) Student Activity Book 3, p. 27 Tracing Cards: *e, g, u, w, j, b, r, n*		2–3 minutes
6. Integrated Phonologic/Alphabetic Practice Session: Spelling	3-Square Strip	Letter Tiles: *j, u, g, w, i, m, n, o*	2–3 minutes
7. Phonologic/Spelling Word Page	Word Page (one per child) Student Activity Book 3, p. 28		6–8 minutes

Activity 1 Introduce Letter Name and Sound

Review e/e/

Objective: Children identify *e*/e/.

Time: 1–2 minutes

	To Do	To Say
Test letter name and sound	Hold up the *e* Alphabet Card.	Test **What is the <u>name</u> of this letter? What is the <u>sound</u> for this letter?**
	Give individual turns.	**Ongoing Assessment** **If...** children make an error, **then...** tell them the letter name or sound, have them repeat the name or sound, and return to the letter a second time.

Activity 2 Isolate Initial Sound

Lesson 84

Hold the Pictures Game with /e/, /o/, and /a/

Objective: Children isolate initial sounds /e/, /o/, and /a/. Time: 4–5 minutes

	To Do	To Say
Introduce the game Hold the Pictures	Give each child an /e/, /o/, and /a/ picture. Place letter cards for *e, o,* and *a* on the table, facing children.	**This is how to play Hold the Pictures. When it's your turn, you'll hold up one of your pictures. You'll say the picture name. Then you'll tell the picture's first sound and place the picture under the letter for that sound.**
Model the game		Model **I'll show you how to play.** Hold up the *ant* Picture Card. **This is *ant*. I'll say the first sound in *ant*: /aaa/. I'll place the picture of *ant* under the letter for /aaa/.** Place the picture under the *a* Letter Card.
Test children on the remaining pictures	Call on individual children.	Test **Hold up one of your pictures. What is it? Say the first sound in _____. Place _____ under the letter for /_/.** Continue the game until all of the pictures have been placed. **Ongoing Assessment** **If...** children make an error in any of the steps, **then...** tell them the answer and have them repeat it. Request that children keep the picture in front of them and try again on another turn.

Activity 3 Build Sounds Fluency

Sounds Dash

Objective: Children increase fluency in identifying letter sounds.

Time: 4–5 minutes

	To Do	To Say
Introduce the activity	Hold up the Sounds Dash.	**We're going to do a Sounds Dash today. I'll point to a letter and you'll say the sound for the letter. Let's see how close we can get to the finish line in one minute. You'll need to be careful because if I hear a mistake, the whole group will go back three letters.**
Model the activity	Review the sounds in the first row of the Sounds Dash. Point to the letter briefly if it has a stop sound. Point to the letter for about two seconds if it has a continuous sound.	**Model** **Let's get warmed up for our Sounds Dash. We'll practice the sounds in the first row. Then we can start the timer for our dash. Remember, some of the sounds you'll have to hold and some will be quick. Say each sound only for as long as I touch the letter.** Point to *a*. **What is the <u>sound</u> for this letter? *Yes,* /aaa/.** Finish the row. **Ongoing Assessment** **If...** children make an error, **then...** tell them the sound, have them repeat it, and move back three letters on the page or repeat the letter if it is at the beginning of the row. **If...** children miss more than two sounds in the first row, **then...** do not proceed with the activity. Instead, provide additional practice on the nine sounds on the page, focusing on the ones children aren't firm on.
Lead the activity	Hold up the Sounds Dash. Set the timer for one minute.	**Lead** **Now you're ready for the Sounds Dash. Everybody, eyes on my finger. On your mark, get set, go!** Point to *a* in the first row. **What is the <u>sound</u> for this letter?** Repeat for each letter in the first row. Then go immediately to the second row, third row, and so on. Stop the activity after exactly one minute. Reinforce children for how far they made it. Tell them that they will have a chance to beat their score in three days when they play again. **Ongoing Assessment** **If...** children make an error, **then...** tell them the sound, have them repeat it, and move back three letters on the page or repeat the letter if it is at the beginning of the row.

Activity 4 Read Words

Word Reading Game

Objective: Children sound out and read words.

Time: 4–5 minutes

	To Do	To Say
Introduce the game	Gather the game board, game markers, and number cube. Place the word cards face down in a pile on the table.	**We're going to play the Word Reading Game. This is how to play. When it's your turn, you'll roll the number cube and pick the top card from the pile of word cards. Then you'll sound out and read the word on the card. If you correctly sound out and read the word, you'll get to move your marker the number of spaces on the number cube. Then you'll place your word card at the bottom of the pile.**
Play the game	Have a child pick a word card. Lead the child to say the sounds slowly.	Lead **Say the sounds slowly.**

Ongoing Assessment

If...	then...
If... the child pauses between sounds,	**then...** model saying the sounds without stopping between them. Have the child sound out the word again. For example: **Remember, don't stop between the sounds. Listen: /uuu/ /sss/. Your turn. Get ready.**
If... the child says the wrong sound,	**then...** keep your finger on the missed sound. Model the correct sound and have the child repeat it. Have the child sound out the word again. For example: **This sound is /sss/; what's the sound? Now say the sounds again. Get ready.**

To Do	To Say
Lead the child to say the sounds quickly to say the word.	Lead **Get ready. Now say the sounds quickly to say the word. What's the word?**

Ongoing Assessment

If...	then...
If... the child says the wrong word when he or she says the sounds quickly,	**then...** model the correct word and have the child repeat it. Have the child say the sounds slowly and quickly again.

If the child says the word correctly, he or she advances the game marker on the game board. If the child makes an error, he or she does not advance. Play the game until one child makes it to the finish line or time runs out.

Activity 5 Writer's Warm-Up

Treasure Hunt

Objective: Children write letters.

Time: 2–3 minutes

	To Do	To Say
Introduce the activity	Give each child a Treasure Hunt.	**We are going on a treasure hunt. I will tell you the name of a letter, and you will write it. Let's see if we can get past the monsters and find the hidden treasure!**
Model the activity	Model writing the first letter.	**Model** **Let's do one together. The first letter is *e*. Watch as I write the letter *e*.** Write an *e* on your sheet. **Now you write the letter *e*. What's the name of the letter you wrote?**
Test children on the remaining letters		**Test** **The next letter is *g*. Write the letter *g* on your paper.** Reinforce the group on the letter name: **Everyone, what's the <u>name</u> of the letter you wrote?** Finish the page with the following letters: *u, w, j, b, r, n.*

Ongoing Assessment

If... children write the wrong letter or don't remember a letter, **then...** show them the tracing card of the correct letter and model tracing the letter.

Connect Sound to Letter

Practice Session: Spelling

Objective: Children segment three-phoneme words and connect sounds to letters.

Time: 2–3 minutes

	To Do	To Say
Introduce the activity	Gather the 3-Square Strip and the Letter Tiles.	**Today we are going to practice spelling some words to get ready for a Word Page.**
Lead the activity	Set out the 3-Square Strip and the letter tiles. Segment the word *jug*.	**Lead** **The first word is *jug*. What is the first word?** Have children hold out three fingers. **Say the sounds in *jug* and touch a finger for each sound.**
	Lay out two letter tiles, *j* and one other. Identify the letter for the first sound in *jug*.	**Does everyone know what the first letter in *jug* is?** Call on a child to choose the correct letter tile and place it in the first square of the strip.
	Isolate the middle sound in *jug*.	**Say the sounds in *jug* again and touch a finger for each sound. Stop when you get to the next sound.**
	Lay out two letter tiles, *u* and one other. Identify the letter for the middle sound in *jug*.	**Does everyone know what the next letter in *jug* is?** Call on a child to choose the correct letter tile and place it in the middle square.
	Isolate the last sound in *jug*.	**Say the sounds in *jug* again and touch a finger for each sound. Stop when you get to the last sound.**
	Lay out two letter tiles, *g* and one other. Identify the letter for the last sound in *jug*.	**Does everyone know what the last letter in *jug* is?** Call on a child to choose the correct letter tile and place it in the last square.
	Confirm the spelling of *jug*.	**Now say each sound in *jug* with me as I point to the letters: /j/ /uuu/ /g/. Now say the sounds quickly to say the word: *jug*. That's right; *j-u-g* spells *jug*. The sounds in *jug* are /j/ /uuu/ /g/.** Practice with *wig, gum, win,* and *jog*, as time allows.

Ongoing Assessment

If... children make an error, **then...** model the answer, have them repeat it, and return to the sound or letter a second time.

Activity 7 Connect Sound to Letter

Word Page

Objective: Children connect sounds to letters to spell words. Time: 6–8 minutes

	To Do	To Say
Introduce the activity	Distribute a Word Page to each child.	**We're going to spell words that go with each picture.**
Model the activity	Identify and write the letter for the initial sound in *gum*.	**Model** **The first picture is *gum*. Listen. I will say the sounds in *gum* and touch a finger for each sound: /g/ /uuu/ /mmm/. I'm going to write the first letter in *gum*.** Write the letter in the first space and show children. **Now you write the first letter in *gum*.**
	Identify and write the letter for the middle sound in *gum*.	**I'll say the sounds in *gum* again and touch a finger for each sound. I'll stop when I get to the next sound: /g/ /uuu/. I'm going to write the middle letter in *gum*.** Write the letter and show children. **Write the next letter in *gum*.**
	Identify and write the letter for the final sound in *gum*.	**I'll say the sounds in *gum* again and touch a finger for each sound. I'll stop when I get to the last sound: /g/ /uuu/ /mmm/. I'm going to write the last letter in *gum*.** Write the letter and show children. **Write the last letter in *gum*.**
	Confirm the spelling of *gum*.	**Now say each sound in *gum* with me and point to your letters as we say each sound: /g/ /uuu/ /mmm/. Now say the sounds quickly to say the word. That's right; /g/ /uuu/ /mmm/ are the sounds in *gum* and *g-u-m* spells *gum*.**
Test children on spelling *nut, fin, run*, and *nap*	Identify and write the letter for the initial sound in *nut*.	**Test** **Look at the next picture. This is *nut*. What is this? Say the sounds in *nut* and touch a finger for each sound. Everyone, write the first letter in *nut* in the first space.**
	Identify and write the letter for the middle sound in *nut*.	**Say the sounds in *nut* again and touch a finger for each sound. Stop when you get to the next sound. Everyone, write the next letter in *nut* in the next space.**
	Identify and write the letter for the final sound in *nut*.	**Say the sounds in *nut* again and touch a finger for each sound. Stop when you get to the last sound. Everyone, write the last letter in *nut* in the last space.**
	Confirm the spelling of *nut*.	**Say each sound in *nut* with me and point to your letters: /nnn/ /uuu/ /t/. Say the sounds quickly to say the word. That's right; *n-u-t* spells nut.** Repeat for *fin, run,* and *nap*.

Ongoing Assessment

If...	then...
If... children make an error,	**then...** model the letter name and sound. Have children repeat the letter name and sound and then write the correct letter.

New Sound /z/
Review Sounds /a/, /o/, /i/, /g/, /u/, /j/, /w/, /e/
Key Reading Skills Letter-Sound Correspondences; Word Reading: VC, CVC

Phonological Awareness and Alphabetic Understanding

Activity	Materials	Time
1. Alphabetic Introduce *z*/z/	Alphabet Card: *z* Letter Card: *z* (one per child)	1–2 minutes
2. Phonologic Does It Begin with /z/?	Picture Cards: *zoo, zebra, elephant, zipper, game, web*	4–5 minutes
3. Alphabetic Sounds	Sounds Teacher Resource Package 3	4–5 minutes
4. Phonologic/Reading Say the Sounds/ Say the Word with Fingers; Regular Words	Regular Words Teacher Resource Package 3 Word Cards: *web, net, am, lid* (Lessons 85–90)	4–5 minutes

Writing and Spelling

Activity	Materials		Time
5. Writer's Warm-Up Introduce *z*	Writer's Warm-Up (one per child) Student Activity Book 3, p. 29 or 30 Tracing Cards: *z, w, g, u, b, n, e, j*		2–3 minutes
6. Integrated Phonologic/Alphabetic Practice Session: Spelling	3-Square Strip	Letter Tiles: *e, a, o, w, m, j, p, g, t*	2–3 minutes
7. Phonologic/Spelling Where's the Letter?	3-Square Strip	Letter Tiles: *e, a, o, w, m, j, p, g, t*	6–8 minutes

Activity 1 Introduce Letter Name and Sound

Introduce z/z/

Objective: Children learn and trace z/z/.

Time: 1–2 minutes

	To Do	To Say	
Introduce letter name	Hold up the *z* Alphabet Card.	**Model**	**The name of this letter is z.**
		Lead	**Say the name of the letter with me: z.**
		Test	**What is the name of this letter?**
Introduce letter sound	Continue holding up the *z* Alphabet Card.	**Model**	**The sound for this letter is /zzz/. When you say /zzz/, the tip of your tongue touches above your top teeth and your voice box is on. Put your hand on your throat to see if your voice box is on when you say /zzz/; /zzz/. Yes, your voice box is on when you say /zzz/.**
		Lead	**Say the sound with me: /zzz/.**
		Test	**What is the sound for this letter?**
Test knowledge of letter name and sound	Continue holding up the *z* Alphabet Card.	**Test**	**What is the name of this letter? What is the sound for this letter?**
	Give individual turns on letter name and sound.		**Ongoing Assessment** **If**...children make an error, **then**...tell them the name or sound, have them repeat the name or sound, and return to the letter a second time.
Model tracing *z*	Distribute the *z* Letter Cards. Hold up the *z* Alphabet Card.	**Model**	**Everyone, watch. I'll trace the letter z.** Have children trace the *z* on their letter cards three times. Tell them to say /zzz/ each time they trace the letter.
			Ongoing Assessment **If**...children make an error, **then**...put your hand over their hand and guide them to trace the letter. Then have them try to trace the letter on their own. Repeat as necessary.

Lesson 85

Activity 2 Isolate Initial Sound

Does It Begin with /z/?

Objective: Children isolate initial /z/.

Time: 4–5 minutes

	To Do	To Say
Model names of pictures	Gather the picture cards. Place the *zoo* Picture Card on the table.	**Model** **This is *zoo*. What is this?** Continue with the remaining cards. Test children on the picture names by placing the cards on the table one at a time and asking: **What is this?**
Introduce the game Does It Begin with /z/?	Practice production of target sound.	**We're going to play a game. I'll show you a picture. You'll tell whether it begins with /zzz/.** **Let's say /zzz/. Remember, when you say /zzz/, the tip of your tongue touches above your top teeth, and your voice box is on. Put your hand on your throat to see if your voice box is on when you say /zzz/; /zzz/. Yes, your voice box is on when you say /zzz/.**
Model the game	Display the *zebra* Picture Card.	**Model** **My turn. I'll say the name of the picture and then tell whether it begins with /zzz/: *zebra*** (exaggerate the first sound). ***Zebra* begins with /zzz/. The tip of my tongue touches above my top teeth, and my voice box is on when I say /zzz/, *zebra*. Next picture: *elephant*** (exaggerate the first sound). ***Elephant* does not begin with /zzz/.**
Play the game to test knowledge of initial /z/	Display the *zipper* Picture Card. Give individual turns.	**Test** **This is *zipper*. What is this? Does *zipper*** (exaggerate the first sound) **begin with /zzz/?** Confirm correct responses and prompt sound production: **Yes, *zipper* begins with /zzz/. Remember, when you say /zzz/, the tip of your tongue touches above your top teeth, and your voice box is on.** Continue with *game* and *web*. **Ongoing Assessment** **If...** children make incorrect responses, **then...** model the correct answer. Review the sound production cue. Have children repeat the correct answer. Go back to the example a second time.

Activity 3 Discriminate Letter Sounds

Sounds

Objective: Children discriminate letter sounds: /o/, /g/, /w/, /e/, /i/, /a/, /j/, /u/.

Time: 4–5 minutes

	To Do	To Say
Introduce the activity	Display the Sounds page.	**I'm going to point to one of the letters on this page. You're going to tell me the sound for the letter. Some of the sounds will be quick sounds. You should say a quick sound only for as long as I touch my finger under the letter.** Point to the letter briefly if it is a stop sound, such as /b/. Hold your finger under the letter for about two seconds if it is a continuous sound, such as /aaa/.
Test knowledge of letter sounds	Continue to display the Sounds page. Point to *o*.	Test **What is the <u>sound</u> for this letter?** Hold your finger under the letter for about two seconds as children say the sound. Confirm correct responses: **Yes, the <u>sound</u> for this letter is /ooo/.** Continue with the remaining letters, moving from left to right across the page.
	Give individual turns.	

Ongoing Assessment

If...	then...
If... children make an error,	**then...** tell them the sound, have them repeat it, and move back two letters on the page or repeat the letter if it is at the beginning of the page.
If... children miss more than two sounds on the page,	**then...** repeat the test for all of the letters on the page.

Activity 4 Read Words

Say the Sounds/Say the Word with Fingers; Regular Words

Objective: Children segment, blend, and read words. Time: 4–5 minutes

	To Do	To Say
Introduce the activity		**It's time to play Say the Sounds/Say the Word with Fingers. I'll say the sounds of a word slowly. You'll slowly repeat each sound as you touch a finger. Then you'll say the sounds quickly to say the word.**
Model the activity	Model segmenting and blending *net.*	**Model** **Let's do a three-sound word together. Hold out three fingers.** Have children hold out three fingers pointed toward you. Have them use the pointer finger of the other hand to touch a finger for each sound, moving from left to right. **Listen to the sounds:** (pause) **/nnn/ /eee/ /t/.** Touch a finger as you say each sound, without stopping between the sounds. **Lead** **Say the sounds slowly with me: /nnn/ /eee/ /t/.** You and children touch a finger for each sound. **Now say the sounds quickly with me to say the word.** Clap with children as you and they say the word: ***net.***
Test knowledge of segmenting and blending	Test children on segmenting *map.*	**Test** **It's your turn to do a three-sound word. Hold out three fingers. Listen to the sounds:** (pause) **/mmm/ /aaa/ /p/.** Touch a finger as you say each sound, without stopping between the sounds. **Say the sounds slowly.** You and they touch a finger for each sound as only children say the sounds slowly. **Ongoing Assessment** **If...**children do not touch the appropriate finger for each sound, **then...**model how to do it. Have children try again. If needed, guide their hands to touch the appropriate fingers. **If...**children stop between the sounds, **then...**model how to say the sounds without stopping between them. Have children say the sounds again.
	Test children on blending *map.*	**Test** **Now say the sounds quickly to say the word.** Clap with children as only they say the word *map.* **Ongoing Assessment** **If...**children have difficulty saying the sounds quickly, **then...**tell them the word. Model how to say the sounds slowly and quickly. Have children segment and blend the word again. Repeat the test with *am, lid, it,* and *web.* For *am* and *it,* have children hold out two fingers. Then give individual turns.

	To Do	To Say
Introduce the activity	Display the Regular Words.	**Let's read some words. First, we'll say the sounds in the word slowly. Then we'll say the sounds quickly to say the word. Some of the words end with quick sounds, so watch my finger.**
Test knowledge of segmenting and blending regular words	Gather the word cards. Display the Regular Words. Test children on sounding out *web*.	**Test** **Now it's your turn to read a word. First, you'll say the sounds slowly. Then you'll say the sounds quickly to say the word. Say the sounds. Get ready.** Move your finger under each letter as children say each sound. Touch under the first two letters for one to two seconds, without pausing between them. Tap your finger under the last letter. **Ongoing Assessment** **If...** children pause between sounds, **then...** model saying the sounds without stopping between them. Have children sound out the word again. **If...** children say the wrong sound, **then...** keep your finger on the missed sound. Model the correct sound and have children repeat it. Have children sound out the word again.
	Test children on reading *web*.	**Now say the sounds quickly to say the word.** Move your finger quickly across the arrow as children quickly say the sounds. **What's the word?** Repeat with *net, am,* and *lid.* **Ongoing Assessment** **If...** children say the wrong word when they say the sounds quickly, **then...** tell them the correct word and have children repeat it. Have children say the sounds slowly and quickly again.
	Test the group.	Point to the words in random order. Have the group say the sounds slowly and then quickly.
	Give individual turns.	Give a child one of the word cards from the Word Page to sound out and read. Have the child touch under each letter while slowly saying the sounds and then move a finger quickly across the arrow while quickly saying the sounds. Provide physical assistance as needed. **Ongoing Assessment** **If...** a child makes an error, **then...** correct the error with the whole group. Have the child who made the error sound out and read the word again. **If...** children make many errors during their individual turns, **then...** model, lead, and test each word again with the whole group. When the group can sound out and read each word, resume individual turns.

Activity 5 Writer's Warm-Up

Introduce z; Review Letters

Objective: Children trace and write *z* and review writing *w, g, u, b, n, e,* and *j*.

Time: 2–3 minutes

	To Do	To Say
Review letter name and sound	Hold up the *z* Tracing Card.	**Test** **What is the <u>name</u> of this letter? What is the <u>sound</u> for this letter?**
Model tracing *z*	Distribute a Writer's Warm-Up to each child. Hold up the *z* Tracing Card. Model tracing *z* again.	**Model** **Everyone, watch as I trace the letter *z* with my finger.** **Lead** **Now use your finger to trace the first two *z*'s on your warm-up sheet.** **Model** **Everyone, watch as I trace *z* again.** **Lead** **Now use your pencil to trace the next two *z*'s.**
Model writing *z*	Hold up the lined side of the *z* Tracing Card.	**Model** **Everyone, watch as I write the letter *z*. I start at the dot and write the letter.** Have children write *z* two times on their warm-up sheets. Remind them to write their letters carefully. **Ongoing Assessment** **If...** children make an error, **then...** put your hand over their hand and guide them to write the letter. Then have them try to write the letter on their own. Repeat as necessary.
Test knowledge of writing *z*	Model writing *z* again.	Have children cover the letters they traced and wrote. Have them write *z* two times from memory. Then have them uncover their papers and compare the letters. **Do your letters look the same? Circle your best *z*.**
Review ***w, g, u, b, n, e, j***		Have children trace and write each review letter on their warm-up sheets. **Ongoing Assessment** **If...** children make an error, **then...** use the tracing card to model tracing the letter and have them write the letter again. If needed, put your hand over their hand and guide them to write the letter. Then have them try to write the letter on their own. Repeat as necessary.

Activity 6 Connect Sound to Letter

Practice Session: Spelling

Objective: Children segment words and connect sounds to letters.

Time: 2–3 minutes

	To Do	To Say
Introduce the activity	Gather the 3-Square Strip and the letter tiles.	**Today we're going to practice spelling some words to get ready for Where's the Letter?**
Lead the activity	Set out the 3-Square Strip and the letter tiles. Segment the word *jet*.	**Lead** **The first word is *jet*. What is the first word?** Have children hold out three fingers. **Say the sounds in *jet* and touch a finger for each sound.**
	Identify the letter for the first sound in *jet*.	**Does everyone know what the first letter in *jet* is?** Call on a child to choose the correct letter tile and place it in the first square.
	Identify the letter for the middle sound in *jet*.	**Does everyone know what the next letter in *jet* is?** Call on a child to choose the correct letter tile and place it in the middle square. **Ongoing Assessment** **If...** children make an error, **then...** have them segment the word again.
	Identify the letter for the last sound in *jet*.	**Does everyone know what the last letter in *jet* is?** Call on a child to choose the correct letter tile and place it in the last square. **Ongoing Assessment** **If...** children make an error, **then...** have them segment the word again.
	Confirm the spelling of *jet*.	**Now say each sound in *jet* with me as I point to the letters: /j/ /eee/ /t/. Now say the sounds quickly to say the word: *jet*. That's right; you spelled *jet*. The sounds in *jet* are /j/ /eee/ /t/.** Practice with *map, jog, jam,* and *wet*, as time allows.

Activity 7 Connect Sound to Letter

Where's the Letter?

Objective: Children segment words and connect sounds to letters.

Time: 6–8 minutes

	To Do	To Say
Introduce the activity	Gather the 3-Square Strip and the letter tiles. Distribute the letter tiles to children, giving each child a different set of letters that includes a vowel.	**Now we're going to play Where's the Letter? We're going to spell some words together. I'll say a word. You'll look at your letter tiles to see if you have one of the letters that will help spell the word. Let's see how many words we can spell together!**
Model the activity	Set out the 3-Square Strip. Model identifying the letter for the first sound in *wet*.	**Model** **The first word is *wet*. Listen. I'll say the sounds in *wet* and touch a finger for each sound: /www/ /eee/ /t/. I'm going to look for the first letter in *wet*.** Take the *w* Letter Tile from a child's set of letters and place it in the first square.
	Model identifying the letter for the middle sound in *wet*.	**Now I'll look for the next letter in *wet*.** Take the *e* Letter Tile from a child's set of letters and place it in the middle square.
	Model identifying the letter for the last sound in *wet*.	**Now I'll look for the last letter in *wet*.** Take the *t* Letter Tile from a child's set of letters and place it in the last square.
	Confirm the spelling of *wet*.	**Lead** **Everyone, say each sound in *wet* with me as I point to the letters: /www/ /eee/ /t/. Now say the sounds quickly to say the word: *wet*. That's right; you spelled *wet*. The sounds in *wet* are /www/ /eee/ /t/.**

	To Do	To Say	
Test knowledge of spelling *top, get, wag, jot,* and *mop*	Test children on identifying the letters for the first and middle sounds in *top*.	**Test**	**The next word is *top*. What is the next word? Say the sounds in *top* and touch a finger for each sound: /t/ /ooo/ /p/. Who has the first letter in *top*?** Have the child who has the *t* Letter Tile place in it the first square. **Who has the next letter in *top*?** Have the child who has the *o* Letter Tile place it in the middle square.
			Ongoing Assessment **If...** children make an error, **then...** have them segment the word again.
	Test children on identifying the letter for the last sound in *top*.	**Test**	**Who has the last letter in *top*?** Have the child who has the *p* Letter Tile place it in the last square.
			Ongoing Assessment **If...** children make an error, **then...** have them segment the word again.
	Confirm the spelling of *top*.	**Lead**	**Now say each sound in *top* with me as I point to the letters: /t/ /ooo/ /p/. Say the sounds quickly to say the word: *top*. That's right; you spelled *top*. The sounds in *top* are /t/ /ooo/ /p/.** Repeat the test for *get, wag, jot,* and *mop*.

New Sound /z/
Review Sounds /k/, /a/, /b/, /i/, /u/, /w/, /e/
Key Reading Skills Letter-Sound Correspondence; Word Reading: VC, CVC

Phonological Awareness and Alphabetic Understanding

Activity	Materials	Time
1. Alphabetic Introduce *z*/z/	Alphabet Card: *z* Letter Card: *z* (one per child)	1–2 minutes
2. Phonologic Which Picture Begins with /z/?	Picture Choices: 86-1, 86-2, 86-3 Teacher Resource Package 3	4–5 minutes
3. Alphabetic Sounds	Sounds Teacher Resource Package 3	4–5 minutes
4. Phonologic/Reading Say the Sounds/ Say the Word with Fingers; Regular Words	Regular Words Teacher Resource Package 3 Word Cards: *mud, not, fan, in* (Lessons 85–90)	4–5 minutes

Writing and Spelling

Activity	Materials		Time
5. Writer's Warm-Up Introduce *z*	Writer's Warm-Up (one per child) Student Activity Book 3, p. 31 or 32 Tracing Cards: *z, a, g, u, j, n, w, r*		2–3 minutes
6. Integrated Phonologic/Alphabetic Practice Session: Spelling	3-Square Strip	Letter Tiles: *o, i, w, f, n, b, g*	2–3 minutes
7. Phonologic/Spelling Word Dictation	Write-On/Wipe-Off Cards (one per child)	markers (not provided)	6–8 minutes

Activity 1 Introduce Letter Name and Sound

Introduce z/z/

Objective: Children learn and trace z/z/.

Time: 1–2 minutes

	To Do	To Say	
Introduce letter name	Hold up the *z* Alphabet Card.	Model	**The name of this letter is z.**
		Lead	**Say the name of the letter with me: z.**
		Test	**What is the name of this letter?**
Introduce letter sound	Continue holding up the *z* Alphabet Card.	Model	**The sound for this letter is /zzz/. When you say /zzz/, the tip of your tongue touches above your top teeth and your voice box is on. Put your hand on your throat to see if your voice box is on when you say /zzz/; /zzz/. Yes, your voice box is on when you say /zzz/.**
		Lead	**Say the sound with me: /zzz/.**
		Test	**What is the sound for this letter?**
Test knowledge of letter name and sound	Continue holding up the *z* Alphabet Card.	Test	**What is the name of this letter? What is the sound for this letter?**
	Give individual turns on letter name and sound.		**Ongoing Assessment** **If...** children make an error, **then...** tell them the name or sound, have them repeat the name or sound, and return to the letter a second time.
Model tracing *z*	Distribute the *z* Letter Cards. Hold up the *z* Alphabet Card.	Model	**Everyone, watch. I'll trace the letter z.** Have children trace the *z* on their letter cards three times. Tell them to say /zzz/ each time they trace the letter.
			Ongoing Assessment **If...** children make an error, **then...** put your hand over their hand and guide them to trace the letter. Then have them try to trace the letter on their own. Repeat as necessary.

Activity 2 Isolate Initial Sound

Which Picture Begins with /z/?

Objective: Children isolate initial /z/.

Time: 4–5 minutes

	To Do	To Say
Model names of pictures	Gather the picture choices. Display Picture Choice 86-1. Point to *web*.	**Model** **This is *web*. What is this?** Continue with the remaining pictures: *zoo, elbow; gum, well, zipper.* Test children on the picture names by pointing to the pictures one at a time and asking: **What is this?**
Introduce the game Which Picture Begins with /z/?		**We're going to play another game with our new sound /zzz/. I'll show you three pictures. You'll tell which picture begins with the sound /zzz/.**
	Practice production of target sound.	**Let's say /zzz/. Remember, when you say /zzz/, the tip of your tongue touches above your top teeth, and your voice box is on. Put your hand on your throat to see if your voice box is on when you say /zzz/; /zzz/. Yes, your voice box is on when you say /zzz/.**
Model the game	Display Picture Choice 86-1. Cover the bottom row.	**Model** **My turn. I'll show you how to play the game. This is *web, zoo, elbow*. I'll find the picture that begins with /zzz/: *zoo*** (exaggerate the first sound). ***Zoo* begins with /zzz/.** Exaggerate the first sound and say the word: **/zzz/, *zoo*.** Model again with the bottom row of pictures: *gum, well, zipper.*
Play the game to test knowledge of initial /z/	Display Picture Choice 86-2. Cover the bottom row.	**Test** Have children name each picture: *zebra, egg, wood.* **Which picture begins with /zzz/?** Confirm correct responses and prompt sound production: **Yes, *zebra* begins with /zzz/. Let's say /zzz/. Remember, when you say /zzz/, the tip of your tongue touches above your top teeth, and your voice box is on.** Continue with the bottom row of pictures *(game, zoo, elephant)* and Picture Choice 86-3 *(envelope, glue, zipper; goose, zebra, wheel).*
	Give individual turns.	**Ongoing Assessment** — **If...** children make incorrect responses, **then...** model the correct answer. Review the sound production cue. Have children repeat the correct answer. Go back to the example a second time.

Activity 3 Discriminate Letter Sounds

Sounds

Objective: Children discriminate letter sounds: *z*/z/, *a*/a/, *e*/e/, *b*/b/, *w*/w/, *c*/k/, *i*/i/, *u*/u/.

Time: 4–5 minutes

	To Do	To Say
Introduce the activity	Display the Sounds page.	**I'm going to point to one of the letters on this page. You're going to tell me the sound for the letter. Some of the sounds will be quick sounds. You should say a quick sound only for as long as I touch my finger under the letter.** (Point to the letter briefly if it is a stop sound such as /b/. Hold your finger under the letter for about two seconds if it is a continuous sound such as /aaa/.)
Test knowledge of letter sounds	Continue to display the Sounds page. Point to *z*.	**Test** **What is the <u>sound</u> for this letter?** Hold your finger under the letter for about two seconds as children say the sound. Confirm correct responses: ***Yes, the <u>sound</u> for this letter is /zzz/.*** Continue with the remaining letters, moving from left to right across the page.
	Give individual turns.	**Ongoing Assessment** **If**...children make an error, **then**...tell them the sound, have them repeat it, and move back two letters on the page or repeat the letter if it is at the beginning of the page. **If**...children miss more than two sounds on the page, **then**...repeat the test for all of the letters on the page.

Activity 4 Read Words

Lesson 86

Say the Sounds/Say the Word with Fingers; Regular Words

Objective: Children segment, blend, and read words. Time: 4–5 minutes

	To Do	To Say
Introduce the activity		**Let's play Say the Sounds/Say the Word with Fingers. I'll say the sounds of a word slowly. *You'll* slowly repeat each sound as you touch a finger. Then you'll say the sounds quickly to say the word.**
Model the activity	Model segmenting and blending *not.*	**Model** **Let's do a three-sound word together. Hold out three fingers.** Have children hold out three fingers pointed toward you. Have them use the pointer finger of the other hand to touch a finger for each sound, moving from left to right. **Listen to the sounds:** (pause) **/nnn/ /ooo/ /t/.** Touch a finger as you say each sound, without stopping between the sounds. **Lead** **Say the sounds slowly with me: /nnn/ /ooo/ /t/.** You and children touch a finger for each sound. **Now say the sounds quickly with me to say the word.** Clap with children as you and they say the word: ***not.***
Test knowledge of segmenting and blending	Test children on segmenting *up*.	**Test** **It's your turn to do a two-sound word. Hold out two fingers. Listen to the sounds:** (pause) **/uuu/ /p/.** Touch a finger as you say each sound, without stopping between the sounds. **Say the sounds slowly.** You and children touch a finger for each sound as only they say the sounds slowly. **Ongoing Assessment** **If...** children do not touch the appropriate finger for each sound, **then...** model how to do it. Have children try again. If needed, guide their hands to touch the appropriate fingers. **If...** children stop between the sounds, **then...** model how to say the sounds without stopping between them. Have children say the sounds again.
	Test children on blending *up*.	**Test** **Now say the sounds quickly to say the word.** Clap with children as only they say the word *up*. Repeat the test with *fan, sun, in*, and *mud*.
	Give individual turns.	**Ongoing Assessment** **If...** children have difficulty saying the sounds quickly, **then...** tell them the word. Model how to say the sounds slowly and quickly. Have them try the word again.

	To Do	To Say
Introduce the activity	Display the Regular Words page.	**Let's read some words. First, you'll say the sounds in the word slowly. Then you'll say the sounds quickly to say the word. Some of the words end with quick sounds, so watch my finger.**
Test knowledge of segmenting and blending regular words	Gather the word cards. Display the Regular Words page. Test children on sounding out *mud*.	Test **Now it's your turn to read a word. First, you'll say the sounds slowly. Then you'll say the sounds quickly to say the word. Say the sounds. Get ready.** Move your finger under each letter as children say the sounds. Touch under the first two letters for one to two seconds, without pausing between them. Tap your finger under the last letter.

Ongoing Assessment

If... children pause between sounds,	**then...** model saying the sounds without stopping between them. Have children sound out the word again.
If... children say the wrong sound,	**then...** keep your finger on the missed sound. Model the correct sound and have children repeat it. Have children sound out the word again.

To Do	To Say
Test children on reading *mud*.	Test **Now say the sounds quickly to say the word.** Move your finger quickly across the arrow as children quickly say the sounds. **What's the word?** Repeat with *not, fan,* and *in*.

Ongoing Assessment

If... children say the wrong word when they say the sounds quickly,	**then...** tell them the correct word and have children repeat it. Have children say the sounds slowly and quickly again.

To Do	To Say
Test the group.	Point to the words in random order. Have the group say the sounds slowly and then quickly.
Give individual turns.	Give a child one of the word cards from the Word Page to sound out and read. Have the child first touch under each letter while slowly saying the sounds and then move a finger quickly across the arrow while quickly saying the sounds. Provide physical assistance as needed.

Ongoing Assessment

If... a child makes an error,	**then...** correct the error with the whole group. Have the child who made the error sound out and read the word again.
If... children make many errors during their individual turns,	**then...** model, lead, and test each word again with the whole group. When the group can sound out and read each word, resume individual turns.

Activity 5 Writer's Warm-Up

Introduce z

Objective: Children trace and write *z* and review writing *a, g, u, j, n, w,* and *r.*

Time: 2–3 minutes

	To Do	To Say
Review letter name and sound	Hold up the *z* Tracing Card.	**Test** **What is the <u>name</u> of this letter? What is the <u>sound</u> for this letter?**
Model tracing *z*	Distribute a Writer's Warm-Up to each child. Hold up the *z* Tracing Card.	**Model** **Everyone, watch as I trace the letter *z* with my finger.** **Lead** **Now you trace the first two *z*'s on your warm-up sheet with your finger.**
	Model tracing *z* again.	**Model** **Everyone, watch as I trace *z* again.** **Lead** **Now use your pencil to trace the next two *z*'s.**
Model writing *z*	Hold up the lined side of the *z* Tracing Card.	**Model** **Everyone watch as I write the letter *z*. I start at the dot and write the letter.** **Lead** **Now you write two *z*'s on your warm-up sheet. Start at the dot like I did. Write your letters carefully.** **Ongoing Assessment** **If...** children make an error, **then...** put your hand over their hand and guide them to write the letter. Then have them write the letter on their own. Repeat as necessary.
Test knowledge of writing *z*	Model writing *z* again.	Have children cover the letters they traced and wrote. Have them write *z* two times from memory. Then have them uncover their papers and compare the letters. **Do your letters look the same? Circle your best *z*.**
Review ***a, g, u, j, n, w, r***		Have children trace and write each review letter on their warm-up sheets. **Ongoing Assessment** **If...** children make an error, **then...** model writing the letter using the tracing card and have children write the letter again. If needed, put your hand over their hand and guide them to write the letter. Then have them write the letter on their own. Repeat as necessary.

Activity 6 Connect Sound to Letter

Practice Session: Spelling

Objective: Children segment words and connect sounds to letters.

Time: 2–3 minutes

	To Do	To Say
Introduce the activity	Gather a 3-Square Strip and the letter tiles.	**Today we're going to practice spelling words to get ready for Word Dictation.** Depending on children's abilities, you may wish to display letter tiles for all letters children have learned. Keep the activity brief so that more time can be spent on Activity 7.
Lead the activity	Set out the 3-Square Strip and the letter tiles. Segment the word *bin*.	Lead **The first word is *bin*. What is the first word?** Have children hold out three fingers. **Say the sounds in *bin* and touch a finger for each sound.**
	Identify the letter for the first sound in *bin*.	**Does everyone know what the first letter in *bin* is?** Call on a child to choose the correct letter tile and place it in the first square.
	Identify the letter for the middle sound in *bin*.	**Does everyone know what the next letter in *bin* is?** Call on a child to choose the correct letter tile and place it in the middle square.
	Identify the letter for the last sound in *bin*.	**Does everyone know what the last letter in *bin* is?** Call on a child to choose the correct letter tile and place it in the last square. **Ongoing Assessment** **If...** children make an error, **then...** have them segment the word again.
	Confirm the spelling of *bin*.	Lead **Now say each sound in *bin* with me as I point to the letters: /b/ /iii/ /nnn/. Now say the sounds quickly to say the word: *bin*. That's right; you spelled *bin*. The sounds in *bin* are /b/ /iii/ /nnn/.** Practice with *fog, win, bog,* and *wig*, as time allows.

Activity 7 Connect Sound to Letter

Word Dictation

Objective: Children connect sounds to letters to spell words. Time: 6–8 minutes

	To Do	To Say
Introduce the activity	Give each child a Write-On/Wipe-Off Card and a marker.	**I'm going to say a word.** ***You're*** **going to spell it. Let's see how many words we can spell!**
Model the activity	Hold up a Write-On/Wipe-Off Card. Model identifying the letter for the first sound in *fib*.	**Model** **The first word is *fib*. Listen. I'll say the sounds in *fib* and touch a finger for each sound: /fff/ /iii/ /b/.** Point to the first finger. **I'm going to write the first letter in *fib*.** Write an *f* on your card.
	Model identifying the letter for the middle sound in *fib*.	**Now I'll write the next letter in *fib*.** Write an *i* on your card and show children.
	Model identifying the letter for the last sound in *fib*.	**Now I'll write the last letter in *fib*.** Write a *b* on your card and show children.
	Confirm the spelling of *fib*.	**Lead** **Everyone, say each sound in *fib* with me and touch a finger as we say each sound: /fff/ /iii/ /b/. Say the sounds quickly to say the word: *fib*. That's right; you spelled *fib*. The sounds in *fib* are /fff/ /iii/ /b/ and *f-i-b* spells *fib*.**

Activity 7 Connect Sound to Letter (continued))

	To Do	To Say	
Test children on spelling *win, big, web, cob,* and *fig*	Test children on identifying the letters for the first and middle sounds in *win*.	**Test**	**The next word is *win*. What is the next word? Say the sounds in *win* and touch a finger for each sound: /www/ /iii/ /nnn/. Now, everyone, write the first letter in *win*.** Watch as children write a *w* on their cards. **Write the next letter in *win*.**
			Ongoing Assessment **If**...children make an error, **then**...have them segment the word again.
	Test children on identifying the letter for the last sound in *win*.	**Test**	**Write the last letter in *win*.**
			Ongoing Assessment **If**...children make an error, **then**...have them segment the word again.
	Confirm the spelling of *win*.	**Lead**	**Now say each sound in *win* with me and point to your letters as we say each sound: /www/ /iii/ /nnn/. Say the sounds quickly to say the word: *win*. That's right; you spelled *win*. The sounds in *win* are /www/ /iii/ /nnn/ and *w-i-n* spells *win*.** Repeat the test for *big, web, cob*, and *fig*.

New Sound /z/
Review Sounds /u/, /f/, /a/, /l/, /i/, /b/, /t/, /g/, /m/
Key Reading Skills Letter-Sound Correspondence; Word Reading: VC, CVC

Phonological Awareness and Alphabetic Understanding

Activity	Materials		Time
1. Alphabetic Introduce *z*/z/	Alphabet Card: *z* Letter Card: *z* (one per child)		1–2 minutes
2. Integrated Phonologic/Alphabetic Which Picture Begins with /z/?	Alphabet Card: *z* Picture Choices: 87-1, 87-2, 87-3 Teacher Resource Package 3		4–5 minutes
3. Alphabetic Sounds Dash	Sounds Dash Teacher Resource Package 3	timer (not provided)	4–5 minutes
4. Phonologic/Reading Say the Sounds/ Say the Word with Fingers; Regular Words	Regular Words Teacher Resource Package 3 Word Cards: *it, leg, ran, at* (Lessons 85–90)		4–5 minutes

Writing and Spelling

Activity	Materials		Time
5. Writer's Warm-Up Memory Review: *e, i, u, w, t, r, s, l, n*	Write-On/Wipe-Off Cards (one per child) markers (not provided)	Tracing Cards: *e, i, u, w, t, r, s, l, n*	2–3 minutes
6. Integrated Phonologic/Alphabetic Practice Session: Spelling	3-Square Strip	Letter Tiles: *e, i, u, w, t, r, n*	2–3 minutes
7. Phonologic/Spelling Rescue the Cat	Rescue the Cat (one per child) Student Activity Book 3, p. 33		6–8 minutes

Activity 1 Introduce Letter Name and Sound

Introduce z/z/

Objective: Children learn and trace z/z/.

Time: 1–2 minutes

	To Do	To Say	
Introduce letter name	Hold up the *z* Alphabet Card.	Model	**The name of this letter is *z*.**
		Lead	**Say the name of the letter with me: *z*.**
		Test	**What is the name of this letter?**
Introduce letter sound	Continue holding up the *z* Alphabet Card.	Model	**The sound for this letter is /zzz/. When you say /zzz/, the tip of your tongue touches above your top teeth and your voice box is on. Put your hand on your throat to see if your voice box is on when you say /zzz/; /zzz/. Yes, your voice box is on when you say /zzz/.**
		Lead	**Say the sound with me: /zzz/.**
		Test	**What is the sound for this letter?**
Test knowledge of letter name and sound	Continue holding up the *z* Alphabet Card.	Test	**What is the name of this letter? What is the sound for this letter?**
	Give individual turns on letter name and sound.		**Ongoing Assessment** — If... children make an error, then... tell them the name or sound, have them repeat the name or sound, and return to the letter a second time.
Model tracing *z*	Distribute the *z* Letter Cards. Hold up the *z* Alphabet Card.	Model	**Everyone, watch. I'll trace the letter *z*.** Have children trace the *z* on their letter cards three times. Tell them to say /zzz/ each time they trace the letter.
			Ongoing Assessment — If... children make an error, then... put your hand over their hand and guide them to trace the letter. Then have them try to trace the letter on their own. Repeat as necessary.

Activity 2 Isolate Initial Sound

Which Picture Begins with /z/?

Objective: Children isolate initial /z/ and connect sound to letter. Time: 4–5 minutes

	To Do	To Say
Model names of pictures	Gather the picture choices. Display Picture Choice 87-1. Point to *apple*.	Model **This is *apple*. What is this?** Continue with the remaining pictures: *zebra, rug; zoo, jam, umbrella.* Test children on the picture names by pointing to the pictures one at a time and asking: **What is this?**
Introduce the game Which Picture Begins with /z/?		**Now we're going to play a game. I'll show you a letter and three pictures. You'll tell me which picture begins with the sound for the letter.**
Model the game	Hold up the *z* Alphabet Card.	Model **The name of this letter is *z*. The sound for this letter is /zzz/. Remember, when you say /zzz/, the tip of your tongue touches above your top teeth, and your voice box is on.**
		Test **What is the <u>sound</u> for this letter?**
	Display Picture Choice 87-1. Cover the bottom row.	Model **My turn. I'll show you how to play the game. This is *apple, zebra, rug*. I'll find the picture that has the first sound /zzz/: *zebra*** (exaggerate the first sound). ***Zebra* has the first sound /zzz/.** Exaggerate the first sound and say the word: **/zzz/, *zebra*.** Model again with the bottom row of pictures: *zoo, jam, umbrella*.
Play the game to test knowledge of initial /z/	Hold up the *z* Alphabet Card.	Test **What is the <u>sound</u> for this letter?**
	Display Picture Choice 87-2. Cover the bottom row.	Have children name each picture: *ant, jeep, zipper*. **Which picture has the first sound /zzz/?** Confirm correct responses and prompt sound production: **Yes, *zipper* has the first sound /zzz/. Let's say /zzz/. Remember, when you say /zzz/, the tip of your tongue touches above your top teeth, and your voice box is on.** Continue with the bottom row of pictures *(zebra, up, run)* and Picture Choice 87-3 *(under, zoo, jet; astronaut, rake, zipper)*.
	Give individual turns.	**Ongoing Assessment** **If...** children make incorrect responses, **then...** model the correct answer. Review the sound production cue. Have children repeat the correct answer. Go back to the example a second time.

Activity 3 Build Sounds Fluency

Sounds Dash

Objective: Children increase fluency in identifying letter sounds.

Time: 4–5 minutes

	To Do	To Say
Introduce the activity	Display the Sounds Dash page.	**Today we're going to have a Sounds Dash. I'll point to a letter. You'll say the sound for the letter. Let's see how close we can get to the finish line in one minute. Be careful, though. If I hear a wrong sound, you'll have to go back three letters. Remember, too, that you will need to hold some of the sounds. Some of the sounds you will say only for as long as I touch under the letter.**
Model the activity	Display the Sounds Dash page.	Model **Let's get warmed up for our Sounds Dash. We'll practice the sounds in the first row. Then we'll start the timer for our dash.** Point to *u.* **What is the sound for this letter?** Hold your finger under the letter for about two seconds as children say the sound. **Yes, the sound for this letter is /uuu/.** **Ongoing Assessment** **If...** children make an error, **then...** tell them the sound, have them repeat it, and move back three letters on the page or repeat the letter if it is at the beginning of the row. Practice the sound of each letter in the first row. If children miss more than two sounds, do not proceed with the activity. Instead, practice the sounds on the page, especially those that children know less well.
Lead the activity	Display the Sounds Dash page. Set the timer for one minute.	Lead **Now you're ready for the Sounds Dash. Everyone, look at my finger. On your mark, get set, go!** Point to *u* in the first row. **What is the sound for this letter?** Repeat for each sound in the first row. Then immediately proceed to the next row, and so on. **Ongoing Assessment** **If...** children make an error, **then...** tell them the sound, have them repeat it, and move back three letters on the page or repeat the letter if it is at the beginning of the row. Stop the activity after exactly one minute. Praise children for how far they went. Tell them that they will have a chance to beat their score in three days when they play again.

Activity 4 Read Words

Say the Sounds/Say the Word with Fingers; Regular Words

Objective: Children segment, blend, and read words.

Time: 4–5 minutes

	To Do	To Say
Introduce the activity		**Let's play Say the Sounds/Say the Word with Fingers. I'll say the sounds of a word slowly. You'll repeat each sound as you touch a finger. Then you'll say the sounds quickly to say the word.**
Model the activity	Model segmenting and blending *it*.	**Model** **Let's do a two-sound word together. Hold out two fingers.** Their fingers should be pointed toward you. **Listen to the sounds:** (pause) **/iii/ /t/.** Touch a finger as you say each sound, moving from left to right, without stopping between the sounds. **Lead** **Say the sounds slowly with me: /iii/ /t/.** You and children touch a finger for each sound, moving from left to right. **Now say the sounds quickly with me to say the word.** Clap with children as you and they say the word: ***it.***
Test knowledge of segmenting and blending	Test children on segmenting *fun*.	**Test** **It's your turn to do a three-sound word. Hold out three fingers. Listen to the sounds:** (pause) **/fff/ /uuu/ /nnn/.** Touch a finger as you say each sound, without stopping between the sounds. **Say the sounds slowly.** You and children touch a finger for each sound as children only say the sounds. **Ongoing Assessment** **If...** children do not touch the appropriate finger for each sound, **then...** model how to do it. Have children try again. If needed, guide their hands to touch the appropriate fingers. **If...** children stop between the sounds, **then . . .** model how to say the sounds without stopping between them. Have children say the sounds again.
	Test children on blending *fun*.	**Test** **Now say the sounds quickly to say the word.** Repeat the test with *leg, at, ran,* and *nod.* Then give individual turns. **Ongoing Assessment** **If...** children have difficulty saying the sounds quickly, **then...** tell them the word. Model how to say the sounds slowly and quickly. Have children segment and blend the word again.

Activity 4 Read Words (continued)

	To Do	To Say
Introduce the activity	Display the Regular Words card.	**Now it's time to read some words. First, we'll say the sounds in the word slowly. Then we'll say the sounds quickly to say the word. Some of the words end with quick sounds, so you'll have to watch my finger carefully.**
Test knowledge of segmenting and blending regular words	Gather the word cards. Display the Regular Words card. Test children on segmenting *it*.	**Test** **Now it's your turn to read a word. First, you'll say the sounds slowly. Then you'll say the sounds quickly to say the word. Say the sounds. Get ready.** Move your finger under each letter as children say the sounds. Touch under the first letter for one to two seconds. Tap your finger under the second letter.

Ongoing Assessment

If... children pause between sounds,	**then...** model saying the sounds without stopping between them. Have children sound out the word again.
If... children say the wrong sound,	**then...** keep your finger on the missed sound. Model the correct sound and have children repeat it. Have children sound out the word again.

To Do	To Say
Test children on blending *it*.	**Test** **Now say the sounds quickly to say the word.** Move your finger quickly across the arrow as only children quickly say the sounds. **What's the word?** Repeat with *leg, ran,* and *at.*

Ongoing Assessment

If... children say the wrong word when they say the sounds quickly,	**then...** tell them the correct word and have children repeat it. Have children say the sounds slowly and quickly again.

To Do	To Say
Test the group.	Point to the words in random order. Have the group say the sounds slowly and quickly.
Give individual turns.	Give a child one of the word cards from the Word Page to sound out and read. Have the child first touch under each letter while slowly saying the sounds and then move a finger quickly across the arrow while quickly saying the sounds. Provide physical assistance as needed.

Ongoing Assessment

If... a child makes an error,	**then...** correct the error with the whole group. Have the child who made the error sound out and read the word again.
If... children make many errors during their individual turns,	**then...** model, lead, and test each word again with the whole group. When the group can sound out and read each word, resume individual turns.

Activity 5 Writer's Warm-Up

Memory Review: e, i, u, w, t, r, s, l, n

Objective: Children practice writing letters. Time: 2–3 minutes

	To Do	To Say
Review letter names	Gather the tracing cards. Hold up the *e* Tracing Card.	**Test** **What is the name of this letter?** Continue with the remaining cards.
Introduce the activity	Give each child a Write-On/Wipe-Off Card and a marker.	**Today you're going to practice writing some of the letters you've learned. I'll say the name of a letter. *You'll* write the letter on your card.**
Model the activity	Hold up a Write-On/Wipe Off Card.	**Model** **My turn. I'll show you how this activity works. The first letter is *n*. Now I'll write the letter *n* on my card.**
Test knowledge of writing *e, i, u, w, t, r, s, l,* and *n*		**Test** Dictate the name of a letter and have children write the letter on their cards. Reinforce the group on the letter name: **Everyone, what's the name of the letter you wrote?** Dictate each letter once, or as time allows. Erase the cards between turns.

Ongoing Assessment

If . . . children write the wrong letter or don't remember a letter, **then . . .** show them the tracing card of the correct letter. Trace the letter and say its name.

Activity 6 Connect Sound to Letter

Practice Session: Spelling

Objective: Children segment words.

Time: 2–3 minutes

	To Do	To Say
Introduce the activity	Gather the 3-Square Strip and the letter tiles.	**Today we're going to practice spelling words to get ready for Rescue the Cat.** Depending on children's abilities, you may wish to display letter tiles for all letters children have learned. Keep the activity brief so that more time can be spent on Activity 7.
Lead the activity	Set out the 3-Square Strip and the letter tiles. Segment the word *rut*.	**Lead** **The first word is *rut*. What is the first word?** Have children hold out three fingers. **Say the sounds in *rut* and touch a finger for each sound.**
	Identify the letter for the first sound in *rut*.	**Does everyone know what the first letter in *rut* is?** Call on a child to choose the correct letter tile and place it in the first square.
	Identify the letter for the middle sound in *rut*.	**Does everyone know what the next letter in *rut* is?** Call on a child to choose the correct letter tile and place it in the middle square. **Ongoing Assessment** **If...** children make an error, **then...** have them segment the word again.
	Identify the letter for the last sound in *rut*.	**Does everyone know what the last letter in *rut* is?** Call on a child to choose the correct letter tile and place it in the last square. **Ongoing Assessment** **If...** children make an error, **then...** have them segment the word again.
	Confirm the spelling of *rut*.	**Say each sound in *rut* with me as I point to the letters: /rrr/ /uuu/ /t/. Now say the sounds quickly to say the word: *rut*. That's right; you spelled *rut*. The sounds in *rut* are /rrr/ /uuu/ /t/ and *r-u-t* spells *rut*.** Practice with *ten, wet, win,* and *net*, as time allows.

7 Connect Sound to Letter

Rescue the Cat

Objective: Children connect sounds to letters to spell words. Time: 6–8 minutes

	To Do	To Say	
Introduce the activity	Distribute Rescue the Cat.		**Today's activity is Rescue the Cat. I'm going to say a word. You're going to spell it. Let's see if we can help the firefighter climb the tree to rescue the cat!**
Model the activity	Hold up a Rescue the Cat. Point to the word space below the firefighter. Model identifying the letter for the first sound.	Model	**We'll write the first word in the word space next to the fire truck. Everyone, find the word space next to the fire truck. The first word is *run*. Listen. I'll say the sounds in *run* and touch a finger for each sound: /rrr/ /uuu/ /nnn/. Now I'm going to write the first letter in *run*.** Write an *r* in the first letter space and show children.
			Now you write the first letter in *run*.
	Model identifying the letter for the middle sound.		**I'm going to write the next letter in *run*.** Write a *u* in the middle letter space and show children.
			Now you write the next letter in *run*.
	Model identifying the letter for the last sound.		**Now I'll write the last letter in *run*.** Write an *n* in the last letter space and show children.
			Now you write the last letter in *run*.
	Confirm the spelling.	Lead	**Everyone, say each sound in *run* with me and point to your letters as we say each sound: /rrr/ /uuu /nnn/. Say the sounds quickly to say the word: *run*. That's right; you spelled *run*. The sounds in *run* are /rrr/ /uuu/ /nnn/ and *r-u-n* spells *run*.**

	To Do	To Say
Test children on spelling *let, tin, sun,* and *win*	Test children on identifying the letter for the first sound.	**Test** **Find your way up the tree to the next word space. The next word is *let*. What is the next word? Say the sounds in *let* and touch a finger for each sound: /lll/ /eee/ /t/. Now write the first letter in *let* in the first letter space.**
	Test children on identifying the letter for the middle sound.	**Write the next letter in *let* in the next letter space.** **Ongoing Assessment** **If**... children make an error, **then**... have them segment the word again.
	Test children on identifying the letter for the last sound.	**Write the last letter in *let* in the last letter space.** **Ongoing Assessment** **If**... children make an error, **then**... have them segment the word again.
	Confirm the spelling.	**Lead** **Now say each sound in *let* with me and point to your letters as we say each sound: /lll/ /eee/ /t/. Say the sounds quickly to say the word: *let*. That's right; you spelled *let*. The sounds in *let* are /lll/ /eee/ /t/ and *l-e-t* spells *let*.** Repeat with *tin, sun,* and *win*.

New Sound /h/
Review Sounds /t/, /o/, /r/, /i/, /u/, /j/, /e/, /z/
Key Reading Skills Letter-Sound Correspondences; Word Reading: VC, CVC

Phonological Awareness and Alphabetic Understanding

Activity	Materials		Time
1. Alphabetic Introduce *h*/h/	Alphabet Card: *h* Letter Card: *h* (one per child)		1–2 minutes
2. Phonologic Does It Begin with /h/?	Picture Cards: *hen, wave, hat, hose, house, jeep*		4–5 minutes
3. Alphabetic Sounds	Sounds Teacher Resource Package 3		4–5 minutes
4. Phonologic/Reading Say the Sounds/ Say the Word with Fingers; Regular Words	Regular Words Teacher Resource Package 3	Word Cards: *wet, up, mop, sit* (Lessons 85–90)	4–5 minutes

Writing and Spelling

Activity	Materials		Time
5. Writer's Warm-Up Introduce *h*	Writer's Warm-Up (one per child) Student Activity Book 3, p. 34 or 35	Tracing Cards: *h, z, g, e, j, n, w, b*	2–3 minutes
6. Integrated Phonologic/Alphabetic Practice Session: Spelling	3-Square Strip	Letter Tiles: *e, u, a, w, t, z, p, c, l*	2–3 minutes
7. Phonologic/Spelling Monster Words	Write-On/Wipe-Off Cards (three) marker (not provided)		6–8 minutes

Activity 1 Introduce Letter Name and Sound

Introduce h/h/

Objective: Children learn and trace *h*/h/.

Time: 1–2 minutes

	To Do	To Say	
Introduce letter name	Hold up the *h* Alphabet Card.	Model	**The name of this letter is *h*.**
		Lead	**Say the name of the letter with me: *h*.**
		Test	**What is the name of this letter?**
Introduce letter sound	Continue holding up the *h* Alphabet Card.	Model	**The sound for this letter is /h/. When you say /h/, air comes out of your mouth. Put your hand in front of your mouth. Say /h/ and feel the air come out of your mouth. Everyone, say /h/.**
		Lead	**Say the sound with me: /h/.**
		Test	**What is the sound for this letter?**
Test knowledge of letter name and sound	Continue holding up the *h* Alphabet Card.	Test	**What is the name of this letter? What is the sound for this letter?**
	Give individual turns on letter name and sound.		**Ongoing Assessment** If... children make an error, then... tell them the name or sound, have them repeat the name or sound, and return to the letter a second time.
Model tracing *h*	Distribute the *h* Letter Cards. Hold up the *h* Alphabet Card.	Model	**Everyone, watch. I'll trace the letter *h*.** Have children trace the *h* on their letter cards three times. Tell them to say /h/ each time they trace the letter.
			Ongoing Assessment If... children make an error, then... put your hand over their hand and guide them to trace the letter. Then have them try to trace the letter on their own. Repeat as necessary.

Activity 2 Isolate Initial Sound

Does It Begin with /h/?

Objective: Children isolate initial /h/.

Time: 4–5 minutes

	To Do	To Say
Model names of pictures	Gather the picture cards. Place the *hen* Picture Card on the table.	Model **This is *hen*. What is this?** Continue with the remaining cards. Test children on the picture names by placing the cards on the table one at a time and asking: **What is this?**
Introduce the game Does It Begin with /h/?	Practice production of target sound.	**Now we're going to play a game. I'll show you a picture. *You'll* tell whether it begins with /h/.** **Let's say /h/. Remember, when you say /h/, air comes out of your mouth. Put your hand in front of your mouth. Say /h/ and feel the air come out. Everyone, say /h/.**
Model the game	Place the *hen* Picture Card on the table.	Model **My turn. I'll say the name of the picture and then tell whether it begins with /h/: *hen*** (exaggerate the first sound). ***Hen* begins with /h/. Feel the air come out of your mouth when you say /h/, *hen*. Next picture: *wave*** (exaggerate the first sound). ***Wave* does not begin with /h/.**
Play the game to test knowledge of initial /h/	Place the *hat* Picture Card on the table. Give individual turns.	Test **What is this? Does *hat*** (exaggerate the first sound) **begin with /h/?** Confirm correct responses and prompt sound production: ***Yes, hat* begins with /h/. Let's say /h/. Remember, when you say /h/, air comes out of your mouth.** Continue with *hose, house,* and *jeep*. **Ongoing Assessment** **If...** children make an error, **then...** model the correct answer. Review the sound production cue. Have children repeat the correct answer. Go back to the example a second time.

Activity 3 Discriminate Letter Sounds

Sounds

Objective: Children discriminate letter sounds: r/r/, t/t/, z/z/, j/j/, o/o/, u/u/, i/i/, e/e/.

Time: 4–5 minutes

	To Do	To Say
Introduce the activity	Display the Sounds page.	**I'm going to point to one of the letters on this page. You're going to tell me the sound for the letter. Some of the sounds will be quick sounds. You should say a quick sound only for as long as I touch under the letter.** Point to the letter briefly if it is a stop sound such as /b/. Hold your finger under the letter for about two seconds if it is a continuous sound such as /aaa/.
Test knowledge of letter sounds	Continue to display the Sounds page. Point to *r*.	**Test** **What is the <u>sound</u> for this letter?** Hold your finger under the letter for about two seconds as children say the sound. Confirm correct responses: **Yes, the <u>sound</u> for this letter is /rrr/.** Continue with the remaining letters, moving from left to right across the page.
	Give individual turns.	**Ongoing Assessment** **If . . .** children make an error, **then . . .** tell them the sound, have them repeat it, and move back two letters on the page or repeat the letter if it is at the beginning of the page. **If . . .** children miss more than two sounds on the page, **then . . .** repeat the test for all of the letters on the page.

Activity 4 Read Words

Say the Sounds/Say the Word with Fingers; Regular Words

Objective: Children segment, blend, and read words. Time: 2–3 minutes

	To Do	To Say
Introduce the activity		**Now we're going to play Say the Sounds/Say the Word with Fingers. I'll say the sounds of a word slowly. You'll slowly repeat each sound as you touch a finger. Then you'll say the sounds quickly to say the word.**
Model the activity	Model segmenting and blending *mop*.	**Model** **Let's do a three-sound word together. Hold out three fingers.** Have children hold out three fingers pointed toward you. Have them use the pointer finger of the other hand to touch a finger for each sound, moving from left to right. **Listen to the sounds:** (pause) **/mmm/ /ooo/ /p/.** Touch a finger as you say each sound, without stopping between the sounds. **Lead** **Say the sounds slowly with me: /mmm/ /ooo/ /p/.** You and children touch a finger for each sound. **Now say the sounds quickly with me to say the word.** Clap with children as you and they say the word: ***mop.***
Test knowledge of segmenting and blending	Test children on segmenting *sit*.	**Test** **It's your turn to do a three-sound word. Hold out three fingers. Listen to the sounds:** (pause) **/sss/ /iii/ /t/.** Touch a finger as you say each sound, without stopping between the sounds. **Say the sounds slowly.** You and children touch a finger as they slowly say each sound. **Ongoing Assessment** **If...** children do not touch the appropriate finger for each sound, **then...** model how to do it. Have children try again. If needed, guide their hands to touch the appropriate fingers. **If...** children stop between the sounds, **then...** model how to say the sounds without stopping between them. Have children say the sounds again.
	Test children on blending *sit*.	**Test** **Now say the sounds quickly to say the word.** Clap with children as only they say the word *sit*. **Ongoing Assessment** **If...** children have difficulty saying the sounds quickly, **then...** tell them the word and then model how to say the sounds slowly and quickly. Have children try again. Repeat the test with *in, up, wet,* and *nap*. For *in* and *up*, have children hold out two fingers. Then give individual turns.

Activity 4 Read Words (continued)

	To Do	To Say
Introduce the activity	Display the Regular Words page.	**Let's read some words. First, we'll say the sounds in the word slowly. Then we'll say the sounds quickly to say the word. Some of the words end with quick sounds, so watch my finger.**
Test knowledge of segmenting and blending regular words	Gather the word cards. Display the Regular Words page. Test children on segmenting *wet*.	Test **Now it's your turn to read a word. First, you'll say the sounds slowly. Then you'll say the sounds quickly to say the word. Get ready. Say the sounds.** Move your finger under each letter as children say the sounds. Touch under the first two letters for one to two seconds. Tap your finger under the last letter.
		Ongoing Assessment **If...** children pause between sounds, **then...** model saying the sounds without stopping between them. Have children sound out the word again. **If...** children say the wrong sound, **then...** keep your finger on the missed sound. Model the correct sound and have children repeat it. Have children sound out the word again.
	Test children on blending *wet*.	Test **Now say the sounds quickly to say the word.** Move your finger quickly across the arrow as children quickly say the sounds. **What's the word?** Repeat the test with *up, mop,* and *sit*.
		Ongoing Assessment **If...** children say the wrong word when they say the sounds quickly, **then...** model the correct word and have children repeat it. Have children say the sounds slowly and quickly again.
	Test the group.	Point to the words in random order. Have children say the sounds slowly and then quickly.
	Give individual turns.	Give a child one of the word cards from the Word Page to sound out and read. Have the child first touch under each letter while slowly saying the sounds and then move a finger across the arrow while quickly saying the sounds. Provide physical assistance as needed.
		Ongoing Assessment **If...** a child makes an error, **then...** correct the error with the whole group. Have the child who made the error sound out and read the word again. **If...** children make many errors during their individual turns, **then...** model, lead, and test each word again with the group. When the group can sound out and read each word, resume individual turns.

Activity 5 Writer's Warm-Up

Introduce h

Objective: Children trace and write *h and review writing z, g, e, j, n, w,* and *b*.

Time: 2–3 minutes

	To Do	To Say
Review letter name and sound	Hold up the *h* Tracing Card.	Test **What is the <u>name</u> of this letter? What is the <u>sound</u> for this letter?**
Model tracing *h*	Distribute a Writer's Warm-Up to each child. Hold up the *h* Tracing Card. Model tracing *h* again.	Model **Everyone, watch as I trace the letter *h* with my finger.** **Use your finger to trace the first two *h*'s on your sheet.** **Everyone, watch as I trace *h* again.** **Now use your pencil to trace the next two *h*'s on your sheet.**
Model writing *h*	Hold up the lined side of the *h* Tracing Card.	Model **Everyone, watch as I write the letter *h*. I start at the dot and write the letter.** **Now you write two *h*'s. Start at the dot like I did. Write your letters carefully.** **Ongoing Assessment** **If...** children make an error, **then...** put your hand over their hand and guide them to write the letter. Then have them try to write the letter on their own. Repeat as necessary.
Test knowledge of writing *h*	Model writing *h* again.	Have children cover the letters they traced and wrote. Have them write the letter two times from memory. Then have them uncover their papers and compare the letters. **Do your letters look the same? Circle your best *h*.**
Review ***z, g, e, j, n, w, b***		Have children trace and write each review letter on their warm-up sheets. **Ongoing Assessment** **If...** children make an error, **then...** use the tracing card to model tracing the letter and have them write the letter again. If needed, put your hand over their hand and guide them to write the letter. Then have them try to write the letter on their own. Repeat as necessary.

Activity 6 Connect Sound to Letter

Practice Session: Spelling

Objective: Children segment words and connect sounds to letters.

Time: 2–3 minutes

	To Do	To Say
Introduce the activity	Gather the 3-Square Strip and the letter tiles.	**Today we're going to practice spelling words to get ready for Monster Words.** Depending on children's abilities, you may wish to display letter tiles for all letters children have learned. Keep the activity brief so that more time can be spent on Activity 7.
Lead the activity	Set out the 3-Square Strip and the letter tiles. Segment the word *wet*.	**Lead** **The first word is *wet*. What is the first word?** Have children hold out three fingers. **Say the sounds in *wet* and touch a finger for each sound.**
	Identify the letter for the first sound in *wet*.	**Does everyone know what the first letter in *wet* is?** Call on a child to choose the correct letter tile and place it in the first square.
	Identify the letter for the middle sound in *wet*.	**Does everyone know what the next letter in *wet* is?** Call on a child to choose the correct letter tile and place it in the middle square. **Ongoing Assessment** **If**... children make an error, **then**... have them segment the word again.
	Identify the letter for the last sound in *wet*.	**Does everyone know what the last letter in *wet* is?** Call on a child to choose the correct letter tile and place it in the last square. **Ongoing Assessment** **If**... children make an error, **then**... have them segment the word again.
	Confirm the spelling of *wet*.	**Say each sound in *wet* with me as I point to the letters: /www/ /eee/ /t/. Now say the sounds quickly to say the word: *wet*. That's right; you spelled *wet*. The sounds in *wet* are /www/ /eee/ /t/ and *w-e-t* spells *wet*.** Practice with *lap, pet, cup,* and *zap,* as time allows.

Activity 7 Connect Sound to Letter

Monster Words

Objective: Children connect sounds to letters to spell words.

Time: 6–8 minutes

	To Do	To Say
Introduce the activity	Set out in a row three Write-On/Wipe-Off Cards.	**Now we're going to write some monster words. I'll say a word. You'll spell the word by writing big, monster letters on these Write-On/Wipe-Off Cards. Let's see how many monster words we can spell!**
Model the activity	Model identifying the letter for the first sound in *let*.	**Model** **The first word is *let*. Listen. I'll say the sounds in *let* and touch a finger for each sound: /lll/ /eee/ /t/. I'm going to write the first letter in *let*.** Write a big *l* on the first card.
	Model identifying the letter for the middle sound in *let*.	**Now I'll write the next letter in *let*.** Write a big *e* on the next card.
	Model identifying the letter for the last sound in *let*.	**Now I'll write the last letter in *let*.** Write a big *t* on the last card.
	Confirm the spelling of *let*.	**Lead** **Everyone, say each sound in *let* with me as I point to the letters: /lll/ /eee/ /t/. Say the sounds quickly to say the word: *let*. That's right; you spelled *let*. The sounds in *let* are /lll/ /eee/ /t/ and *l-e-t* spells *let*.**

	To Do	To Say
Test children on spelling *tap, pup, wet, cap,* and *zap*	Test children on identifying the letter for the first sound.	**Test** **The next word is *tap*. What is the next word? Say the sounds in *tap* and touch a finger for each sound: /t/ /aaa/ /p/. Write the first letter in *tap* on the first card.** Call on a child to write the first letter in *tap* on the first card.
	Test children on identifying the letter for the middle sound.	**Write the next letter in *tap* on the next card.** Call on a child to write the next letter in *tap* on the next card. **Ongoing Assessment** **If**... children make an error, **then**... have them segment the word again.
	Test children on identifying the letter for the last sound.	**Write the last letter in *tap* on the last card.** Call on a child to write the last letter in *tap* on the last card. **Ongoing Assessment** **If**... children make an error, **then**... have them segment the word again.
	Confirm the spelling.	**Lead** **Now say each sound in *tap* with me as I point to the letters: /t/ /aaa/ /p/. Say the sounds quickly to say the word: *tap*. That's right; you spelled *tap*. The sounds in *tap* are /t/ /aaa/ /p/ and *t-a-p* spells *tap*.** Repeat the test with *pup, wet, cap,* and *zap*.

New Sound /h/
Review Sounds /a/, /o/, /i/, /g/, /u/, /e/, /z/
Key Reading Skills Letter-Sound Correspondences; Word Reading: VC, CVC

Phonological Awareness and Alphabetic Understanding

Activity	Materials		Time
1. Alphabetic Introduce *h*/h/	Alphabet Card: *h* Letter Card: *h* (one per child)		1–2 minutes
2. Phonologic Which Picture Begins with /h/?	Picture Choices: 89-1, 89-2, 89-3 Teacher Resource Package 3		4–5 minutes
3. Alphabetic Sounds	Sounds Teacher Resource Package 3		4–5 minutes
4. Phonologic/Reading Say the Sounds/ Say the Word with Fingers; Regular Words	Regular Words Teacher Resource Package 3	Word Cards: *us, sad, lip, met* (Lessons 85–90)	4–5 minutes

Writing and Spelling

Activity	Materials		Time
5. Writer's Warm-Up Introduce *h*	Writer's Warm-Up (one per child) Student Activity Book 3, p. 36 or 37	Tracing Cards: *h, z, g, u, j, n, w, r*	2–3 minutes
6. Integrated Phonologic/Alphabetic Practice Session: Spelling	3-Square Strip	Letter Tiles: *e, u, o, w, f, t, b, g*	2–3 minutes
New **7. Phonologic/Spelling** Silly Words	Silly Words (one per child) Student Activity Book 3, p. 38		6–8 minutes

Activity 1 Introduce Letter Name and Sound

Introduce h/h/

Objective: Children learn *h*/h/.

Time: 1–2 minutes

	To Do	To Say
Introduce letter name	Hold up the *h* Alphabet Card.	Model **The name of this letter is *h*.** Lead **Say the name of the letter with me: *h*.** Test **What is the name of this letter?**
Introduce letter sound	Continue holding up the *h* Alphabet Card.	Model **The sound for this letter is /h/. When you say /h/, air comes out of your mouth. Put your hand in front of your mouth. Say /h/ and feel the air come out. Everyone, say /h/.** Lead **Say the sound with me: /h/.** Test **What is the sound for this letter?**
Test knowledge of letter name and sound	Continue holding up the *h* Alphabet Card. Give individual turns on letter name and sound.	Test **What is the name of this letter? What is the sound for this letter?** **Ongoing Assessment** **If...** children make an error, **then...** tell them the name or sound, have them repeat the name or sound, and return to the letter a second time.
Model tracing *h*	Distribute the *h* Letter Cards. Hold up the *h* Alphabet Card.	Model **Everyone, watch. I'll trace the letter *h*.** Have children trace the *h* on their letter cards three times. Tell them to say /h/ each time they trace the letter. **Ongoing Assessment** **If...** children make an error, **then...** put your hand over their hand and guide them to trace the letter. Then have them try to trace the letter on their own. Repeat as necessary.

Activity 2 Isolate Initial Sound

Lesson **89**

Which Picture Begins with /h/?

Objective: Children isolate initial /h/.

Time: 4–5 minutes

	To Do	To Say
Model names of pictures	Gather the picture choices. Display Picture Choice 89-1. Point to *bone*.	**Model** **This is *bone*. What is this?** Continue with the remaining pictures: *hair, wave; hay, web, zipper.* Then test children on the picture names by pointing to the pictures one at a time and asking: **What is this?**
Introduce the game Which Picture Begins with /h/?	Practice production of target sound.	**We're going to play another game with our new sound /h/. I'll show you three pictures. You'll find the picture that begins with /h/.** **Let's say /h/. When you say /h/, air comes out of your mouth. Put your hand in front of your mouth. Say /h/ and feel the air come out.**
Model the game	Display Picture Choice 89-1. Cover the bottom row.	**Model** **My turn. I'll show you how to play the game. This is *bone, hair, wave*. I'll find the picture that begins with /h/: *hair*** (exaggerate the first sound). ***Hair* begins with /h/.** Exaggerate the first sound and say the word: **/h/, *hair*.** Model again with the bottom row of pictures: *hay, web, zipper.*
Play the game to test knowledge of initial /h/	Display Picture Choice 89-2. Cover the bottom row. Give individual turns.	Have children name each picture: *wall, bat, hat.* **Which picture begins with /h/?** Confirm correct responses and prompt sound production: **Yes, *hat* begins with /h/. Let's say /h/. Remember, when you say /h/, air comes out of your mouth.** Continue with the bottom row of pictures *(box, hug, zoo)* and Picture Choice 89-3 *(hoe, wheel, zebra; well, bee, hook)*. **Ongoing Assessment** **If...** children make incorrect responses, **then...** model the correct answer. Review the sound production cue. Have children repeat the correct answer. Go back to the example a second time.

Discriminate Letter Sounds

Lesson
89

Sounds

Objective: Children discriminate letter sounds: *e*/e/, *g*/g/, *h*/h/, *a*/a/, *z*/z/, *i*/i/, *o*/o/, *u*/u/.

Time: 4–5 minutes

	To Do	To Say
Introduce the activity	Display the Sounds page.	**I'm going to point to one of the letters on this page. You're going to tell me the sound for the letter. Some of the sounds will be quick sounds. You should say a quick sound only for as long as I touch under the letter.** Point to the letter briefly if it is a stop sound such as /b/. Hold your finger under the letter for about two seconds if it is a continuous sound such as /aaa/.
Test knowledge of letter sounds	Continue to display the Sounds page. Point to *e*.	**Test** **What is the sound for this letter?** Hold your finger under the letter for about two seconds as children say the sound. Confirm correct responses: **Yes, the sound for this letter is /eee/.** Continue with the remaining letters, moving from left to right across the page.
	Give individual turns.	**Ongoing Assessment** **If...** children make an error, **then...** tell them the sound, have them repeat it, and move back two letters on the page or repeat the letter if it is at the beginning of the page. **If...** children miss more than two sounds on the page, **then...** repeat the test for all of the letters on the page.

Activity 4 Read Words

Say the Sounds/Say the Word with Fingers; Regular Words

Objective: Children segment, blend, and read words. Time: 4–5 minutes

	To Do	To Say
Introduce the activity		**It's time to play Say the Sounds/Say the Word with Fingers. I'll say the sounds of a word slowly. You'll slowly repeat each sound as you touch a finger. Then you'll say the sounds quickly to say the word.**
Model the activity	Model segmenting and blending *met*.	**Model** **Let's do a three-sound word together. Hold out three fingers.** Children hold out three fingers and use the pointer finger of the other hand to touch a finger for each sound, moving from left to right. **Listen to the sounds:** (pause) **/mmm/ /eee/ /t/.** Touch a finger as you say each sound, without stopping between the sounds. **Lead** **Say the sounds slowly with me: /mmm/ /eee/ /t/.** You and children touch a finger for each sound. **Now say the sounds quickly with me to say the word.** Clap with children as you and they say the word: ***met.***
Test knowledge of segmenting and blending	Test children on segmenting *sad*.	**Test** **It's your turn to do a three-sound word. Hold out three fingers. Listen to the sounds:** (pause) **/sss/ /aaa/ /d/.** Touch a finger as you say each sound, without stopping between them. **Say the sounds slowly.** You and children touch a finger for each sound as only they say each sound. **Ongoing Assessment** **If . . .** children do not touch the appropriate finger for each sound, **then . . .** model how to do it. Have children try again. If needed, guide their hands to touch the appropriate fingers. **If . . .** children stop between the sounds, **then . . .** model how to say the sounds without stopping between them. Have children say the sounds again.
	Test children on blending *sad*.	**Now say the sounds quickly to say the word.** Clap with children as only they say the word *sad*. **Ongoing Assessment** **If . . .** children have difficulty saying the sounds quickly, **then . . .** tell them the word and model saying the sounds slowly and quickly. Have them try the word again. Repeat the test with *lip, us, fat,* and *mow*. For *us* and *mow*, have children hold out two fingers. Then give individual turns.

	To Do	To Say
Introduce the activity	Display the Regular Words card.	**Let's read some words. First, you'll say the sounds in the word slowly. Then you'll say the sounds quickly to say the word. Some of the words end with quick sounds, so watch my finger.**
Test knowledge of segmenting and blending regular words	Gather the word cards. Display the Regular Words card. Test children on segmenting *us*.	Test **Now it's your turn to read a word. First, you'll say the sounds slowly. Then you'll say the sounds quickly to say the word. Say the sounds. Get ready.** Move your finger under each letter as children say each sound. Touch under each letter for one to two seconds, without pausing between them.

Ongoing Assessment

If... children pause between sounds,	**then...** model saying the sounds without stopping between them. Have children sound out the word again.
If... children say the wrong sound,	**then...** keep your finger on the missed sound. Model the correct sound and have children repeat it. Have children sound out the word again.

To Do	To Say
Test children on blending *us*.	**Now say the sounds quickly to say the word.** Move your finger quickly across the arrow as children quickly say the sounds. **What's the word?** Repeat the test with *sad, lip,* and *met*.

Ongoing Assessment

If... children say the wrong word when they say the sounds quickly,	**then...** tell them the correct word and have children repeat it. Have children say the sounds slowly and quickly again.

To Do	To Say
Test the group.	Point to the words in random order. Have the group say the sounds slowly and then quickly.
Give individual turns.	Give a child one of the word cards to sound out and read. Have the child first touch under each letter while slowly saying the sounds and then move a finger quickly across the arrow while quickly saying the sounds. Provide physical assistance as needed.

Ongoing Assessment

If... a child makes an error,	**then...** correct the error with the whole group. Have the child who made the error sound out and read the word again.
If... children make many errors during their individual turns,	**then...** model, lead, and test each word again with the group. When the group can sound out and read each word, resume individual turns.

Activity 5 Writer's Warm-Up

Introduce h

Objective: Children trace and write *h* and review writing *z*, *g*, *u*, *j*, *n*, *w*, and *r*.

Time: 2–3 minutes

	To Do	To Say
Review letter name and sound	Hold up the *h* Tracing Card.	**Test** **What is the <u>name</u> of this letter? What is the <u>sound</u> for this letter?**
Model tracing *h*	Distribute a Writer's Warm-Up to each child. Hold up the *h* Tracing Card. Model tracing *h* again.	**Model** **Everyone, watch as I trace the letter *h* with my finger.** **Now you trace the first two *h*'s on your warm-up sheet with your finger.** **Everyone, watch as I trace *h* again.** **Now use your pencil to trace the next two *h*'s on your warm-up sheet.**
Model writing *h*	Hold up the lined side of the *h* Tracing Card.	**Model** **Everyone, watch as I write the letter *h*. I start at the dot and write the letter.** **Now you write two *h*'s. Start at the dot like I did. Write your letters carefully.** **Ongoing Assessment** **If...** children make an error, **then...** put your hand over their hand and guide them to write the letter. Then have them try to write the letter on their own. Repeat as necessary.
Test knowledge of writing *h*	Model writing *h* again.	**Watch as I write *h* again.** Have children cover their letters. Have them write *h* twice from memory. Then have them uncover their papers and compare. **Do your letters look the same? Circle your best *h*.**
Review *z, g, u, j, n, w, r*		Have children trace and write each review letter on their warm-up sheets. **Ongoing Assessment** **If...** children make an error, **then...** use the tracing card to model tracing the letter and have children write the letter again. If needed, put your hand over their hand and guide them to write the letter. Then have them try to write the letter on their own. Repeat as necessary.

Connect Sound to Letter

Practice Session: Spelling

Objective: Children segment words and connect sounds to letters.

Time: 2–3 minutes

	To Do	To Say
Introduce the activity	Gather the 3-Square Strip and the letter tiles.	**Today we're going to practice spelling words to get ready for Silly Words.** Depending on children's abilities, you may wish to display letter tiles for all letters children have learned. Keep the activity brief so that more time can be spent on Activity 7.
Lead the activity	Set out the 3-Square Strip and the letter tiles. Segment the word *bet*.	**Lead** **The first word is *bet*. What is the first word?** Have children hold out three fingers. **Say the sounds in *bet* and touch a finger for each sound.**
	Identify the letter for the first sound in *bet*.	**Does everyone know what the first letter in *bet* is?** Call on a child to choose the correct letter tile and place it in the first square.
	Identify the letter for the middle sound in *bet*.	**Does everyone know what the next letter in *bet* is?** Call on a child to choose the correct letter tile and place it in the middle square. **Ongoing Assessment** **If...** children make an error, **then...** have them segment the word again.
	Identify the letter for the last sound in *bet*.	**Does everyone know what the last letter in *bet* is?** Call on a child to choose the correct letter tile and place it in the last square. **Ongoing Assessment** **If...** children make an error, **then...** have them segment the word again.
	Confirm the spelling of *bet*.	**Say each sound in *bet* with me as I point to the letters: /b/ /eee/ /t/. Now say the sounds quickly to say the word: *bet*. That's right; you spelled *bet*. The sounds in *bet* are /b/ /eee/ /t/ and *b-e-t* spells *bet*.** Practice with *fog, get, bug,* and *wet*, as time allows.

Connect Sound to Letter

Silly Words

Objective: Children connect sounds to letters to spell nonsense words.

Time: 6–8 minutes

	To Do	To Say
Introduce the activity	Distribute the Silly Words sheets.	**Today we're going to spell silly words. I'm going to say a silly, or nonsense word. *You're* going to spell it. Let's see how many silly words we can spell!**
Model the activity	Hold up a Silly Words sheet. Model identifying the letter for the first sound in *mog*.	Model **The first word is *mog*. Listen. I'll say the sounds in *mog* and touch a finger for each sound: /mmm/ /ooo/ /g/. I'm going to write the first letter in *mog*.** Write an *m* on your sheet and show children. **Now you write the first letter in *mog*.**
	Model identifying the letter for the middle sound in *mog*.	**Now I'll write the next letter in *mog*.** Write an *o* on your sheet and show children. **Now you write the next letter in *mog*.**
	Model identifying the letter for the last sound in *mog*.	**Now I'll write the last letter in *mog*.** Write a *g* on your sheet and show children. **Now you write the last letter in *mog*.**
	Confirm the spelling of *mog*.	**Everyone, say each sound in *mog* with me and point to your letters as we say each sound: /mmm/ /ooo/ /g/. Say the sounds quickly to say the word: *mog*. That's right; you spelled *mog*. The sounds in *mog* are /mmm/ /ooo/ /g/.**

Activity 7 Connect Sound to Letter (continued)

	To Do		To Say
Test children on spelling *tef, sot, gub, wem,* and *bof*	Test children on identifying the letter for the first sound.	**Test**	**The next word is *tef*. What's the next word? Say the sounds in *tef* and touch a finger for each sound: /t/ /eee/ /fff/. Now, everyone, write the first letter in *tef*.**
	Test children on identifying the letter for the middle sound.		**Write the next letter in *tef*.**
			Ongoing Assessment — **If...** children make an error, **then...** have them segment the word again.
	Test children on identifying the letter for the last sound.		**Write the last letter in *tef*.**
			Ongoing Assessment — **If...** children make an error, **then...** have them segment the word again.
	Confirm the spelling.	**Lead**	**Now say each sound in *tef* with me and point to your letters as we say each sound: /t/ /eee/ /fff/. Say the sounds quickly to say the word: *tef*. That's right; you spelled *tef*. The sounds in *tef* are /t/ /eee/ /fff/ and *t-e-f* spells *tef*.** Repeat the test for *zot, gub, wem,* and *bof.*

New Sound /h/
Review Sounds /p/, /k/, /n/, /u/, /s/, /d/, /a/, /o/, /r/
Key Reading Skills Letter-Sound Correspondences; Word Reading: VC, CVC

Phonological Awareness and Alphabetic Understanding

Activity	Materials		Time
1. Alphabetic Introduce *h*/h/	Alphabet Card: *h* Letter Card: *h* (one per child)		1–2 minutes
2. Integrated Phonologic/Alphabetic Which Picture Begins with *h*?	Alphabet Card: *h* Picture Choices: 90-1, 90-2, 90-3 Teacher Resource Package 3		4–5 minutes
3. Alphabetic Sounds Dash	Sounds Dash Teacher Resource Package 3	timer (not provided)	4–5 minutes
4. Reading Word Reading Game	Word Cards: all cards for Lessons 85–90 Game Board 3	game markers (one per child/ not provided) number cube (not provided)	4–5 minutes

Writing and Spelling

Activity	Materials		Time
5. Writer's Warm-Up Ready, Set, Go!	Writer's Warm-Up (one per child) Student Activity Book 3, p. 39 or 40	Tracing Cards: *h, e, g, a, w, j, z, n, r, o, d, i*	2–3 minutes
6. Integrated Phonologic/Alphabetic Practice Session: Spelling	3-Square Strip	Letter Tiles: *e, a, i, w, z, d, r, n, p*	2–3 minutes
New **7. Phonologic/Spelling** Missing Letters	Missing Letters (one per child) Student Activity Book 3, p. 41		6–8 minutes

Activity 1 Introduce Letter Name and Sound

Introduce h/h/

Objective: Children learn and trace *h*/h/.

Time: 1–2 minutes

	To Do	To Say	
Introduce letter name	Hold up the *h* Alphabet Card.	Model	**The name of this letter is *h*.**
		Lead	**Say the name of the letter with me: *h*.**
		Test	**What is the name of this letter?**
Introduce letter sound	Continue holding up the *h* Alphabet Card.	Model	**The sound for this letter is /h/. When you say /h/, air comes out of your mouth. Put your hand in front of your mouth. Say /h/ and feel the air come out. Everyone, say /h/.**
		Lead	**Say the sound with me: /h/.**
		Test	**What is the sound for this letter?**
Test knowledge of letter name and sound	Continue holding up the *h* Alphabet Card.	Test	**What is the name of this letter? What is the sound for this letter?**
	Give individual turns on letter name and sound.		**Ongoing Assessment** If... children make an error, then... tell them the name or sound, have them repeat the name or sound, and return to the letter a second time.
Model tracing *h*	Distribute the *h* Letter Cards. Hold up the *h* Alphabet Card.	Model	**Everyone, watch. I'll trace the letter *h*.** Have children trace the *h* on their letter cards three times. Tell them to say /h/ each time they trace the letter.
			Ongoing Assessment If... children make an error, then... put your hand over their hand and guide them to trace the letter. Then have them try to trace the letter on their own. Repeat as necessary.

Activity 2 Isolate Initial Sound

Which Picture Begins with h?

Objective: Children isolate initial /h/ and connect sound to letter.

Time: 4–5 minutes

	To Do	To Say
Model names of pictures	Gather the picture choices. Display Picture Choice 90-1. Point to *goose*.	**Model** **This is *goose*. What is this?** Continue with the remaining pictures: *soap, hook; zipper, hen, sun.* Test children on the picture names by pointing to the pictures one at a time and asking: **What is this?**
Introduce the game Which Picture Begins with *h*?		**Now we're going to play a game. I'll show you a letter and three pictures. You'll find the picture that begins with the sound for the letter.**
Model the game	Hold up the *h* Alphabet Card. Display Picture Choice 90-1. Cover the bottom row.	**Model** **The <u>name</u> of this letter is *h*. The <u>sound</u> for this letter is /h/. Remember, when you say /h/, air comes out of your mouth.** **What is the <u>sound</u> for this letter?** **My turn. I'll show you how to play the game. This is *goose, soap, hook*. I'll find the picture that has the first sound /h/: *hook*** (exaggerate the first sound). ***Hook* has the first sound /h/.** Point to the letter *h*. Exaggerate the first sound and say the word: **/h/, *hook*.** Model again with the bottom row of pictures: *zipper, hen, sun.*
Play the game to test knowledge of initial /h/	Hold up the *h* Alphabet Card. Display Picture Choice 90-2. Cover the bottom row. Give individual turns.	**Test** **What is the <u>sound</u> for this letter?** Have children name each picture: *hat, seal, gum.* **Which picture has the first sound /h/?** Confirm correct responses and prompt sound production: ***Yes, hat* has the first sound /h/. Remember, when you say /h/, air comes out of your mouth.** Continue with the bottom row of pictures *(glue, zoo, hat)* and Picture Choice 90-3 *(sock, hug, goal post; house, zebra, inch)*. **Ongoing Assessment** **If...** children make incorrect responses, **then...** model the correct answer. Review the sound production cue. Have children repeat the correct answer. Go back to the example a second time.

3 Build Sounds Fluency

Sounds Dash

Objective: Children increase fluency in identifying letter sounds.

Time: 4–5 minutes

	To Do	To Say
Introduce the activity	Display the Sounds Dash.	**Today we're going to have a Sounds Dash. I'll point to a letter. You'll say the sound for the letter. Let's see how close we can get to the finish line in one minute. Be careful, though. If I hear a wrong sound, you'll have to go back three letters. Remember, too, that you will need to hold some of the sounds. Some of the sounds you will say only for as long as I touch under the letter.**
Model the activity	Display the Sounds Dash.	**Model** **Let's get warmed up for our Sounds Dash. We'll practice the sounds in the first row. Then we'll start the timer for our dash.** Point to *p*. **What is the <u>sound</u> for this letter?** Tap your finger under the letter as children say the sound. **Yes, the <u>sound</u> is /p/.** **Ongoing Assessment** **If...**children make an error, **then...**tell them the sound, have them repeat it, and move back three letters on the page or repeat the letter if it is at the beginning of the row. Practice the sound of each letter in the first row. If children miss more than two sounds, do not proceed with the activity. Instead, practice the sounds on the page, especially those that children know less well.
Lead the activity	Display the Sounds Dash. Set the timer for one minute.	**Lead** **Now you're ready for the Sounds Dash. Everyone, look at my finger. On your mark, get set, go!** Point to *p* in the first row. **What is the <u>sound</u> for this letter?** Repeat for each sound in the first row. Then immediately proceed to the next row, and so on. **Ongoing Assessment** **If...**children make an error, **then...**tell them the sound, have them repeat it, and move back three letters on the page or repeat the letter if it is at the beginning of the row. Stop the activity after exactly one minute. Praise children for how far they went. Tell them that they will have a chance to beat their score in three days when they play again.

Activity 4 Read Words

Word Reading Game

Objective: Children sound out and read review words. Time: 4–5 minutes

	To Do	To Say
Introduce the game	Gather Game Board 3, the word cards, the game markers, and a number cube. Place the word cards face down in a pile on the table.	**Now we're going to play the Word Reading Game. First, you'll roll the number cube. Then you'll choose the top card from the pile. You'll sound out and read the word on the card. Then, if you have correctly sounded out and read the word, you'll move your marker on the game board. You'll move the number of spaces that you rolled. Then you'll place your word card at the bottom of the pile.**
Play the game		Have children take turns rolling the number cube and choosing a word card. Have each child sound out and read the word on the word card: **Say the sounds. Get ready. Now say the sounds quickly to say the word. What's the word?** Play the game until one child reaches the finish line or time runs out.

Ongoing Assessment

If . . . a child pauses between sounds,	**then . . .** model saying the sounds without stopping between them. Have the child sound out the word again. Do not have the child advance a marker on the game board.
If . . . a child says the wrong sound,	**then . . .** keep your finger on the missed sound. Model the correct sound and have the child repeat it. Have the child sound out the word again. Do not have the child advance a marker on the game board.
If . . . a child says the wrong word when he or she says the sounds quickly,	**then . . .** model the correct word and have the child repeat it. Have the child say the sounds slowly and quickly again. Do not have the child advance a marker on the game board.

Activity 5 Writer's Warm-Up

Ready, Set, Go!

Objective: Children practice writing *h, e, g, a, w, j, z, n, r, o, d,* and *i.*

Time: 2–3 minutes

	To Do	To Say
Introduce the activity	Give each child a Writer's Warm-Up.	**Today you're going to practice writing some of the letters you've learned. You're going to write your best letters as fast as you can.**
Model the activity	Hold up a Writers Warm-Up sheet. Point to the first row.	**Model** **My turn. I'll show you how this activity works. The letters in the first row are *h, e, g,* and *a*. Watch as I trace each letter with my pencil.** Trace each letter in the first row. **Now it's your turn to trace the letters in the first row.** Watch as children trace the letters. **After I say "Ready, set, go," I'll write my best *h, e, g,* and *a* as fast as I can on the second row. Watch me try. Ready, set, go!** Write the letters on the second row and then put your pencil down. **Now it's your turn to write your best *h, e, g,* and *a* as fast as you can. Ready, set, go!** Tell children to put their pencils down when they have finished.
Test knowledge of writing *w, j, z, n, r, o, d,* and *i*	Point to the next row.	**Test** **The letters in the next row are *w, j, z,* and *n*. Warm up by tracing each letter with your pencil. Put your pencil down when you have finished. Now it's your turn to write your best *w, j, z,* and *n* as fast as you can. Ready, set, go!** Remind children to put their pencils down when they have finished. Repeat for the last row of letters. **Ongoing Assessment** **If...** children write the wrong letter or don't remember how to write a letter, **then...** show them the tracing card for the letter. Trace the letter and say its name. **Now look over your paper and circle your very best letters.**

Activity 6 Connect Sound to Letter

Practice Session: Spelling

Objective: Children segment words and connect sounds to letters.

Time: 2–3 minutes

	To Do	To Say
Introduce the activity	Gather the 3-Square Strip and the letter tiles.	**Today we're going to practice spelling words to get ready for Missing Letters.** Depending on children's abilities, you may wish to display letter tiles for all letters children have learned. Keep the activity brief so that more time can be spent on Activity 7.
Lead the activity	Set out the 3-Square Strip and the letter tiles. Segment the word *ran*.	**Lead** **The first word is *ran*. What is the first word?** Have children hold out three fingers. **Say the sounds in *ran* and touch a finger for each sound.**
	Identify the letter for the first sound in *ran*.	**Does everyone know what the first letter in *ran* is?** Call on a child to choose the correct letter tile and place it in the first square.
	Identify the letter for the middle sound in *ran*.	**Does everyone know what the next letter in *ran* is?** Call on a child to choose the correct letter tile and place it in the middle square. **Ongoing Assessment** **If...** children make an error, **then...** have them segment the word again.
	Identify the letter for the last sound in *ran*.	**Does everyone know what the last letter in *ran* is?** Call on a child to choose the correct letter tile and place it in the last square. **Ongoing Assessment** **If...** children make an error, **then...** have them segment the word again.
	Confirm the spelling of *ran*.	**Say each sound in *ran* with me as I point to the letters: /rrr/ /aaa/ /nnn/. Now say the sounds quickly to say the word: *ran*. That's right; you spelled *ran*. The sounds in *ran* are /rrr/ /aaa/ /nnn/ and *r-a-n* spells *ran*.** Practice with *den, wed, zip,* and *nap*, as time allows.

Activity 7 Connect Sound to Letter

Missing Letters

Objective: Children connect sounds to letters to spell words.

Time: 6–8 minutes

	To Do	To Say
Introduce the activity	Distribute a Missing Letters sheet to each child.	**Look at your sheet. It looks as if some of the words are missing letters. We're going to finish spelling the words by writing the missing letters. Let's see if we can figure out how to spell all of the words!**
Model the activity	Hold up a Missing Letters sheet. Point to the first word.	Model **The first word is *pen*. Listen. I'll say the sounds in *pen* and touch a space for each sound: /p/ /eee/ /nnn/. Now I'll say the sounds in *pen* again and stop when I get to the missing sound: /p/ /eee/. I'm going to write the missing letter in *pen*.** Write an *e* in the middle letter space and show children.
	Confirm the spelling of *pen*.	**Now say each sound in *pen* with me as I point to the letters: /p/ /eee/ /nnn/. Say the sounds quickly to say the word: *pen*. That's right; you spelled *pen*. The sounds in *pen* are /p/ /eee/ /nnn/ and *p-e-n* spells *pen*.**
Test children on spelling *zap*, *win*, *dad*, *den*, *zip*, and *fad*	Continue to hold up a Missing Letters sheet. Point to the second word.	Test **The next word is *zap*. What is the next word? Say the sounds in *zap* and touch a space for each sound: /zzz/ /aaa/ /p/. Now say the sounds in *zap* again and stop when you get to the missing sound: /zzz/. Write the missing letter in *zap*.** **Ongoing Assessment** **If...** children make an error, **then...** have them segment the word again.
	Confirm the spelling.	**Now say each sound in *zap* with me as I point to the letters: /zzz/ /aaa/ /p/. Now say the sounds quickly to say the word: *zap*. That's right; you spelled *zap*. The sounds in *zap* are /zzz/ /aaa/ /p/ and *z-a-p* spells *zap*.** Repeat the test for *win, dad, den, zip,* and *fad*.

New Sound /y/
Review Sounds /a/, /i/, /n/, /u/, /j/, /e/, /z/, /h/
Key Reading Skills Letter-Sound Correspondences; Word Reading: VC, CVC

Phonological Awareness and Alphabetic Understanding

Activity	Materials		Time
1. Alphabetic Introduce *y*/y/	Alphabet Card: *y*	Letter Card: *y* (one per child)	1–2 minutes
2. Phonologic Does It Begin with /y/?	Picture Cards: *yard, zebra, yellow, yarn, yo-yo, hat*		4–5 minutes
3. Alphabetic Sounds	Sounds Teacher Resource Package 3		4–5 minutes
4. Phonologic/Reading Say the Sounds/ Say the Word with Fingers; Regular Words	Regular Words Teacher Resource Package 3	Word Cards: *Diz, tub, Sam, if* (Lessons 91–96)	4–5 minutes

Writing and Spelling

Activity	Materials		Time
5. Writer's Warm-Up Introduce *y*	Tracing Card: *y* Writer's Warm-Up (one per child) Student Activity Book 3, p. 42 or 43		2–3 minutes
6. Integrated Phonologic/Alphabetic Practice Session: Spelling	3-Square Strip	Letter Tiles: *a, o, i, z, s, j, g, b, p*	2–3 minutes
7. Phonologic/Spelling Guess What I Am	Guess What I Am (one per child) Student Activity Book 3, p. 44		6–8 minutes

Activity 1 Introduce Letter Name and Sound

Introduce y/y/

Objective: Children learn and trace *y*/y/.

Time: 1–2 minutes

	To Do	To Say
Introduce letter name	Hold up the *y* Alphabet Card.	**Model** **The <u>name</u> of this letter is *y*.** **Lead** **Say the <u>name</u> with me: *y*.** **Test** **What is the <u>name</u> of this letter?**
Introduce letter sound	Continue holding up the *y* Alphabet Card.	**Model** **This is the letter for the sound /y/. When you say /y/, your tongue is behind your lower teeth, and your mouth is open. Say /y/ and feel your tongue behind your lower teeth.** **Lead** **Say the sound with me: /y/.** **Test** **What is the <u>sound</u> for this letter?**
Test letter name and sound	Continue holding up the *y* Alphabet Card. Give individual turns on letter name and sound.	**Test** **What is the <u>name</u> of this letter? What is the <u>sound</u> for this letter?** **Ongoing Assessment** **If**...children make an error, **then**...tell them the name or sound, have them repeat the name or sound, and return to the letter a second time.
Model tracing *y*	Model tracing *y* on your Alphabet Card. Distribute a letter card to each child.	**Model** **Watch. I'll trace the letter *y*.** Have children trace the letter *y* on their letter cards three times and say /y/ each time they trace the letter. **Ongoing Assessment** **If**...children make an error, **then**...put your hand over their hand and guide the tracing of the letter. Then have children try to trace the letter on their own. Repeat as necessary.

Activity 2 Isolate Initial Sound

Does It Begin with /y/?

Objective: Children isolate initial /y/.

Time: 4–5 minutes

	To Do	To Say
Model names of pictures	Gather Pictures Cards. Put the *yard* picture on the table.	**Model** Model names of all pictures. **This is ____.** Have children repeat them. **Test** **What is this?** Continue with the remaining pictures.
Introduce the game Does It Begin with /y/?	Practice production of the target sound.	Tell children they will play a game. They need to find pictures that begin with /y/. **Model** **When you say /y/, your tongue is behind your lower teeth, and your mouth is open. Say /y/ and feel your tongue behind your lower teeth.**
Model the game	Model two examples. Exaggerate the first sound of each word.	**Model** **It's my turn. I'll say the name of the picture and then tell whether it begins with /y/; *yard. Yard* begins with /y/. Your tongue is behind your lower teeth, and your mouth is open when you say *yard*. Next picture. *Zebra. Zebra* does not begin with /y/.**
Test knowledge of /y/	Test children with more examples: *yellow, yarn, yo-yo, hat.* Give individual turns.	**Test** **What is this? Does *yellow* begin with /y/?** Confirm correct responses and prompt sound production. **Yes, *yellow* begins with /y/. Remember, when you say /y/, your tongue is behind your lower teeth, and your mouth is open; /y/, *yellow*.** **Ongoing Assessment** **If...** children make an error, **then...** model the correct answer. Then review the sound production cue. Have children repeat the correct answer. Go back to the example a second time.

Activity 3 Discriminate Letter Sounds

Sounds

Objective: Children connect sound to letter.

Time: 4–5 minutes

	To Do	To Say
Introduce the activity	Display the Sounds page.	**I'll point to a letter and you'll say the sound for the letter. Some sounds will be quick sounds. You'll need to say each sound only for as long as I touch the letter.**
Test the sounds	Point to each letter on the Sounds Page. Note: If the letter has a stop sound, like /b/, point to the letter briefly. If the letter has a continuous sound, like /a/, hold your finger under the sound for about two seconds. Give individual turns.	**Test** **What is the <u>sound</u> for this letter?** Point to *i* and hold your finger under the letter for about two seconds as children say the sound. **Yes, /iii/.** Repeat the test with each letter.

Ongoing Assessment

If... children make an error,	**then...** tell them the sound, have them repeat it, and move back two letters on the page or repeat the letter if at the beginning of the page.
If... children miss more than two sounds on the page,	**then...** repeat the test for all letters on the page.

Activity 4 Read Words

Say the Sounds/Say the Word with Fingers; Regular Words

Objective: Children segment, blend, and read words.

Time: 4–5 minutes

	To Do	To Say
Introduce the activity		**It's time to play Say the Sounds/Say the Word with Fingers. I'll say the sounds of a word slowly. You will repeat each sound slowly as you touch a finger for each sound. Then you will say the sounds quickly to say the word.**
Lead the activity	Lead segmenting *Diz.*	**Lead** **Let's do a three-sound word together. Hold out three fingers.** Have each child hold out three fingers pointed toward you. Then have them use the pointer finger of the other hand to touch a finger for each sound moving from left to right. **Listen to the quick sound at the beginning of the word. For the quick sound, we'll touch our first finger just for a second. Then we'll move on to the next sound. Listen.** Pause. Touch a finger for each sound, pausing briefly after /d/, since it's a stop sound. Don't stop between the other sounds: **/d/ /iii/ /zzz/.**
	Lead segmenting and blending *Diz.*	**Say the sounds slowly with me: /d/ /iii/ /zzz/.** Remind children to touch fingers from left to right. **Say the sounds quickly with me.** Clap with children as you and they say the word: *Diz.*
Test knowledge of segmenting and blending words	Test segmenting and blending *if.*	**Test** **It's your turn to do a two-sound word. Hold out two fingers. Listen;** (pause) **/iii/ /fff/.** Touch a finger for each sound. **Say the sounds slowly.** Teacher and children touch their fingers. Only children say the sounds. **Say the sounds quickly.** All clap hands as children say the word: *if.* Repeat test for *zip, us, Sam,* and *tub.* Point out that children will need to hold out two fingers for *us. Tub* begins with a quick sound, so they will need to touch the first finger very quickly.
	Give individual turns.	**Ongoing Assessment** (see below)

Ongoing Assessment

If... children do not touch the appropriate finger for each sound,	**then...** model how to do it. Then have them try again. If necessary, guide children's hands to touch fingers correctly.
If... children stop between the sounds,	**then...** model how to say the sounds without stopping betweem them. Then have children try the word again.
If... children have trouble saying the word quickly,	**then...** tell them the word and then say it slowly and quickly before having them try again.

Activity 4 Read Words (continued)

	To Do	To Say
Introduce the activity	Display the Regular Words card.	**Today we will read some words. First, you will say each sound slowly. Then you'll say the sounds quickly to read the word. Some of the words begin with a quick sound, so watch my finger carefully.**
Model the activity	Model sounding out *Diz*.	**Model** **It's my turn to read a word.** Point to the capital *D* in *Diz* on the Regular Words card. **This word begins with a capital *D* because this word is someone's name. Names always begin with a capital letter.** You may want to point out *Dd* displayed together in your classroom. **Let's see whose name this is.** **This word begins with a quick sound. Watch my finger. I'll touch the quick sound at the beginning of the word just for a second, and then I'll move on. Each time I touch a letter, I'll say its sound. I won't stop between the other sounds.** Point to *Diz* on the word card: **/d/ /iii/ /zzz/.** Tap under the *D* and then immediately move on. Touch under the last two letters for one to two seconds each.
	Model reading *Diz*.	**Now I'll say it quickly: *Diz*.** Move your finger beneath the word. **The word is *Diz*.**
Lead the activity	Lead sounding out and reading *Diz*. Use the same finger movements you modeled with.	**Lead** **Now let's read this word together. Watch my finger because this word begins with a quick sound. Say the sounds. Get ready: /d/ /iii/ /zzz/. Now let's say the sounds quickly: *Diz*. What's the word? *Diz*. Yes, *Diz* is the name of our dinosaur puppet.**

	To Do	To Say	
Test children on the activity	Test sounding out and reading *Diz*.	Test	**Now it's your turn to read the word. First, you'll say the sounds slowly. Then you'll say them quickly. Look out for that quick sound at the beginning. Say the sounds. Get ready.** Touch under the stop sound just for an instant and immediately move on. Children should not pause between the other sounds in the word. **Now say it quickly.** Move your finger quickly under the word as children say it. **What's the word?**

Repeat the cycle to model, lead, and test the word *tub*.

Then test children on sounding out and reading the words *Sam* and *if*. Before testing children on *Sam*, point to the capital *S* and say: **This word begins with a capital *S* because this word is someone's name. Remember, a name always begins with a capital letter.** You may want to point out *Ss* displayed together in your classroom.

Test the group on all the words again in random order. Have the group say the sounds slowly and then quickly. Point out words that begin with a stop sound.

Give individual turns by handing out the word cards from the word page to individuals. Ask each child to sound out and read his or her word: **_______, it's your turn. Say the sounds. Get ready. Now say the sounds quickly. What's the word?** If necessary, assist children in making finger movements.

Ongoing Assessment

If... children pause between sounds,	**then...** model sounding out the word without stopping between sounds, and have children sound it out again.
If... children say the wrong sound,	**then...** keep your finger on the missed sound, model it correctly, and have children repeat the sound. Then have them sound out the word again.
If... children say the wrong word when they say it quickly,	**then...** model the correct word and have children repeat it. Then have children say the sounds slowly again and then say them quickly.
If... a child makes an error on an individual turn,	**then...** have the whole group say the word, say the sounds, and say it quickly. If there are many errors on individual turns, model, lead, and test each word again with the whole group before providing individual turns again.

	To Do	To Say
Introduce Sentence Reading Warm-Up	Display the Regular Words card.	**Soon you will begin to read sentences and stories. Today I will show you how to read words when they are in a sentence.**
Model reading words in sentences	Point to *Sam* on the Regular Words card.	**Everybody, eyes on this word. This is how we'll read this word when we see it in a sentence. I'll touch under the word.** Touch under the word, just to the left of the box. **Now I'll say the sounds. Watch my finger.** Move your finger below each sound as you say it. **First sound /sss/, next sound /aaa/, last sound /mmm/. Now I'll say it quickly.** Slash your finger under the word box: ***Sam.*** **Now I'll say the word.** Slash your finger under the word again: ***Sam.***
Test the activity	Test children on how to read a word in a sentence.	**Your turn.** Point to the word *Sam* on the word card. **Remember how we'll read this word when we see it in a sentence. We'll touch under the word and then we'll say the sounds. We won't stop between the sounds. Watch my finger.** Move your finger under each letter as children say the sounds. **First sound. Next sound. Last sound. Now say it quickly.** Slash your finger under the word box. **What's the word?** Slash your finger under the word box again. Repeat the test with the word *if*. If time permits, give individual turns with the word cards for *Sam* and *if*. Tell the child to touch under the word. **Say the sounds. First sound, next sound, last sound. Say it quickly. What's the word?** Provide physical guidance if needed.

Ongoing Assessment

If... children pause between sounds,	**then...** model sounding out the word, without stopping between sounds, and have children sound it out again.
If... children say the wrong sound,	**then...** keep your finger on the missed sound, model it correctly, and have children repeat the sound. Then have them sound out the word again.
If... children say the wrong word when they say it quickly,	**then...** model the correct word and have children repeat it. Have children say the sounds again slowly and then quickly.
If... children have difficulty following the new cues,	**then...** model and lead them through the word. Then try the test.

Activity 5 Writer's Warm-Up

Lesson 91

Introduce y

Objective: Children trace and write *y* and review writing *z, e, j, g, h, w,* and *u*.

Time: 2–3 minutes

	To Do	To Say
Review letter name and sound	Display the *y* Tracing Card.	**What is the name of this letter?** **What is the sound for this letter?**
Model tracing *y*	Distribute Writer's Warm-Up.	Model **Watch as I trace the letter *y* with my finger.** Have children trace the first two letters on their sheets with their finger. Repeat the model and have children trace the next two letters with their pencils.
Model writing *y*	Model writing the new letter using the lined side of the tracing card.	Model **Watch as I write the letter *y*. I start at the dot and write the letter.** Have children write the letter twice on their sheet. Remind them to start at the dot and write carefully. **Ongoing Assessment** **If...** children make an error, **then...** put your hand over their hand and guide them to write the letter. Then have them write the letter on their own. Repeat as necessary.
 ***z, e, j, g, h, w, u***		Test Model writing *y* again on the lined side of the tracing card. Have children cover their letters and write the letter twice from memory on their sheets. **Do your letters look the same? Circle the letter that is your best work.** Then have children trace and write each review letter one time each. **Ongoing Assessment** **If...** children make an error, **then...** use the tracing card to model writing the letter and have children write the letter again. If needed, put your hand over theirs and guide the writing of the letter. Have children write the letter on their own. Repeat as necessary.

Activity  Connect Sound to Letter

Practice Session: Spelling

Objective: Children segment sounds to spell words.

Time: 2–3 minutes

	To Do	To Say
Introduce the activity	Gather the 3-Square Strip and letter tiles.	**We are going to practice spelling for "Guess What I Am."**
Lead the activity	Segment the word jog.	**The first word is *jog*. What word?** Have children hold out three fingers. **Say the sounds in *jog* and touch a finger for each sound.**
	Identify the first letter. Depending on ability level, display all the letter tiles or just two at a time.	Point to the first square of the 3-Square Strip. **Does everyone know what the first letter in *jog* is?** Call on a child to choose the correct letter and place it on the first square. **Ongoing Assessment** **If...** children make an error, **then...** have them segment the word again.
	Identify the middle letter.	**Does everyone know what the next letter in *jog* is?** Call on a child to choose and place the next letter.
	Identify the last letter.	**Do you know what the last letter in *jog* is?** Call on a child to choose and place the letter.
	Confirm the spelling.	**Say each sound in *jog* with me as I point to the letters: /j/ /ooo/ /g/. Now say it quickly. That's right, you spelled *jog;* /j/ /ooo/ /g/ are the sounds in *jog*.** Practice with at least two more words, as time allows: *zip, sob, pig, bag.*

Activity 7 Connect Sound to Letter

Guess What I Am

Objective: Children connect sounds to letters to spell words.

Time: 6–8 minutes

	To Do	To Say
Introduce the activity	Distribute Guess What I Am.	**We're going to play a guessing game. I will give you a clue about something, and you will guess what it is. Then we will spell the word. Let's see if we can guess all the words!**
Lead the activity	Segment the word *pig*.	**Here's the first clue: I'm a farm animal. I like to wallow in mud and oink. Guess what I am! That's right; the word is *pig*. Listen. I'll touch a finger as I say each sound in *pig:* /p/ /iii/ /g/.**
	Model writing the word *pig*.	**Now I'll write the first letter in *pig*.** Write *p* in the first box and show children. **Now you write the first letter in *pig*.** Continue this procedure for the rest of the word.
	Confirm the spelling.	**Let's point to each letter as we say the sounds in *pig:* /p/ /iii/ /g/. Say it quickly. *Yes,* you spelled *pig;* /p/ /iii/ /g/ are the sounds in *pig*.** Give the next clue from the Clue Bank.
	Test segmenting the next word.	**That's right. The word is *big*. What word? Touch a finger as you say each sound in *big*.**
	Test writing the next word.	**Now write the first letter in *big*.** Point to your first finger. Have children finish writing the word: **Write the next letter in *big*. Write the last letter in *big*.** Confirm the spelling.
		Ongoing Assessment **If...** children make an error, **then...** have them segment the word again.
	Continue using the same procedure.	**Clue Bank** After giving each clue say: **Guess what I am?** 2. I'm not small. I'm very, very ______. (*big*) 3. I'm not a big gulp of water, I'm just a little ______. (*sip*) 4. You put groceries in me. I'm a paper ______. (*bag*) 5. Let's get our running shoes and take a ______. (*jog*) 6. Before you go, ______ up your coat. (*zip*) 7. Mom put her arms around me and gave me a ______. (*hug*) 8. I have a pillow and blanket and you sleep in me. (*bed*)

New Sound /y/
Review Sounds /o/, /i/, /n/, /u/, /e/, /z/, /h/
Key Reading Skills Letter-Sound Correspondences; Word Reading: VC, CVC

Phonological Awareness and Alphabetic Understanding

Activity	Materials		Time
1. Alphabetic Introduce *y*/y/	Alphabet Card: *y*	Letter Card: *y* (one per child)	1–2 minutes
2. Phonologic Which Picture Begins with /y/?	Picture Choice: 92-1, 92-2, 92-3 Teacher Resource Package 3		4–5 minutes
3. Alphabetic Sounds	Sounds Teacher Resource Package 3		4–5 minutes
4. Phonologic/Reading Say the Sounds/ Say the Word with Fingers; Regular Words	Regular Words Teacher Resource Package 3	Word Cards: *jam, sun, an, big* (Lessons 91–96)	4–5 minutes

Writing and Spelling

Activity	Materials		Time
5. Writer's Warm-Up Introduce *y*	Writer's Warm-Up Student Activity Book 3, p. 45 or 46	Tracing Cards: *y, z, e, j, r, h, w, b*	2–3 minutes
6. Integrated Phonologic/Alphabetic Practice Session: Spelling	3-Square Strip	Letter Tiles: *u, e, n, d, l, m, r, g*	2–3 minutes
7. Phonological/Spelling Where's the Letter?	3-Square Strip	Letter Tiles: *m, u, d, e, n, i, t, r, b, g, p, j, o*	6–8 minutes

Activity 1 Introduce Letter Name and Sound

Introduce y

Objective: Children learn and trace *y*/y/.

Time: 1–2 minutes

	To Do	To Say
Introduce letter name	Hold up the *y* Alphabet Card.	**Model** **The <u>name</u> of this letter is *y*.** **Lead** **Say the <u>name</u> with me: *y*.** **Test** **What is the <u>name</u> of this letter?**
Introduce letter sound	Continue holding up the *y* Alphabet Card.	**Model** **This is the letter for the <u>sound</u> /y/. When you say /y/, your tongue is behind your lower teeth, and your mouth is open. Say /y/ and feel your tongue behind your lower teeth.** **Lead** **Say the <u>sound</u> with me: /y/.** **Test** **What is the <u>sound</u> for this letter?**
Test letter name and sound	Continue holding up the *y* Alphabet Card. Give individual turns on letter name and sound.	**Test** **What is the <u>name</u> of this letter? What is the <u>sound</u> for this letter?** **Ongoing Assessment** **If...** children make an error, **then...** tell them the name or sound, have them repeat the name or sound, and return to the letter a second time.
Model tracing *y*	Model how to trace *y* using your Alphabet Card.	**Model** **Watch. I'll trace the letter *y*.** Have children trace the letter *y* on their Letter Cards three times and say /y/ each time they trace the letter. **Ongoing Assessment** **If...** children make an error, **then...** Put your hand over their hand and guide the tracing of the letter. Then have children try to trace the letter on their own. Repeat as necessary.

Activity 2 | Lesson 92

Isolate Initial Sound

Which Picture Begins with /y/?

Objective: Children isolate initial /y/.

Time: 4–5 minutes

	To Do	To Say
Model names of pictures	Display Picture Choice 92-1.	**Model** Model names of pictures and have children repeat them *(wave, yo-yo, hat; yarn, hug, zebra)*: **This is ____. What is this?** **Test** **What is this?**
Introduce the game Which Picture Begins with /y/?	Practice production of the target sound.	Tell children they will play another game with /y/. You will show them three pictures. They will find the one with the first sound /y/. (Cover one picture if children have difficulty.) **Let's say /y/. When you say /y/, your tongue is behind your lower teeth, and your mouth is open. Say /y/ and feel your tongue behind your lower teeth.**
Model the game	Model two examples.	**Model** **It's my turn to show you how to play the game.** Display the Picture Choice 92-1: *wave, yo-yo, hat.* Cover other pictures. **This is *wave, yo-yo,* and *hat. Yo-yo* has the first sound /y/; /y/, yo-yo.** Model one more example with *yarn, hug,* and *zebra.*
Test knowledge of /y/	Test children with four other examples. Cover the row not in use. Display Picture Choices 92-2 *(wig, gum, yell; game, yarn, zoo)* and 92-3 *(yawn, zipper, house; goal post, hook, yarn).* Give individual turns.	**Test** Display the remaining Picture Choices, one at a time, covering pictures not in use. Ask children to tell the name of each picture in the row: **What is this?** Have them find the picture that has the first sound /y/. Confirm correct responses and prompt sound production cue. For example, **Yes, *yell* has the first sound /y/. Let's say /y/. Remember, when you say /y/, your tongue is behind your lower teeth, and your mouth is open.** **Ongoing Assessment** **If . . .** children make incorrect responses, **then . . .** model the correct answer. Then review the sound production cue. Have children repeat the answer. Go back to the example a second time.

Activity 3 Discriminate Letter Sounds

Sounds

Objective: Children discriminate letter sounds.

Time: 4–5 minutes

	To Do	To Say
Introduce the activity	Display Sounds so all children can see.	Tell children that you will point to a letter. They will say the sound for that letter. Remind children that they will say quick sounds only for as long as you touch the letter.
Test the activity	Test children on each sound. Note: If the letter has a stop sound, like /b/, point to the letter briefly. If the letter has a continuous sound, like /a/, hold your finger under the sound for about two seconds. Give individual turns.	**Test** **What is the <u>sound</u> for this letter?** Point to *y* and hold your finger under the letter for about two seconds as children say the sound. **Yes, /y/.** Repeat the test with each letter.

Ongoing Assessment

If... children make an error,	**then...** tell them the sound, have them repeat it, and move back two letters on the page or repeat the letter if at the beginning of the page.
If... children miss more than two sounds on the page,	**then...** repeat the test for all letters on the page.

Lesson 92

Activity 4 Read Words

Say the Sounds/Say the Word with Fingers; Regular Words

Objective: Children segment, blend, and read words.

Time: 4–5 minutes

	To Do	To Say
Introduce the activity		**It's time to play Say the Sounds/Say the Word with Fingers. I will say the sounds of a word slowly. You will repeat each sound slowly and touch a finger as you say each sound. Then you will say the sounds quickly to figure out the word.**
Lead the activity	Lead segmenting *dad*.	**Lead** **Let's do a three-sound word together. Hold out three fingers.** Have each child hold out three fingers pointed toward you. Then have them use the pointer finger of the other hand to touch a finger for each sound moving from left to right. **Listen carefully to the quick sound at the beginning of the word. When we say the quick sound, we'll touch our first finger just for a second. Then we'll move on to the next sound. Listen, /d/ /aaa/ /d/.** Pause briefly after touching your first finger and saying the initial stop sound, but do not pause between the other sounds.
	Lead blending *dad*.	**Say it slowly with me: /d/ /aaa/ /d/.** All touch fingers from left to right. **Say it quickly with me and clap your hands, *dad*.**
Test knowledge of segmenting and blending words	Test segmenting and blending.	**Test** **It's your turn to do a two-sound word. Hold out two fingers. Listen, /iii/ /t/.** Teacher and children touch a finger for each sound. Only children say the sounds slowly. **Say it quickly.** All clap hands as children say the word. Repeat the test for *big, an, jam,* and *sun*. Point out that *an* is a two-sound word, so children will need to hold out two fingers. Point out that *big* and *jam* begin with a quick sound, so they will need to touch the first finger quickly for these words. Then give individual turns.

Ongoing Assessment

If... children do not touch the appropriate finger for each sound.	**then...** model how to do it. Then have them try again. If necessary, guide children's hands to touch fingers correctly.
If... children stop between the sounds,	**then...** model sounding out the word without stopping between sounds. Then have children try the word again.
If... children have trouble saying the word quickly,	**then...** tell them the word and say it slowly and quickly. Have them try again.

	To Do	To Say	
Introduce the activity	Display the Regular Words card.	Tell children that today they will read some words. Some of them begin with quick sounds, so they will have to watch your finger closely.	
Model the activity	Model sounding out *jam*.	**Model**	**My turn to read a word that begins with a quick sound. Watch my finger. I'll touch the quick sound at the beginning of the word just for a second, and then I'll move on. Each time I touch a letter, I'll say its sound. I won't stop between the other sounds.** Point to *jam* on the word card: **/j/ /aaa/ /mmm/.** Tap under the *j* and immediately move on. Touch under the last two squares for one to two seconds each.
	Model reading *jam*.		**Now I'll say it quickly, *jam*.** Move your finger beneath the word as you say it. **The word is *jam*.**
Lead the activity	Lead sounding out and reading *jam*. Use the same finger movements you used to model.	**Lead**	**Let's read this word together. Watch my finger because this word begins with a quick sound! Say the sounds. Get ready: /j/ /aaa/ /mmm/. Now let's say it quickly, *jam*. What's the word? *Yes*, *jam*.**

	To Do	To Say	
Test the activity	Test sounding out and reading *jam*.	Test	**Now it's your turn to read the word. First you'll say the sounds slowly. Then you'll say them quickly. Look out for that quick sound at the beginning. Say the sounds. Get ready.** Touch under the stop sound just for an instant and immediately move on. Children should not pause between the other sounds in the word. **Now say it quickly.** Move your finger quickly under the word as children say the word fast. **What's the word?**

Repeat the cycle to model, lead, and test the word *big*.

Then only test children in sounding out and reading *sun* and *an*.

Next, point to each word in random order. Children say the sounds slowly and then quickly. Point out words that begin with a stop sound.

Hand out word cards from today's word page to individuals. Ask each child to sound out and read his or her word: ______**, it's your turn. Say the sounds. Get ready. Now say the sounds quickly. What's the word?** If necessary, provide physical assistance in making finger movements.

Ongoing Assessment

If...children pause between sounds,	**then**...model sounding out the word and have children sound it out again.
If...children say the wrong sound,	**then**...keep your finger on the missed sound, model it correctly, and have children repeat the sound. Then have them sound out the word again.
If...children say the wrong word when they say it quickly,	**then**...model the correct word and have children repeat it. Have children say the sounds again slowly and then quickly.
If...a child makes an error on an individual turn,	**then**...have the whole group say the word, say the sounds, and say it quickly. If there are many errors on individual turns, model, lead, and test each word again with the whole group before providing individual turns again.

	To Do	To Say
Introduce Sentence-Reading Warm-Up	Display the Regular Words card.	**Soon you will begin to read sentences and stories. Today I will show you how to read words when they are in a sentence.**
Model reading words in sentences	Point to *an* on the Regular Words card.	**Model** **Everybody, look at this word. This is how we'll read this word when we see it in a sentence. I'll touch under the word.** Touch under the word, just to the left of the box. **Now I'll say the sounds. Watch my finger.** Move your finger below each letter as you say it. **First sound /aaa/, last sound /nnn/. Now I'll say it quickly.** Slash your finger under the word box: ***an*. Now I'll say the word.** Slash finger under the word box: ***an*.**
Test the activity	Test children on how to read a word in a sentence.	**Test** **Everybody, your turn to try this word.** Point to the word *an* on the Regular Words card. **Remember how we'll read this word when we see it in a sentence. First touch under the word. Now say the sounds. Don't stop between the sounds. Watch my finger.** Move your finger under each letter as children say the sounds. **First sound. Last sound. Now say it quickly.** Slash your finger under the word box. **What's the word?** Slash your finger under the word box. Repeat the test with the word *big*. Remind them that *big* begins with a quick sound, but they should not stop between the other sounds. If time permits, give individual children a word card for *an* or *big*. Tell the child to touch under the word. **Say the sounds. First sound, (next sound,) last sound. Say it quickly. What's the word?** Provide physical guidance if necessary.

Ongoing Assessment

If... children pause between sounds,	**then...** model sounding out the word and have children sound it out again.
If... children say the wrong sound,	**then...** keep your finger on the missed sound, model it correctly, and have children repeat the sound. Then have them sound out the word again.
If... children say the wrong word when they say it quickly,	**then...** model the correct word and have children repeat it. Have children say the sounds again slowly and then quickly.
If... children have difficulty following the new cues,	**then...** model and lead them through the word. Then try the test.

Activity 5 Writer's Warm-Up

Lesson 92

Introduce y

Objective: Children trace and write *y* and review writing *z*, *e*, *j*, *r*, *h*, *w*, and *b*.

Time: 2–3 minutes

	To Do	To Say
Review letter name and sound	Display the *y* Tracing Card.	Ask children to tell you the letter name and sound of *y*.
Model tracing *y*	Distribute a Writer's Warm-Up to each child. Model tracing *y*.	**Model** **Watch as I trace the letter *y* with my finger.** Have children trace the first two letters on their sheets with their finger. Repeat the model and have children trace the next two letters with their pencils.
Model writing *y*	Model writing *y* using the lined side of the tracing card.	**Model** **Watch as I write the letter *y*. I start at the dot and write the letter.** Have children write the letter twice on their sheets. Remind them to start at the dot and write carefully. **Ongoing Assessment** **If...** children make an error, **then...** put your hand over their hand and guide the writing of the letter. Then have children try to write the letter on their own. Repeat as necessary.
 Review ***z, e, j, r, h, w, b***	Model writing *y* again on the lined side of the tracing card.	**Test** Have children cover their letters and write the letter twice from memory on their sheets. **Do your letters look the same? Circle the letter that is your best work.** Then have children trace and write each review letter one time each. **Ongoing Assessment** **If...** children make an error, **then...** use the tracing card to model writing the letter and have children write the letter again. If needed, put your hand over the children's hands and guide the writing of the letter. Then have children try to write the letter on their own. Repeat as necessary.

Activity 6 Connect Sound to Letter

Practice Session: Spelling

Objective: Children segment sounds to spell words. Time: 2–3 minutes

	To Do	To Say
Introduce the activity	Gather the 3-Square Strip and letter tiles.	**We are going to practice spelling for "Where's the Letter?"**
Lead the activity	Segement the word *red.* Identify the first letter. Depending on ability level, display all the letter tiles or just two at a time.	**Lead** **The first word is *red.* What word?** Have children hold out three fingers. **Say the sounds in *red* and touch a finger for each sound.** Point to the first square of the 3-Square Strip. **Does everyone know what the first letter in *red* is?** Call on a child to choose the correct letter and place it on the first square. **Ongoing Assessment** **If**...children make an error, **then**...have them segment the word again.
	Identify the middle letter.	**Does everyone know what the next letter in *red* is?** Call on a child to choose and place the next letter.
	Identify the last letter.	**Do you know what the last letter in *red* is?** Call on a child to choose and place the letter.
	Confirm the spelling.	**Say each sound in *red* with me as I point to the letters: /rrr/ /eee/ /d/. Now say it quickly. That's right, you spelled *red;* /rrr/ /eee/ /d/ are the sounds in *red.*** Practice with at least two more words, as time allows: *leg, mud, run, men.*

Activity 7 Connect Sound to Letter

Where's the Letter?

Objective: Children connect sound to letter.

Time: 6–8 minutes

	To Do	To Say
Introduce the activity	Distribute letter tiles randomly to children. Each child should have a different set of tiles, including one vowel.	**We're going to spell some words together. I'm going to say a word and you are going to look at your letter tiles to see if you have a letter that will help spell the word. Let's see how many words we can spell together.**
Model the activity	Model segmenting the word *mud.*	**The first word is *mud.* Listen. I'll touch a finger as I say each sound in *mud:* /mmm/ /uuu/ /d/.**
	Model spelling the word *mud.* Display a 3-Square Strip.	**Now I'm going to look for the first letter in *mud.*** Take an *m* from a child's pile and place it in the first box on the 3-Square Strip. Use this procedure for the remaining letters in the word.
	Confirm the spelling of *mud.*	**Now, say each sound in *mud* with me while I point to the letters: /mmm/ /uuu/ /d/. Say it quickly. That's right. We spelled *mud;* /mmm/ /uuu/ /d/ are the sounds in *mud.***
Test the activity	Test segmenting the word *den.*	**The next word is *den.* What's the word? Say the sounds in *den* and touch a finger for each sound.**
	Test spelling the word *den.*	**Who has the first letter in *den?*** Have the child place the letter in the first box on the 3-Square Strip. Use this procedure for the remaining letters in the word.
		Ongoing Assessment **If**... children make an error, **then**... have them segment the word again. **Say the sounds in _____ again and touch a finger for each sound. Stop when you get to the _____ sound.**
	Confirm the spelling of *den.*	**Now, say each sound in *den* with me while I point to the letters: /d/ /eee/ /nnn/. Say it quickly. That's right. We spelled *den;* /d/ /eee/ /nnn/ are the sounds in *den.***
	Test the words *red, bug, jot,* and *pin.*	Use the same test procedure you used for *den.* Confirm the spelling of each word before testing the next word.

New Sound /y/
Review Sounds /w/, /f/, /t/, /j/, /l/, /u/, /b/, /i/, /g/
Key Reading Skills Letter-Sound Correspondences; Word Reading: VC, CVC

Phonological Awareness and Alphabetic Understanding

Activity	Materials		Time
1. Alphabetic Introduce *y*	Alphabet Card: *y*	Letter Card: *y* (one per child)	1–2 minutes
2. Integrated Phonologic/Alphabetic Which Picture Begins with /y/?	Alphabet Card: *y* Picture Choice: 93-1, 93-2, 93-3 Teacher Resource Package 3		4–5 minutes
3. Alphabetic Sounds Dash	Sounds Dash Teacher Resource Package 3	timer (not provided)	4–5 minutes
4. Phonologic/Reading Say the Sounds/ Say the Word with Fingers; Regular Words; Warm-Up for Sentence Reading	Regular Words Teacher Resource Package 3 Word Cards: *pan, am, did, him* (Lessons 91–96)		4–5 minutes

Writing and Spelling

Activity	Materials		Time
5. Writer's Warm-Up Memory Review	Write-On/Wipe-Off Cards markers (one per child/not provided)	Tracing Cards: *i, e, a, z, p, c, t, j, s*	2–3 minutes
6. Integrated Phonologic/Alphabetic Practice Session: Spelling	3-Square Strip	Letter Tiles: *i, e, a, z, p, c, t, j, s*	2–3 minutes
7. Phonologic/Spelling Word Page	Word Page (one per child) Student Activity Book 3, p. 47		6–8 minutes

Activity 1 Introduce Letter Name and Sound

Introduce y

Objective: Children learn and trace *y*/y/.

Time: 1–2 minutes

	To Do	To Say	
Introduce letter name	Hold up the *y* Alphabet Card.	Model	**The name of this letter is *y*.**
		Lead	**Say the name with me.**
		Test	**What is the name of this letter?**
Introduce letter sound	Continue holding up the *y* Alphabet Card.	Model	**This is the letter for the sound /y/. When you say /y/, your tongue is behind your lower teeth, and your mouth is open. Say /y/ and feel your tongue behind your lower teeth.**
		Lead	**Say the sound with me, /y/.**
		Test	**What is the sound for this letter?**
Test letter name and sound	Continue holding up the *y* Alphabet Card.	Test	**What is the name of this letter? What is the sound for this letter?**
	Give individual turns.		**Ongoing Assessment** — **If**...children make an error, **then**...tell them the name or sound, have them repeat the name or sound, and return to the letter a second time.
Model tracing *y*	Model how to trace *y* using your Alphabet Card.	Model	**Watch. I'll trace the letter *y*.** Have children trace the letter *y* on their Letter Cards three times and say /y/ each time they trace the letter.
			Ongoing Assessment — **If**...children make an error, **then**...Put your hand over their hand and guide the tracing of the letter. Then have children try to trace the letter on their own. Repeat as necessary.

Activity 2 Isolate Initial Sound

Lesson **93**

Which Picture Begins with /y/?

Objective: Children isolate initial /y/ and connect sound to letter.

Time: 4–5 minutes

	To Do	To Say
Model names of pictures	Display Picture Choice 93-1.	**Model** Model names of pictures and have children repeat them: *apple, yell, rake; yarn, jump, zebra.* . **This is _____. What is this?** **Test** **What is this?**
Introduce the game Which Picture Begins with /y/?	Practice production of the target sound. Hold up the *y* Alphabet Card.	**I will show you a letter. You will find the picture that begins with the sound for that letter.** **It's my turn. The <u>name</u> of this letter is *y*. The <u>sound</u> for this letter is /y/. Remember, when you say /y/, your tongue is behind your lower teeth, and your mouth is open.** **What is the <u>sound</u> for this letter?**
Model the game	Model two examples.	Display the first Picture Choice: *apple, yell, rake.* Cover the other pictures. **This is *apple, yell,* and *rake*. It's my turn to find the picture that has the first sound /y/.** Point to the letter. ***Yell, yell* has the first sound /y/.** Exaggerate the first sound, then say the word: ***/y/, yell.*** Model one more example with *yarn, jump,* and *zebra*.
Test knowledge of /y/	Test children with Picture Choice 93-2 *(jeep, astronaut, yawn; rug, yo-yo, jam)* and 93-3 *(rain, jet, yo-yo; yell, boat, ant)*. Give individual turns.	**Test** Display the remaining Picture Choices, one at a time, covering pictures not in use. Hold up Alphabet Card *y*: **What is the <u>sound</u> for this letter?** Ask children to tell the name of each picture in the row: **What is this?** Have them find the picture that has the first sound /y/ (point to the alphabet card). Confirm correct responses and prompt sound production cue. **Yes, *yawn* has the first sound /y/. When you say /y/, your tongue is behind your lower teeth, and your mouth is open.** **Ongoing Assessment** **If...** children make incorrect responses, **then...** model the correct answer. Then review the sound production cue. Have children repeat the answer. Go back to the example a second time.

Activity 3 Build Sound Fluency

Sounds Dash

Objective: Children increase fluency in identifying letter sounds.

Time: 4–5 minutes

	To Do	To Say
Introduce Sounds Dash	Display Sounds Dash.	**Today we will do a Sounds Dash. I will point to a letter, and you will say the sound for that letter. Get as close to the finish line as possible in one minute. Be careful! If I hear a mistake, the group will go back three letters. Also, remember to say a sound only as long as I touch the letter. Some sounds will be quick.**
Review Sounds of Letters	Review the sounds in the first row of the Sounds Dash page.	**Model** **Let's get warmed up for our game. We will practice the sounds in the first row.** Point to *w*. **What is the sound for this letter?** Hold your finger under the letter *w* for one to two seconds. **Yes, /w/.** Practice the sound of each letter in the first row.
Play the game	Display the Sounds Dash page. Set the timer for one minute.	**Test** **Now you're ready for the Sounds Dash. Everybody, look at my finger. On your mark, get set, go!** Point to *w* in the first row. **What is the sound for this letter?** Repeat with each sound in the first row. Then go immediately to the second row and so on, until one minute is up. Reinforce children's progress in the Sounds Dash and tell them they will have a chance to beat their score when they play again in three days.

Ongoing Assessment (Review Sounds of Letters)

If...children make an error,	**then**...tell them the sound, have them repeat it, and move back three letters on the page or repeat the letter if at the beginning of the row.
If...children miss more than two sounds in the first row,	**then**...provide additional practice on the nine sounds on the page instead of doing the Sounds Dash. Emphasize sounds children are unsure of.

Ongoing Assessment (Play the game)

If...children make an error,	**then**...tell them the sound, have them repeat it, and move back three letters or repeat the letter if at the beginning of a row.

Activity 4 Read Words

Say the Sounds/Say the Word with Fingers; Regular Words

Objective: Children segment, blend, and read words.

Time: 4–5 minutes

	To Do	To Say
Introduce the activity		**It's time to play Say the Sounds/Say the Words with Fingers. I will say the sounds of a word slowly. You will repeat each sound slowly and touch a finger as you say each sound. Then you will say the sounds quickly to say the word.**
Lead the activity	Segment the word *him*.	**Lead** **Let's do a three-sound word together. Hold out three fingers. Listen carefully to the quick sound at the beginning of the word. When we say the quick sound, we'll touch our first finger just for a second. Then we'll move on to the next sound.**
	Blend the word *him*.	Check to be sure children point fingers toward you, not up. Remind them to get their pointer finger ready. **Listen: /h/ /iii/ /mmm/.** Pause briefly after touching your first finger and saying the initial stop sound, but do not pause between other sounds. **Say it slowly with me, /h/ /iii/ /mmm/.** All touch fingers from left to right. **Say it quickly with me and clap your hands: *him*.**
Test the activity	Segment and blend *up*.	**Test** **Your turn to do a two-sound word. Hold out two fingers. Listen: /uuu/ /p/.** Touch a finger as you say each sound. **Say it slowly.** Teacher and children touch a finger for each sound. Only children say the sounds slowly. **Say it quickly.** All clap hands as children say the word. Repeat test for *mug, pan, did,* and *am.* Point out that *am* is a two-sound word, so children will need to hold out two fingers. Tell children that *pan* and *did* begin with a quick sound, so they will need to touch the first finger quickly for these words.
	Give individual turns.	See Ongoing Assessment below.

Ongoing Assessment

If... children do not touch the appropriate finger for each sound.	**then...** model how to do it. Then have them try again. If necessary, guide children's hands to touch fingers correctly.
If... children stop between the sounds,	**then...** model sounding out the word without stopping between the sounds. Then have children try the word again.
If... children have trouble saying the word quickly,	**then...** tell them the word and then say it slowly and quickly before having them try again.

	To Do	To Say
Introduce the activity	Display the Regular Words card.	**Today you will read some words. Some of them begin with quick sounds, so you will have to watch my finger closely.**
Model the activity	Segment *pan*. Blend *pan*.	**Model** **It's my turn to read a word that begins with a quick sound. Watch my finger. I'll touch the quick sound at the beginning of the word just for a second, and then I'll move on. Each time I touch a letter, I'll say its sound. I won't stop between the other sounds.** Point to *pan* on the Regular Words card: **/p/ /aaa/ /nnn/.** Tap under the square for *p* and then immediately move on. Touch under the last two squares for one to two seconds each, without pausing between sounds. **Now I'll say it quickly, *pan*.** Sweep your finger beneath the word. **The word is *pan*.**
Lead the activity	Lead segmenting and blending *pan*. Use the same finger movements you used to model.	**Lead** **Let's read this word together. Watch my finger because this word begins with a quick sound! Say the sounds. Get ready: /p/ /aaa/ /nnn/. Now let's say it quickly, *pan*. What's the word? *Pan*. The word is *pan*.**
Test children on the activity	Segment and blend *pan*.	**Test** **Now it's your turn to read the word. First, say the sounds slowly. Then say them quickly. Look out for the quick sound at the beginning. Say the sounds. Get ready.** Touch under the letters as the sounds indicate. **Now say it quickly.** Move your finger quickly under the word. **What's the word?** Repeat only the test procedure for the word *am*. Repeat the model, lead, and test procedures for *did* and *him*.

Ongoing Assessment

If... children have difficulty following the new cues,	**then...** model and lead them through the word. Then try the test.
If... children pause between sounds,	**then...** model sounding out the word and have children sound it out again.
If... children say the wrong sound,	**then...** keep your finger on the missed sound, model it correctly, and have children repeat the sound. Then have them sound out the word again.
If... children say the wrong word when they say it quickly,	**then...** model the correct word and have children repeat it. Have children say the sounds again slowly and then quickly.

	To Do	To Say	
Test the group	Test the group.	**Test**	Point to each word in random order. Have children say the sounds slowly and then quickly. Alert children to words that begin with a stop sound.
	Provide individual turns.		Hand out word cards from today's words to individuals. Ask each child to sound out and read his or her word: ______**, your turn. Say the sounds. Get ready. Now say it fast. What's the word?** If necessary, assist children in making finger movements.

Ongoing Assessment

If... children pause between sounds,	**then...** model sounding out the word and have children sound it out again.
If... children say the wrong sound,	**then...** keep your finger on the missed sound, model it correctly, and have children repeat the sound. Then have them sound out the word again.
If... children say the wrong word when they say it quickly,	**then...** model the correct word and have children repeat it. Then have children say the sounds slowly again and then say them quickly.
If... a child makes an error on an individual turn,	**then...** have the whole group say the word, say the sounds, and say it quickly. If there are many errors on individual turns, model, lead, and test each word again with the whole group before providing individual turns again.

	To Do	To Say
Introduce Sentence-Reading Warm-Up	Display the Regular Words page.	**Soon you will begin to read sentences and stories. Today I will show you how to read words when they are in a sentence.**
Model reading words in sentences	Model how students will read a word in a sentence.	**Model** **Everybody, look at this word.** Point to *did* on the Regular Words card. **This is how we'll read this word when we see it in a sentence. I'll touch under the word.** Touch under the word, just to the left of the box. **Now I'll say the sounds. Watch my finger.** Move your finger below each sound as you say it. **First sound /d/, next sound /iii/, last sound /d/. Now I'll say it quickly.** Slash your finger under the word box: ***did*. Now I'll say the word.** Slash your finger under the word box: ***did*.**
Test the activity	Test children on how to read a word in a sentence.	**Test** **Everybody, it's your turn to try this word. Point to the word *did*. Remember how we'll read this word when we see it in a sentence. First touch under the word.** Touch under the word, just to the left of the box. **Now say the sounds. This word starts with a quick sound. Don't stop between the other sounds. Watch my finger.** Move your finger under each sound as children say the sounds. **First sound. Next sound. Last sound. Now say it quickly.** Slash your finger under the word box. **What's the word?** Slash your finger under the word box. Repeat the test with the word *him*. If time permits, provide individual turns by giving individual children a Word Card for *him* or *did*. Tell the child to touch under the word. **Say the sounds. First sound, next sound, last sound. Say it quickly. What's the word?** Provide physical guidance if necessary.

Ongoing Assessment

If... children pause between sounds,	**then...** model sounding out the word and have children sound it out again.
If... children say the wrong sound,	**then...** keep your finger on the missed sound, model it correctly, and have children repeat the sound. Then have them sound out the word again.
If... children say the wrong word when they say it quickly,	**then...** model the correct word and have children repeat it. Have children say the sounds again slowly and then quickly.
If... children have difficulty following the new cues,	**then...** model and lead them through the word. Then try the test.

Activity 5 Writer's Warm-Up

Memory Review

Objective: Children write review letters *i, e, a, z, p, c, t, j,* and *s.*

Time: 2–3 minutes

	To Do	To Say
Review letter names	Display the tracing cards.	**What is the name of this letter?**
Model writing letters	Distribute the Write-On/ Wipe-Off Cards and markers. Model one example.	**Model** **I'll show you how this activity works. The first letter is *s*. Now I'll write the letter *s* on my Write-On/ Wipe-Off Card. What is the name of the letter I wrote?**
Test writing letters	Test children on writing review letters.	**Test** Dictate letter names in the following order: *i, e, a, z, p, c, t, j,* and *s.* Have children write the correct letter on their cards. Reinforce the letter name: **Everyone, what's the name of the letter you wrote?** Then have them erase their cards. Dictate the next letter. **Ongoing Assessment** **If...** children write the wrong letter or don't remember a letter, **then...** show them the tracing card for the correct letter, model tracing the letter, and say the letter name.

Connect Sound to Letter

Practice Session: Spelling

Objective: Children segment words and connect sounds to letters.

Time: 2–3 minutes

	To Do	To Say
Introduce the activity	Gather the 3-Square Strip and letter tiles.	**We are going to practice spelling for a word page.**
Lead the activity	Segment the word *set.*	**Lead** **The first word is *set*. What word?** Have children hold out three fingers. **Say the sounds in *set* and touch a finger for each sound.**
	Identify the first letter. Depending on ability level, display all the letter tiles or just two at a time.	Point to the first square of the 3-Square Strip. **Does everyone think they know what the first letter in *set* is?** Call on a child to choose the correct letter and place it on the first square.
		Ongoing Assessment **If...** children make an error, **then...** have them segment the word again.
	Identify the middle letter.	**Does everyone know what the next letter in *set* is?** Call on a child to choose and place the next letter.
	Identify the last letter.	**Do you know what the last letter in *set* is?** Call on a child to choose and place the letter.
	Confirm the spelling.	**Say each sound in *set* with me as I point to the letters: /sss/ /eee/ /t/. Now say it quickly. That's right, you spelled *set;* /sss/ /eee/ /t/ are the sounds in *set*.** Practice with at least two more words, as time allows: *zap, sit, cap, jet.*

Activity 7 Connect Sound to Letter

Word Page

Objective: Children connect sound to letter.

Time: 6–8 minutes

	To Do	To Say
Introduce the activity	Distribute Word Page.	**We're going to spell words that go with each picture. Let's spell words for all the pictures on this page!**
Model the activity	Model segmenting the word *cap*.	**Model** **The first picture is *cap.* Listen. I'll touch a finger as I say each sound in *cap:* /k/ /aaa/ /p/.**
	Model writing the word *cap*.	**Now I'm going to write the first letter in *cap.*** Write a *c* under *cap* on the activity sheet and show children. **Now you write the first letter in *cap.*** Continue this procedure for the rest of the word.
	Confirm the spelling of *cap*.	**Now, say each sound in *cap* with me and point to the letters: /k/ /aaa/ /p/. Say it quickly. That's right. We spelled *cap;* /k/ /aaa/ /p/ are the sounds in *cap,* and *c-a-p* spells *cap.***
Test the activity	Test segmenting the word *sit*.	**Test** **Look at the next picture. This is *sit.* What is this? Touch a finger as you say each sound in *sit.***
	Test spelling the word *sit*.	**Everyone, write the first letter in *sit.* Write the next letter in *sit.* Write the last letter in *sit.***
		Ongoing Assessment **If**...children make an error, **then**...have them segment the word again: **Say the sounds in _____ again and touch a finger for each sound. Stop when you get to the _____ sound.**
	Confirm the spelling of *sit*.	**Now say each sound in *sit* with me while you point to the letters: /sss/ /iii/ /t/. Say it quickly. That's right. You spelled *sit;* /s/ /iii/ /t/ are the sounds in *sit,* and *s-i-t* spells *sit.***
	Test the words *jet, pan,* and *pen.*	Use the same test procedure you used for *sit.* Confirm the spelling of each word before testing the next word.

Review Sounds /a/, /o/, /n/, /j/, /e/, /z/, /h/, /y/

Key Reading Skills Letter-Sound Correspondences; Word Reading: VC, CVC

Phonological Awareness and Alphabetic Understanding

Activity	Materials	Time
1. **Alphabetic** Review *y*/y/	Alphabet Card: *y*	1–2 minutes
2. **Integrated Phonologic/Alphabetic** First Sound Mix-Up Game with /y/ and /e/	Letter Cards: *y* and *e* Picture Cards: *yarn, yak, yard, yo-yo, escalator, elbow, egg, elephant*	4–5 minutes
3. **Alphabetic** Sounds	Sounds Teacher Resource Package 3	4–5 minutes
New 4. **Reading** Irregular Words; Regular Words; Sentence Reading Warm-Up	Irregular Words Teacher Resource Package 3 Regular Words Teacher Resource Package 3 Word Cards: *bed, cup, it, had* (Lessons 91–96) Diz Puppet	4–5 minutes

Writing and Spelling

Activity	Materials	Time
5. **Writer's Warm-Up** Writer's Warm-Up	Writer's Warm-Up (one per child) Student Activity Book 3, p. 48 or 49 Tracing Cards: *z, y, w, f, r, h, e, m, t, u*	2–3 minutes
6. **Integrated Phonologic/Alphabetic** Practice Session: Spelling	3-Square Strip Letter Tiles: *e, u, a, y, m, f, l, n, g*	2–3 minutes
7. **Phonologic/Spelling** Missing Letters	Missing Letters (one per child) Student Activity Book 3, p. 50	6–8 minutes

Activity 1 Review Letter Name and Sound

Review y/y/

Objective: Children review *y*/y/.

Time: 1–2 minutes

	To Do	To Say	
Test letter name and sound	Hold up the *y* Alphabet Card.	Test	**What is the <u>name</u> of this letter? What is the <u>sound</u> for this letter?**
	Give individual turns on letter name and sound.		

Ongoing Assessment

If...children make an error,	**then**...tell them the name or sound, have them repeat the name or sound, and return to the letter a second time.

Activity 2 Isolate Initial Sound

Lesson **94**

First Sound Mix-Up Game with /y/ and /e/

Objective: Children isolate initial sounds.

Time: 4–5 minutes

	To Do	To Say
Review names of pictures	Display the picture cards.	**This is ______. What is this?** Repeat for the remaining picture cards.
Introduce the game First Sound Mix-Up	Mix the picture cards and place them in a pile. Have *egg* and then *yarn* on top. Place Letter Cards *y* and *e* on the table facing children.	**You are going to play First Sound Mix-Up. I will hold up a picture. You will say the name of the picture and then tell the first sound. Some of the pictures begin with /y/ and some with /eee/.**
Model the game	Display the *egg* picture card.	Model **I'll show you how to play the game. This is *egg*. I'll say the first sound in *egg*, /eee/. Now I'll put *egg* by the letter for the sound /eee/. Remember, the name of this letter is *e*. The sound for *e* is /eee/.**
Test knowledge of /y/ and /e/	Test children.	Test Display the next picture in the pile. **What is this? Say the first sound in _____.** Confirm correct responses and prompt sound production cue. **Yes, the first sound in *yarn* is /y/. When you say /y/, your tongue is behind your lower teeth, and your mouth is open. Put your tongue behind your lower teeth. *Yarn*. Put *yarn* by the letter that stands for the sound /y/.** Repeat with remaining Picture Cards. (Sound production cue for /e/: **When you say /eee/, your mouth is open and your tongue is behind your bottom teeth. Put your tongue behind your bottom teeth.)**
	Give individual turns.	**Ongoing Assessment** **If...** children make an error, **then...** tell them the answer and have them repeat it. Put the picture back into the pile so you can return to it a second time.

Activity 3 Discriminate Letter Sounds

Sounds

Objective: Children discriminate letter sounds.

Time: 4–5 minutes

	To Do	To Say
Introduce Sounds	Display Sounds.	**I will point to a letter. Then you will say the sound for that letter. Say a sound only for as long as I touch the letter. Some sounds will be quick.**
Test the activity	Test children on each sound. Note: If the letter has a stop sound, like /b/, point to the letter briefly. If the letter has a continuous sound, like /a/, hold your finger under the sound for about two seconds. Give individual turns.	**Test** Point to *a*. **The name of this letter is *a*. What is the sound for this letter?** Hold your finger under the letter for about two seconds as children say the sound. **Yes, /aaa/.** Repeat with each letter.

Ongoing Assessment

If...children make an error,	**then**...tell them the sound, have them repeat it, and move back two sounds or repeat the letter if at the beginning of a page.
If...children miss more than two sounds on the page,	**then**...repeat the test for all letters on the page.

Activity 4 Read Words

Regular Words; Irregular Words; Sentence Reading Warm-Up

Objective: Children read regular and irregular words. Time: 4–5 minutes

	To Do	To Say
Introduce the activity	Display the Irregular Words card.	**Today you will learn to read a new Dizzy word.**
	Introduce new irregular word *the*.	**Lead** **Here is the new word. Let's have Diz try to say the sounds slowly and then say them quickly.** Touch under the box just to the left of the word.
	Place the Diz puppet on your hand.	**Diz, say the sounds. Get ready.** Make the puppet say the sounds slowly. **/t/ /h/ /eee/. Now say it quickly, Diz: /t/ /h/ /eee/; /t/ /h/ /eee/ isn't a real word. It's a Dizzy word. Remember we don't sound out Dizzy words. We spell them out.**
Lead children in the activity	Point to *the* on the Irregular Words card.	**This word is really *the*. What's the word?** Slash your finger under the word as children say it quickly. **Spell *the, t-h-e*.** Touch under each letter as children name each letter. **What word did you spell?** Slash your finger under the word as children say it. **Yes, *the*. This Dizzy word is *the*.**
Introduce the activity	Display the Regular Words card.	**Today you will read some words that begin with quick sounds. You will have to watch my finger closely.**
Model the activity	Sound out and read *bed*.	**Model** **It's my turn to read a word that begins with a quick sound. Watch my finger. I'll touch the quick sound at the beginning of the word just for a second, and then I'll move on. Each time I touch a letter, I'll say its sound. I won't stop between the sounds.** Point to *bed* on the word page: **/b/ /eee/ /d/.** Tap under *b* and then immediately move on. Do not pause between the other sounds. **Now I'll say the sounds quickly, *bed*.** Move your finger quickly beneath the word as you say it. **The word is *bed*.**

	To Do	To Say	
Lead the activity	Sound out and read *bed*. Repeat your finger movements from the model.	**Lead**	**Let's read this word together. Watch my finger because this word begins with a quick sound! Say the sounds. Get ready; /b/ /eee/ /d/. Now let's say it quickly, *bed*. What's the word? *Bed*. Yes, *bed*.**
Test the activity	Sound out and read *bed*.	**Test**	**Now it's your turn to read the word. First, you'll say the sounds slowly. Then you'll say them quickly. Look out for the quick sound at the beginning. Say the sounds. Get ready.** Touch under the letters as the sounds indicate. **Now say it quickly.** Move your finger quickly under the word. **What's the word?**
			Repeat the model, lead, and test procedures with *cup* and *had*. Then repeat the test procedure only with *it*.
	Test the group.		Point to each word in random order. Have children say the sounds slowly and then quickly. Alert children to words that begin with a stop sound.
	Provide individual turns.		Hand out the Word Cards. Ask each child to sound out and read his or her word: **______, it's your turn. Say the sounds. Get ready. Now say the sounds quickly. What's the word?** If necessary, provide physical assistance in making finger movements.

Ongoing Assessment

If... children pause between sounds,	**then...** model sounding out the word and have children sound it out again.
If... children say the wrong sound,	**then...** keep your finger on the missed sound, model it correctly, and have children repeat the sound. Then have them sound out the word again.
If... children say the wrong word when they say it quickly,	**then...** model the correct word and have children repeat it. Then have children say the sounds slowly again and then say them quickly.
If... a child makes an error on an individual turn,	**then...** have the whole group say the word, say the sounds, and say them quickly. If there are many errors on individual turns, model, lead, and test each word again with the whole group before providing individual turns again.

	To Do	To Say
Introduce Sentence Reading Warm-Up	Display the Regular Words card.	**In a few days you will begin to read sentences and stories. Today I will show you how to read words when they are in a sentence.**
Model reading words in sentences	Point to *it* on the Regular Words card.	**Everybody, look at this word. This is how we'll read this word when we see it in a sentence. I'll touch under the word.** Touch under the word, just to the left of the box. **Now I'll say the sounds. Watch my finger.** Move your finger underneath each sound as you say it. **First sound /iii/, last sound /t/. Now I'll say it quickly.** Slash your finger under the word box: ***it*. I'll say the word, *it*.** Slash your finger under the word again as you say it.
Test the activity	Test children on how to read a word in a sentence.	**Everybody, it's your turn to try this word.** Point to the word *it*. **Remember how we'll read this word when we see it in a sentence. First touch under the word. Now say the sounds. Don't stop between the sounds. Watch my finger.** Move your finger under each sound as children say the sounds. **First sound. Last sound. Now say it quickly.** Slash your finger under the word box. **What's the word?** Slash your finger under the word box. Repeat the test with the word *had*. Remind children that *had* begins with a quick sound, but that they shouldn't stop between the other sounds. If time permits, provide individual turns by giving individual children a Word Card for *it* or *had*. Tell the child to touch under the word. **Say the sounds. First sound, next sound, last sound. Say it quickly. What's the word?** Provide physical guidance if necessary.

Ongoing Assessment

If... children pause between sounds,	**then...** model sounding out the word and have children sound it out again.
If... children say the wrong sound,	**then...** keep your finger on the missed sound, model it correctly, and have children repeat the sound. Then have them sound out the word again.
If... children say the wrong word when they say it quickly,	**then...** model the correct word and have children repeat it. Have children say the sounds slowly again and then say them quickly.
If... children have difficulty following the new cues,	**then...** model and lead them through the word. Then try the test.

Activity 5 Writer's Warm-Up

Review Letters: z, y, w, f, r, h, e, m, t, u

Objective: Children trace and write review letters.

Time: 2–3 minutes

	To Do	To Say
Review letter names	Display the *z* Tracing Card.	**What is the <u>name</u> of this letter?** Continue with remaining tracing cards.
Complete the activity	Trace and write letters.	**Trace and write each review letter one time. When you finish writing all the letters, circle your best letters.**

Ongoing Assessment

If... children make an error,	**then...** use the tracing card to model writing the letter and ask them to write the letter again. If necessary, put your hand over their hands and guide the writing of the letter. Then have children try to write the letter on their own. Repeat as necessary.

Activity 6 Connect Sound to Letter

Practice Session: Spelling

Objective: Children segement sounds to spell words.

Time: 2–3 minutes

	To Do	To Say
Introduce the activity	Gather the 3-Square Strip and letter tiles.	**We are going to practice spelling for Missing Letters.**
Lead the activity	Segment the word *leg*.	**Lead** **The first word is *leg*. What word?** Have children hold out three fingers. **Say the sounds in leg and touch a finger for each sound.**
	Identify the first letter. Depending on ability level, display all the letter tiles or just two at a time.	Point to the first square of the 3-Square Strip. **Does everyone think they know what the first letter in *leg* is?** Call on a child to choose the correct letter and place it on the first square.
		Ongoing Assessment If... children make an error, then... have them segment the word again.
	Identify the middle letter.	**Does everyone know what the next letter in *leg* is?** Call on a child to choose and place the next letter.
	Identify the last letter.	**Do you know what the last letter in *leg* is?** Call on a child to choose and place the letter.
	Confirm the spelling.	**Say each sound in *leg* with me as I point to the letters: /lll/ /eee/ /g/. Now say it quickly. That's right, you spelled *leg*; /lll/ /eee/ /g/ are the sounds in *leg*.**
		Practice with at least two more words, as time allows: *yum, mug, fan, gal.*

Activity 7 Connect Sound to Letter

Lesson **94**

Missing Letters

Objective: Children connect sound to letter.

Time: 6–8 minutes

	To Do	To Say
Introduce the activity	Distribute Missing Letters.	**Look at your activity sheet. Some of the words are missing letters. We are going to help finish spelling the words by writing in the missing letters. Let's see if we can figure out the spellings for all the words!**
Model the Activity	Model the word *mug*.	**Model** **The first word is *mug.* Listen. I'll touch a space as I say each sound in *mug:* /mmm/ /uuu/ /g/. Now I'll say the sounds in *mug* again and stop when I get to the missing sound: /mmm/ /uuu/. I'm going to write the missing letter in *mug.*** Show children your activity sheet after you've written the letter.
	Confirm the spelling of *mug*.	**Now, say each sound in *mug* with me while I point to the letters: /mmm/ /uuu/ /g/. Say it quickly. That's right. We spelled *mug;* /mmm/ /uuu/ /g/ are the sounds in *mug*.**
Test the activity	Test the words *log, yum, gal, fun, fog,* and *gum.*	**Test** Use the following procedure for *log* and *fog:* **The next word is ______. What's the word? Touch a space as you say each sound in ______. Now write the missing letter in ______.** Confirm the spelling of the word. Use the following procedure for *yum, gal, fun,* and *gum:* **The next word is ______. What's the word? Touch a space as you say each sound in ______. Say the sounds again and stop when you get to the missing sound. Now write the missing letter in ______.** Confirm the spelling of the word.

Ongoing Assessment

If... children make an error, **then**... have them segment the word again. **Say the sounds in _____ again and touch a finger for each sound. Stop when you get to the missing sound.**

Review Sounds /b/, /i/, /n/, /u/, /e/, /z/, /h/, /y/
Key Reading Skills Letter-Sound Correspondences; Word Reading: VC, CVC

Phonological Awareness and Alphabetic Understanding

Activity	Materials		Time
1. Alphabetic Review *y*/y/	Alphabet Card: *y*		1–2 minutes
2. Integrated Phonologic/Alphabetic Hold the Pictures Game with /y/, /e/, and /o/	Letter Cards: *y, e, o* Picture Cards: *ox, otter, olive, octopus, yarn, yak, yo-yo, egg, elbow, escalator, elephant*		4–5 minutes
3. Alphabetic Sounds	Sounds Teacher Resource Package 3		4–5 minutes
4. Reading Irregular Words; Regular Words, Sentence Reading Warm-Up	Irregular Words Teacher Resource Package 3 Regular Words Teacher Resource Package 3	Word Cards: *bug, nap, dog, mat* (Lessons 91–96)	4–5 minutes

Writing and Spelling

Activity	Materials		Time
5. Writer's Warm-Up Treasure Hunt	Treasure Hunt (one per child) Student Activity Book 3, p. 51	Tracing Cards: *y, b, z, j, g, e, w, u*	2–3 minutes
6. Integrated Phonologic/Alphabetic Practice Session: Spelling	3-Square Strip	Letter Tiles: *i, u, e, y, c, t, d, r, p*	2–3 minutes
7. Phonologic/Spelling Monster Words	3 Write-On/Wipe-Off Cards marker (not provided)		6–8 minutes

Lesson 95

Activity 1 Review Letter Name and Sound

Review y/y/

Objective: Children review *y/y/*.

Time: 1–2 minutes

	To Do	To Say
Test letter name and sound	Hold up the *y* Alphabet Card.	Test **What is the name of this letter? What is the sound for this letter?**
	Give individual turns on letter name and sound.	**Ongoing Assessment** **If...** children make an error, **then...** tell them the name or sound, have them repeat the name or sound, and return to the letter a second time.

Activity 2 Isolate Initial Sound

Hold the Pictures Game with /y/, /e/, and /o/

Objective: Children isolate sounds and connect to letters. Time: 4–5 minutes

	To Do	To Say
Review names of pictures	Display the picture cards.	**This is *yarn*. What is this?** Repeat for the remaining picture cards.
Introduce the game Hold the Pictures with /y/, /e/, and /o/	Mix the picture cards. Give each child three cards. Place Letter Cards *y, e,* and *o* on the table facing children.	**You are going to play Hold the Pictures with /y/, /eee/, and /ooo/. You will take turns holding up a picture. You will say the picture name and the picture's first sound. Then you will place the picture next to the letter for the first sound.**
Model the game	Display the *ox* Picture Card.	Model **I'll show you how to play the game.** (Hold up the picture of *ox*.) **This is *ox*. I'll say the first sound in *ox*, /ooo/. Now I'll put *ox* by the letter for /ooo/.**
Play the game	Give individual turns.	Play **Hold up a picture. What is it? Say the first sound in ____. Put ____ by the letter for /_/.** Continue the game until all pictures have been shown. **Ongoing Assessment** **If...** children make an error in any of the steps, **then...** tell them the answer and have them repeat it. Children keep the picture in front of them and try again on another turn.

Activity 3 Discriminate Letter Sounds

Sounds

Objective: Children connect sound to letter.

Time: 4–5 minutes

	To Do	To Say
Introduce Sounds	Display Sounds.	**I will point to a letter and you will say the sound for that letter. Say a sound only for as long as I touch the letter. Some sounds will be quick.**
Test the activity	Test children on each sound. Note: If the letter has a stop sound, like /b/, point to the letter briefly. If the letter has a continuous sound, like /a/, hold your finger under the sound for about two seconds. Give individual turns.	**Test** Point to *n*. **What is the <u>sound</u> for this letter?** Hold your finger under the letter for about two seconds as children say the sound. **Yes, /nnn/.** Repeat with each letter.

Ongoing Assessment

If... children make an error,	**then...** tell them the sound, have them repeat it, and move back two sounds or repeat the letter if at the beginning of a page.
If... children miss more than two sounds on the page,	**then...** repeat the test for all letters on the page.

Activity 4 Read Words

Irregular Words; Regular Words; Sentence Reading Warm-Up

Objective: Children read regular and irregular words. Time: 4–5 minutes

	To Do		To Say
Reintroduce the Irregular Word	Display the Irregular Words card.		**Everybody, we are going to read the Dizzy word we learned yesterday. Remember, some of the words that you will learn to read will be Dizzy words. We won't sound them out. We will spell them out.**
		Lead	**This Dizzy word is *the*.** Point to the word. **What's the word?** Move your finger quickly under the word as children say it. **Spell *the*.** Touch under each letter as children name each one. **What word did you spell?** Slash your finger under the word as children say it. ***Yes, the*. This Dizzy word is *the*.**
Introduce the activity	Display the Regular Words card.		**Today you will read some words that begin with quick sounds. Watch my finger closely.**
Model the activity	Sound out *hug*.	Model	**It's my turn to read a word that begins with a quick sound. Watch my finger. I'll touch the quick sound at the beginning of the word just for a second, and then I'll move on. Each time I touch a letter, I'll say its sound. I won't stop between the sounds.** Point to *hug* on the Regular Words card: **/h/ /uuu/ /g/.** Tap under the *h* and then immediately move on. Do not pause between sounds.
	Read *hug*.		**Now I'll say it quickly, /h/ /uuu/ /g/.** Move your finger quickly beneath the word as you say it. **The word is *hug*.**

 Read Words (continued)

	To Do	To Say	
Lead the activity	Lead sounding out and reading *hug*. Use the same routine finger movements.	**Lead**	**Let's read this word together. Watch my finger because this word begins with a quick sound! Say the sounds. Get ready: /h/ /uuu/ /g/. Now let's say it quickly, *hug*. What's the word? *Hug;* yes, *hug*.**
Test the activity	Sound out and read *hug*.	**Test**	**Now it's your turn to read the word. First, you'll say the sounds slowly. Then you'll say them quickly. Look out for the quick sound at the beginning. Say the sounds. Get ready.** Touch under the letters as the sounds indicate. **Now say it quickly.** Move your finger quickly under the word. **What's the word?**

Then use the model, lead, and test procedures with the word *dog*. Use only the test procedure with the words *nap* and *mat*.

Point to each word in random order. Have children say the sounds slowly and then quickly. Alert children to words that begin with a stop sound.

Provide individual turns by handing out the Word Cards. Ask each child to sound out and read his or her word: ______, **it's your turn. Say the sounds. Get ready. Now say it quickly. What's the word?** If necessary, provide physical assistance in making finger movements.

Ongoing Assessment

If... children pause between sounds,	**then...** model sounding out the word and have children sound it out again.
If... children say the wrong sound,	**then...** keep your finger on the missed sound, model it correctly, and have children repeat the sound. Then have them sound out the word again.
If... children say the wrong word when they say it quickly,	**then...** model the correct word and have children repeat it. Then have children say the sounds slowly again and then say them fast.
If... a child makes an error on an individual turn,	**then...** have the whole group say the word, say the sounds, and say it quickly. If there are many errors on individual turns, model, lead, and test each word again with the whole group before providing individual turns again.

	To Do	To Say
Introduce Sentence Reading Warm-Up	Display the Regular Words card.	**In a few days you will begin to read sentences and stories. Today I will show you how to read words when they are in a sentence.**
Model reading words in sentences	Model how children will read a word in a sentence.	**Model** **Everybody, look at this word.** Point to *dog* on the word page. **This is how we'll read this word when we see it in a sentence. I'll touch under the word.** Touch under the word, just to the left of the box. **Now I'll say the sounds. Watch my finger.** Move your finger underneath each sound as you say it. **First sound /d/, next sound /ooo/, last sound /g/. Now I'll say it fast.** Slash your finger under the word box, ***dog*****. Now I'll say the word.** Slash finger under the word box, **dog.**
Test children on the activity	Test children on how to read a word in a sentence.	**Test** **Everybody, it's your turn to try this word.** Point to the word *dog.* **Remember how we'll read this word when we see it in a sentence. First touch under the word.** Touch under the word, just to the left of the box. **Now say the sounds. This word starts with a quick sound. Don't stop between sounds. Watch my finger.** Move your finger under each sound as children say the sounds. **First sound. Next sound. Last sound. Now say it quickly.** Slash your finger under the word box. **What's the word?** Slash your finger under the word box. Repeat the test with the word *mat.* If time permits, provide individual turns by giving individual children a Word Card for *dog* or *mat.* Tell the child to touch under the word. **Say the sounds. First sound, next sound, last sound. Say it quickly. What's the word?** Provide physical guidance if necessary.

Ongoing Assessment

If . . . children pause between sounds,	**then . . .** model sounding out the word and have children sound it out again.
If . . . children say the wrong sound,	**then . . .** keep your finger on the missed sound, model it correctly, and have children repeat the sound. Then have them sound out the word again.
If . . . children say the wrong word when they say it quickly,	**then . . .** model the correct word and have children repeat it. Then have children say the sounds slowly again and then fast.
If . . . children have difficulty following the new cues,	**then . . .** model and lead them through the word. Then try the test.

Activity 5 Writer's Warm-Up

Treasure Hunt

Objective: Children write letters from memory: *h, z, j, g, e, w,* and *u*.

Time: 2–3 minutes

	To Do	To Say
Introduce the activity	Distribute Treasure Hunt.	**We are going to go on a treasure hunt. I'm going to tell you the name of a letter, and you are going to write it. Let's see if we can get past the monsters and find the hidden treasure.**
Lead the activity	Lead writing the first letter.	**Lead** **Let's do one together. The first letter is *y*. Watch as I write the letter *y*.** Write the letter on your sheet. **Now you write the letter *y*. Write the letter.**
Test the activity	Test children on writing letters.	**Test** Say the name of each letter, one at a time: *h, z, j, g, e, w, u*. After you've said the name of a letter have children write it. Then, reinforce the letter name. **Everyone, what's the name of the letter you wrote?**

Ongoing Assessment

If... children write the wrong letter or don't remember a letter, **then...** show them the tracing card of the correct letter and model tracing the letter.

Lesson 95

Activity 6 Connect Sound to Letter

Practice Session: Spelling

Objective: Children segment sounds to spell words.

Time: 2–3 minutes

	To Do	To Say
Introduce the activity	Gather the 3-Square Strip and letter tiles.	**We are going to practice spelling for Monster Words.**
Lead the activity	Segment the word *yet*	**Lead** **The first word is *yet*. What word?** Have children hold out three fingers. **Say the sounds in *yet* and touch a finger for each sound.**
	Identify the first letter. Depending on ability level, display all the letter tiles or just two at a time.	Point to the first square of the 3-Square Strip. **Does everyone know what the first letter in *yet* is?** Call on a child to choose the correct letter and place it on the first square.
		Ongoing Assessment **If**... children make an error, **then**... have them segment the word again.
	Identify the middle letter.	**Does everyone know what the next letter in *yet* is?** Call on a child to choose and place the next letter.
	Identify the last letter.	**Do you know what the last letter in *yet* is?** Call on a child to choose and place the letter.
	Confirm the spelling.	**Say each sound in *yet* with me as I point to the letters: /yyy/ /eee/ /t/. Now say it quickly. That's right, you spelled *yet*; /yyy/ /eee/ /t/ are the sounds in *yet*.** Practice with at least two more words, as time allows: *rut, dip, cup, pet.*

Activity 7 Connect Sound to Letter

Monster Words

Objective: Children connect sound to letter.

Time: 6–8 minutes

	To Do	To Say
Introduce the activity	Place three Write-On/ Wipe-Off Cards in a row on the table facing children.	**We are going to spell some Monster Words. I will say a word, and you will spell the word by writing big monster letters on the Write-On/Wipe-Off Cards. Let's see how many monster words we can spell!**
Model the Activity	Model segmenting the word *rut*.	**The first word is *rut*. Listen. I'll touch a finger as I say each sound in *rut*: /rrr/ /uuu/ /t/.**
	Model spelling the word *rut*.	**Now I'm going to write the first letter in *rut*.** Write the letter on the first card, filling the whole card. Continue with the remaining letters in this fashion. As you write the letters, keep the cards in a horizontal row.
	Confirm the spelling of *rut*.	**Now, say each sound in *rut* with me while I point to the letters: /rrr/ /uuu/ /t/. Say it quickly. That's right. We spelled *rut*; /rrr/ /uuu/ /t/ are the sounds in *rut*.**
Test the activity	Test segmenting the word *pot*.	**The next word is *pot*. What's the word? Say the sounds in *pot* and touch a finger for each sound.**
	Test spelling the word *pot*.	Choose a child to write the first letter on the first card: ______, **please write the first letter in *pot* on the first card.** Continue this procedure to finish writing the word. **Ongoing Assessment** **If...** children make an error, **then...** have them segment the word again. **Say the sounds in ___ again and touch a finger for each sound. Stop when you get to the missing sound.**
	Confirm the spelling of *pot*.	**Now, say each sound in *pot* with me while I point to the letters: /p/ /ooo/ /t/. Say it quickly. That's right. We spelled *pot*; /p/ /ooo/ /t/ are the sounds in *pot*.**
	Test segmenting and spelling the remaining words.	Repeat the same test procedures with *wag, not, jug,* and *tan*. Confirm the spelling of each word before testing the next word.

New Sound /m/, /k/, /s/, /a/, /o/, /i/, /n/, /u/, /w/, /y/
Key Reading Skills Letter-Sound Correspondences; Word Reading: VC, CVC

Phonological Awareness and Alphabetic Understanding

Activity	Materials		Time
1. Alphabetic Review *y*/y/	Alphabet Card: *y*		1–2 minutes
2. Alphabetic Sounds Dash	Sounds Dash Teacher Resource Package 3	timer (not provided)	2–3 minutes
3. Reading Irregular Words	Irregular Words Teacher Resource Package 3		2–3 minutes
4. Reading Word Reading Game	Game Board 3 game marker (one per child/not provided) number cube (not provided)	Word Cards: *Diz, tub, Sam, if, jam, sun, an, big, pan, am, did, him, bed, cup, it, had, hug, nap, dog, mat* (Lessons 91–96)	6–8 minutes

Writing and Spelling

Activity	Materials		Time
5. Writer's Warm-Up Ready, Set, Go!	Writer's Warm-Up (one per child) Student Activity Book 3, p. 52 or 53	Tracing Cards: *y, b, n, w, z, g, h, r, e, j, i, a*	2–3 minutes
6. Integrated Phonologic/Alphabetic Practice Session: Spelling	3-Square Strip	Letter Tiles: *e, a, i, y, z, p, t, s, b*	2–3 minutes
7. Phonologic/Spelling Spell Check	Write-On/Wipe-Off Card marker (not provided)		6–8 minutes

Activity 1 Review Letter Name and Sound

Review y/y/

Objective: Children review *y*/y/.

Time: 1–2 minutes

	To Do	To Say
Test letter name and sound	Hold up the *y* Alphabet Card.	Test **What is the <u>name</u> of this letter? What is the <u>sound</u> for this letter?**
	Give individual turns on letter name and sound.	**Ongoing Assessment** — **If...** children make an error, **then...** tell them the name or sound, have them repeat the name or sound, and return to the letter a second time.

Activity 2 Build Sounds Fluency

Sounds Dash

Objective: Children increase fluency in identifying letter sounds.

Time: 2–3 minutes

	To Do	To Say
Introduce the game	Display Sounds Dash.	**Today you will do a Sounds Dash. I will point to a letter, and you will say the sound for that letter. Get as close to the finish line as possible in one minute. Be careful! If I hear a mistake, the group will go back three letters. Also, remember to say a sound only as long as I touch the letter. Some sounds will be quick.**
Review Letter Sounds	Review the sounds in the first row.	**Let's get warmed up for our Sounds Dash game. We will practice the sounds in the first row.** Point to *m*. **What is the sound for this letter?** Hold your finger under the letter *m* for one to two seconds. **Yes, /mmm/.** Practice the sound of each letter in the first row.
Play the game	Display the Sounds Dash page. Set the timer for one minute.	Test **Now you're ready for Sounds Dash. Everybody, look at my finger. On your mark, get set, go!** Point to *m* in the first row. **What is the sound for this letter?** Repeat with each sound in the first row. Then go immediately to the second row and so on until one minute is up. Reinforce children's progress in the Sounds Dash and tell them they will have a chance to beat their score when they play again in three days.

Ongoing Assessment (Review Letter Sounds)

If... children make an error,	**then...** tell them the sound, have them repeat it, and move back three letters on the page or repeat the letter if at the beginning of the row.
If... children miss more than two sounds in the first row,	**then...** provide additional practice on the nine sounds on the page instead of doing the Sounds Dash. Emphasize sounds children are unsure of.

Ongoing Assessment (Play the game)

If... children make an error,	**then...** tell them the sound, have them repeat it, and move back three letters or repeat the letter if at the beginning of a row.

Activity 3 Read Words

Lesson **96**

Irregular Words

Objective: Children practice irregular word *the*.

Time: 2–3 minutes

	To Do	To Say
Introduce the activity	Display the Irregular Words card.	**Today you will practice reading a Dizzy word.**
Lead the activity	Reintroduce irregular word *the*.	**Lead** **Everybody, we're going to read the Dizzy word we learned yesterday. Remember, some of the words that you will learn to read will be Dizzy words. We won't sound them out. We will spell them out.** Point to *the*. **This Dizzy word is *the*. What's the word?** Move your finger quickly under the word as children say it. **Spell *the*.** Children name each letter as you touch under it. **What word did you spell?** Move your finger quickly under the word as children say it. ***Yes, the.*** **This Dizzy word is *the*.**

Activity 4 Read Words

Word Reading Game

Objective: Children read words.

Time: 6–8 minutes

	To Do	To Say
Introduce the game Word Reading	Gather Game Board 3, a marker for each child, and a number cube. Put the Word Cards facedown in a pile on the middle of the table.	**You are going to play the Word Reading Board Game.** **Each of you will get a turn to roll the number cube, pick up the top Word Card, and sound out and read the word on the card. If a person correctly sounds out and reads the word, he or she moves his or her marker the number of spaces rolled on the number cube and then places the Word Card at the bottom of the pile.**
Model the game	Display the *tub* Word Card.	**I will show you how to play. First I will roll the number cube. Then I will take the first Word Card from the pile.**
	Segment the word *tub.*	**I am going to say the sounds slowly. I see there's a quick sound at the beginning: /t/ /uuu/ /b/.**
	Blend the word *tub.*	**Now I am going to say the sounds quickly: /t/ /uuu/ /b/. The word is *tub.* Now I will move my marker the number of spaces shown on the number cube.**
Play the game	Choose a child to begin the game.	**Remember when it is your turn, say the sounds, then say the sounds quickly to say the word. Watch out for any quick sounds.** Play the game until one child makes it to the finish line or time runs out. If a child makes an error, he or she does not get to move the marker.

Ongoing Assessment

If . . . children pause between sounds,	**then . . .** model sounding out the word and have children sound it out again.
If . . . children say the wrong sound,	**then . . .** keep your finger on the missed sound, model it correctly, and have children repeat the sound. Then have them sound out the word again.
If . . . children say the wrong word when they say it quickly,	**then . . .** model the correct word and have children repeat it. Then have children say the sounds slowly again and then say them fast.

Activity 5 Writer's Warm-Up

Ready, Set, Go!

Objective: Children practice writing letters.

Time: 2–3 minutes

	To Do	To Say
Introduce the activity	Distribute Writer's Warm-Up.	**You will write your letters the best you can and as quickly as you can.**
Model the activity	Model tracing letters. Model writing letters.	**Model** **I'll show you how this activity works. The letters in the first row are *y, b, n,* and *w.* Watch as I trace each of the letters.** Trace the first row of letters. **It's your turn to trace the letters in the first row on your sheet.** Wait until children finish. **After I say "Ready, Set, Go!" I'll write *y, b, n,* and *w* as best and as quickly as I can on the second row. Watch me try. Ready, Set, Go!** When you finish, put your pencil down. **It's your turn to write *y, b, n,* and *w* as best and as quickly as you can. Ready, Set, Go!** Tell children to put their pencils down when they finish.
Test the activity	Test children on tracing and writing letters.	**Test** **The letters in the next group are *z, g, h, r.* For warm-up, trace each of the letters. Put your pencil down when you finish. Now write *z, g, h,* and *r* as best and as quickly as you can. Ready, Set, Go!** Remind children to put their pencil down when they finish. **Now look over your paper and circle your best letters.** Repeat procedure for *e, j, i, a.*

Ongoing Assessment

If... children write the wrong letter or don't remember how to write a letter, **then...** show them the tracing card of the correct letter, model tracing the letter, and say the letter name.

Activity 6 Connect Sound to Letter

Practice Session: Spelling

Objective: Children segment sounds to spell words.

Time: 2–3 minutes

	To Do	To Say
Introduce the activity	Gather a 3-Square Strip and letter tiles.	**We are going to practice spelling for Spell Check.**
Lead the activity	Segment the word *yip*.	**Lead** **The first word is *yip*. What word?** Have children hold out three fingers. **Say the sounds in *yip* and touch a finger for each sound.**
	Identify the first letter. Depending on ability level, display all the letter tiles or just two at a time.	Point to the first square of the 3-Square Strip. **Does everyone think they know what the first letter in *yip* is?** Call on a child to choose the correct letter and place it on the first square.
		Ongoing Assessment — **If...** children make an error, **then...** have them segment the word again.
	Identify the middle letter.	**Does everyone know what the next letter in *yip* is?** Call on a child to choose and place the next letter.
	Identify the last letter.	**Do you know what the last letter in *yip* is?** Call on a child to choose and place the letter.
	Confirm the spelling.	**Say each sound in *yip* with me as I point to the letters: /yyy/ /iii/ /p/. Now say it quickly. That's right, you spelled *yip*; /yyy/ /iii/ /p/ are the sounds in *yip*.**
		Practice with at least two more words, as time allows: *tab, sip, yet, zap.*

Lesson 96

Activity 7 Connect Sound to Letter

Spell Check

Objective: Children correct the spelling of words.

Time: 6–8 minutes

	To Do	To Say
Introduce the activity	Display the Write-On/Wipe-Off Card. Write *baz* on the card.	**I'm having trouble spelling today. I keep making mistakes. Will you help me fix my mistakes?**
Model the activity	Model segmenting *bat*.	**Model** **This word is supposed to be *bat*. What word? Let's see if I can fix it. Listen. I'll touch a finger as I say each sound in *bat:* /b/ /aaa/ /t/.**
	Model checking the letters.	**The first sound is /b/ and I wrote *b*.** Point to the letter. **This letter is okay.** Repeat the same procedure for the middle sound and letter. Then continue: **The last sound is /t/ and I wrote *z*.** Point to the letter. **I'll change *z* to *t*.**
	Confirm the spelling.	**Now, let's see if we fixed the word. Say each sound in *bat* with me while I point to the letters: /b/ /aaa/ /t/. Say it quickly. That's right; /b/ /aaa/ /t/ are the sounds in *bat* and *b-a-t* spells *bat*.**
Test the activity	Write *sep* on the card. Test segmenting *sip*.	**Test** **This word is supposed to be *sip*, but I think I made a mistake. What word should this be? Let's see if you can fix it. Touch a finger as you say each sound in *sip*.**
	Test spelling *sip*.	**What's the first sound in *sip*? What letter did I write?** Point to the letter. **Is this letter okay?** Continue this procedure for the rest of the word. When a letter is incorrect, ask a child to fix it: **Can you fix this letter? That's right, *i* is the letter for /iii/, like the /iii/ in *sip*.** Then confirm the spelling. Continue with the following words: *set/yet; tay/tap, pat/pet.*

Ongoing Assessment

If . . . children make an error, **then . . .** model the letter name and sound, have children repeat the letter name and sound, and have children write the correct letter.